GREGG BRADEN

Walking Between The Worlds
The Science of Compassion

OM Mani Padme Hum
Translation of Tibetan mantra,
"May the Jewel of the Lotus descend into your heart."

GREGG BRADEN

Walking Between The Worlds
The Science of Compassion

"...and this message was for the ears of man alone,
they who walk between the worlds of earth and heaven. And unto
the ears of man was whispered this message..."

EXCERPT FROM THE DEAD SEA SCROLLS

A Sacred Spaces/Ancient Wisdom Book

PUBLISHED BY
RADIO BOOKSTORE PRESS
BELLEVUE, WASHINGTON, U.S.A.

Walking Between the Worlds
C/o Radio Bookstore Press
P.O. Box 3010
Bellevue, Wa. 98009-3010

Radio Bookstore Press books and related information may be purchased for educational, business, sales or promotional use. For information and a free catalog, please write:
Radio Bookstore Press, P.O. Box 3010, Bellevue, Wa. 98009-3010.

Cover Concept: Gregg Braden
Book Design and Composition: Webb Design Inc., Taos, New Mexico
Chapter Illustrations and Concepts: Melissa Ewing Sherman

FIRST U.S. EDITION

9 8 7 6 5 4 3 2 1 • 96 97 98 99 00 01 02

ISBN 1-889071-05-6

Printed in the United States of America

DEDICATION

With blessings of the highest knowledge,
In loving wisdom,
From a place of the deepest compassion,
I dedicate this work to you,
the last generation to mature before the close
of this grand cycle of experience.

It is you whose lives are bridging the time
that the ancients called "no time."
It is you who will anchor a new wisdom
rooted in compassion,
laying the foundation for those
with the courage to follow.
It is you who are asked to remember
love, compassion and trust
while living in a world that has
hated, judged and feared.

You will transcend these polarities,
while still living within the polarities.

This book is written and dedicated to
"You Who Walk Between the Worlds."

CHAPTER ART

For centuries the people of the East have had a profound influence on Western culture. Philosophy, breath, meditation, the techniques of Japanese Sumi-e and Chinese brush painting, are examples of the gifts that continue to inspire our lives. The art of oriental ink painting is as much influenced by philosophy and chi, or life energy, as by visual interpretation. Poets, authors and artists were among the first to recognize the various qualities represented in the living elements of the landscape. The following interpretations provide insights into the chapter illustrations of "Walking Between the Worlds."

TECHNICAL ILLUSTRATIONS

LIST OF TABLES

TABLE OF CONTENTS

ACKNOWLEDGMENTS

In his book, *The Prophet,* Kahlil Gibran states that "work is love made visible."[1] I feel truth in Gibran's passage, I know it to be true in my life. Completing this work, my "love made visible," is like the completion of a sentence that began with the *Awakening to Zero Point* text. In the completion I find tremendous peace.

I would like to say thank you and express my deepest gratitude to all who have contributed to Walking Between the Worlds, some without even knowing of their contribution.

Laura and Paul, thank you for your friendship and support.

Mark, many thanks to you for your artistic vision.

Gwynne for your guidance and inspiration in the editing process.

Special thanks to the researchers at the Institute of HeartMath. Your vision provides a foundation for hope and new possibilities, and for remembering our relationship to one another and our earth.

Additionally, I would like to thank Dan Winter for graciously allowing me to share his research validating the resonant relationship between our bodies and our earth. Dan, your work brings a tangible link to the inner knowing for all whose lives you touch.

To everyone who has ever taken a *Zero Point* or *Science of Compassion* workshop, thank you for teaching me the words that are meaningful for you to hear, as these sometimes esoteric and nebulous concepts were offered. If the message of this text is meaningful to you in any way, then you and I have done our "work" well together.

Melissa, thank you for sharing your life with me. Your willingness to have a "virtual" home, with virtual pets and plants has allowed me to create this work, touch the lives of many people and you and I to see beauty in places that few have had the opportunity to travel. As you so often say to me, beauty is just a reflection of the beholder. The beauty that you see in this world is just that; your beauty demonstrated as trust, patience, love and endless support.

To our little feline friend, Sik (pronounced "seek," Tibetan for "Snow Leopard") who disappeared during the early stages of this writing. Thank you for your friendship, companionship, late nights curled up on the couch with me, walking across the pages as I proofread this text.

We miss your upside down glances from the kiva ladder, your smoked almond hockey games across the kitchen floor and your thoughtful stare into our eyes, always at just the right moments.

From you we have learned the lesson of the stewardship of life. I know that you were never ours to begin with. We happened to be the lucky ones that you chose to live with for the nine months of your earthly life.

Strength and blessings to you, as we release you to your journey of exploration and discovery.

Thank you for sharing your wisdom with us.

Thank you for our time together.

PREFACE

B y now you have read the books, heard the predictions, seen the media specials and experienced the workshops. Thanks to national prime time television you have had the opportunity to see an alien autopsy televised into your living room, witness reports of UFO crash sites, view television's "Ancient Prophecies I," "Ancient Prophecies II" and mysterious glyphs occurring in every major crop producing nation of the world. You have seen the predicted maps of change for North America and proposed "safe spots" for you and your families. You have heard channeled angels, archangels and ascended masters. Off planet guides and the spiritual hierarchy of a multitude of well intentioned beings have offered messages ranging from warnings of doom to the antici- pation of ecstasy. Many have offered specifics of diet, breath, exercise and a barrage of "shoulds" and "should nots" regarding the manner in which you live your life. Within this lifetime you have had the opportunity to hear, see and experience tremendous vol- umes of information detailing unprecedented change within your world and your life.

Still, in the back of your mind the questions may linger.

"What does all of this mean to me?

How do I know what is right for me, my family, my life?"

For many, the awareness of the above mentioned information has had the effect of triggering anxiety, even to the point of fear. Why would we expect anything less? Hearing of this tremendous change without context certainly can be frightening. Of even more concern is the feeling of helplessness upon hearing of change, with no apparent power to do anything about it. In some instances, changes appear to just happen. Our predicted earth changes are a good example. Should I move to a safe area away from coasts? Careers: Should I leave my real job and pursue spiritual interests? Concern for others: What will become of my family during and after the Shift of the Ages? How do we defend our bodies against new viruses and disease never seen before in our world?

Clearly, the quality of your life does not hinge upon privileged information regard- ing secret drinks discovered in the Ukraine, exposing government cover ups, 50 year old conspiracies, or whose angel channeled what to whom. You do not need to know of someone else's material regarding a timetable of falling magnetics or global catastrophe to bring healthy, life-giving relationships into the lives of you and your families.

Without context, well intentioned forecasts and warnings may serve to frighten and promote change based in fear rather than heartfelt choice. The reason for the fear is that each prediction and warning is viewed from the perspective of a paradigm that you have outgrown. The questions remain:

"What do I do in these days of unprecedented change?"

"How do I know what is right?"

The momentum of change within your body reflects the pace of change within your world. That mirror promises that during times of intense and rapid shifts of reality, you are not the same person, viewing the same reality, from the same place, as a year ago, two days ago, or even yesterday. This is the one factor that is not accounted for in so many of the predictions and future scenarios. Rather than viewing change remotely and comparing the new to all that you know today, you have become the change.

Herein lives your opportunity to choose a path, the Second Path, laying the foundation for a new wisdom that has no name as yet. This time in our lives is less about what we "do" and more about what we become. Through our culture conditioned to do, I am often posed the question,

"What must I do to learn compassion?"

In its simplicity, the answer to this question has often been a challenge for me to convey. I have also found that the challenge has diminished each time I answer. How do I offer you a science that is not about what you do? What words do I use to convey to you the simplicity of allowing and being rather than doing and making something happen? It is certainly possible to offer meditations, prayers and techniques providing you the sensations of forgiveness and compassion. These feelings are a point of reference, however, for something that you have already become. Your path is to remember your truest nature and live that nature in the challenges of life, regardless of how life is shown to you.

Compassion is an awareness that you become, rather than something that you do on occasion.

Unquestionably, the physical phenomenon mentioned previously, and many more, may be occurring now and are of tremendous interest. The question:

"Is it necessary that you know of the phenomenon or understand them?" The answer:

"Probably not."

What is necessary is that your life work for you. Your life and the opportunity to express whatever it is that your life has come to mean to you is necessary. There is a good chance that most, if not all, of the above mentioned events are, in fact, unfolding within our lifetime. I would ask you to consider, however, each event plays a healthy, natural role within a process far greater than the event itself.

As outrageous as each may appear, the aforementioned phenomenon are by-products of something much more significant. Each phenomenon reflects a change in creation that is mirrored within your body. Of great significance to you is that you feel good about each day, regardless of the outcome of each day. The feeling is your signal, to yourself, regarding how you have resolved each choice within the day.

As others have so graciously reminded us, it is less important what we accomplish as opposed to how we accomplish it. Consider digging ditches, frying hamburgers, healing the sick or writing computer software. None of these can be a better or worse task until we, or someone whose opinion we value, place a judgment upon it. Until our efforts are compared to those of another, our efforts are simply us expressing, creating and being.

You have arrived at a time in your life history where it may serve you to acknowledge that you are you are capable only of life choices and the outcome of those choices, without judgment of good, bad, right, or wrong. In the absence of judgment your expressions simply are, without failure, in career, relationships, families or tasks. How may you fail when your purpose is to experience?

Ancient tools were left to you, for this time in history, for the very purpose of mastering your life at this time, in these days. Those tools are alive within you, encoded within you, available now in this moment. You may know of this coding in your mind, do you remember in your body? Possibly dormant, certainly living within you, is the capability to shift the pattern of life within your body, as well as the manner in which you see that life. That change may occur within the space of a heartbeat as you remember to allow it.

Shifting your body chemistry by shifting your viewpoint is perhaps the single most powerful tool that you have available to you for the remainder of this lifetime.

Researchers have recently demonstrated to the western world a phenomenon that has been taught through the mystery schools for thousands of years. New data now supports the idea that human emotion determines the actual patterning of DNA within the body.[1] Furthermore, laboratory demonstrations have shown that DNA determines how patterns of light, expressed as matter, surround the human body.[2] Imagine the implications.

Stated another way, researchers have discovered that the arrangement of matter (atoms, bacteria, viruses, climate, even other people) surrounding your body, is directly linked to the feeling and emotion from within your body!

Allowing yourself to remember signals a high level of personal mastery that has been sought after by many, and achieved by relatively few, in the past. Do you know how powerful this is? Beyond microcircuit technology, beyond genetic splicing and drug induced engineering, without exception this relationship between your physical body (DNA) and emotion represents the single most sophisticated technology to ever grace this world through the expression of our bodies.

Our own science now has demonstrated that DNA, your DNA, is directly tied to your ability to forgive, allow and love through the expression of your life. The science of loving, forgiving and allowing is nothing new. The technology underlying love and forgiveness is an ancient as well as universal science, known today as compassion. Your ability to express forgiveness, allowing others the outcome of their own experience, without changing the nature of who you are, is a hallmark of the highest levels of life mastery. The quality of your life is directly tied to, and intimately entwined with the personal mastery of what your life means to you.

As a form of love, the mastery of compassion is where your true power lives. What may stand between you and your true power are your emotions and your feelings, interpreted through the lens of what your life has told you that they mean. Within the life giving fields of compassion, debilitating disease is not possible, immune compromising viruses are not possible, your body turning upon itself is not possible. Through mastery, illness is redefined. Through your mastery expressed as forgiveness and compassion, disease and even death become choices rather than chances. Your body is the biological mirror, an indicator, of your level of personal memory.

My intent in offering *Walking Between the Worlds* at this time, is to offer a context within which each moment of each day plays a powerful role toward preparing you to gracefully accept tremendous and accelerated change in your life. It is not necessary that you know this is a lifetime of Bodhisattva, that you are living a process of initiation demonstrated over six thousand years ago or that emotion is your forgotten technology of change. However, you are experiencing life. Your life does have to work for you.

Through simply allowing the resolution of each relationship in your life, whether it is the two minute relationship in the checkout line of a grocery store, or the twenty year relationship of marriage, you are awakening fragments of your soul that allow your body health, vitality and life giving relationships. In this awakened state, change comes gracefully. The key to allowing your awakening, as well as the change, is the ancient science of compassion. Your truest nature, compassion, is your goal of experience in this lifetime. Compassion is your birthright. It is compassion that will carry you gracefully through these times of tremendous change that the ancients called The Shift of the Ages.

I am often asked with whom am I affiliated? What group, what course provides the basis of my offering? By choice, I am affiliated with no organization, group or path. The words that I offer in these pages, or through any of the seminars, are my words reflecting my path, unless I indicate otherwise. It is because we have all arrived at this point in time, together, from our own unique perspectives of viewpoint and experience, that I ask you to look beyond the words of this text if my words are not your words. Please feel the underlying intent of the words and the context within which the offering is made.

My greatest teachers have been those with whom I have shared time in my life. Every relationship, each friendship, whether it lasted forty years or three minutes, has shown me something of myself. It is those understandings that I offer to you, in the hope that they may be of service to you at this point in your lifetime. At times the lesson was not acknowledged until I had achieved the foundation to understand. Sometimes that foundation has come years or even decades later!

Intentionally, I have refrained from reading any books, attending lectures, workshops or retreats while this body of information has unfolded. My choice is to present *Walking Between the Worlds* within the context of its uniqueness untainted by the language, concepts or descriptions of others. The subtle triggers of memory are found in our language. Through our language of spoken and unspoken words, we mirror relationships between the words themselves and subsequent brain chemistry producing varied states of awareness.

When asked to identify a formal path that closely reflects the concepts of my offering, I reference the Essene traditions of the Qumran scrolls, the Nag Hammadi library and their derivations from the Egyptian, Aramaic, Ethiopian and Tibetan texts, as well as the oral traditions of many indigenous cultures. At least two Native American groups have confided in me that their traditions are traced back to those of the ancient Essenes. Dating to nearly five hundred years before Jesus of Nazareth, these Essene teachings are the forerunners of many later beliefs, including the Christian and indigenous traditions of the West. Through these traditions, we are shown codes of conduct that mirror the very patterns of the life that surrounds us. Our path is not found in the scriptures, texts or temples of those who have come before us. These relics are the artifacts of our search to remember ourselves. My beliefs and life history have demonstrated to me that, ultimately, all paths regardless of their outward expression, lead to the One. The codes of the One are mirrored to us daily as the world of life that surrounds us. The very law that allows life to pulse through each organism, every plant, insect and human, is the same law that we seek in texts, forgotten words and oral traditions of antiquity.

While I may reference the script of an ancient text for purposes of clarity or to illustrate a principle, clearly I believe that the time of our outer scriptures, temples, grids and technology is behind us. In reminding us of our holy relationship with all of life, as well as one another, these sacred guides have served us well. I believe that we are living the days when we have outgrown the doing of the ancient references. Today, within the last few years before the close of this great cycle of experience, we are asked to become the hopes, dreams and lives that we have seen as visions of prophecy and scripture. Today you are asked to become the greatest gift that you could ever offer to yourself, your creator and those that you hold most dear. Today, you are asked to become compassion.

Gregg Braden
August, 1996

INTRODUCTION

Plate I: *Plum Blossom*
Sanskrit symbol represents Tree of Wisdom

LONG AGO

Our life on earth was very different from the life on earth of today. Land was plentiful, there were few people to occupy the land, and we remembered...

We remembered the true nature of the compassion that was our lives. We remembered the beauty of this world, our relationship with this world and the gift that we call life.

Then something began to happen. Our lives changed as the memory of our gift began to fade. Feeling separate from the very world that we had come to experience, we began to build machines, extensions of our senses, to explore our world and once again, remember.

Deep into the quantum world of the sub-atom we have traveled. Into the furthest reaches of interstellar space we probe, sending devices, surrogates of our perceptions, to explore. Now a mystery unfolds, as our own science seeks the memory of ourselves. From the far reaches of space, from the deepest realms of the atom, we find that there is a force that cannot be measured or engineered. That force, the intelligence that binds all in its creation, the ancients simply called Spirit. All of the data, each measurement, all of the information points back to us, asking us to remember the mystery within. Collectively, as we approach the time in history that the ancients called the Shift of the Ages, our own science is directing us back to ourselves, back to the most sophisticated technology ever to grace this world with its presence, the mystery of you and me. Through this mysterious force expressing as our lives, we will know ourselves. In the knowing, once again we remember.

EXCERPT FROM THE VIDEO
AWAKENING TO ZERO POINT
BY GREGG BRADEN.

Almost immediately following the release of the book *Awakening to Zero Point: The Collective Initiation,* I was asked for more. Readers asked for a greater understanding and deeper insights into how the material was presented to me. Where did *Awakening to Zero Point* come from? What events had transpired within my life allowing me the opportunity to weave a continuity between deep interpersonal relationships, obscure and ancient texts and the magnetic fields of the earth? What had happened to me on Mt. Sinai in 1987, the Andes mountains of Peru in 1994? Why have I chosen to live in the high deserts of the American Southwest?

Walking Between the Worlds: The Science of Compassion in part, is my response to these questions. It is from a place of graceful urgency that I offer this work now, at this time. When I ask myself the question:

If I were given one day in this world, to leave with those that I love and hold most dear the message that I believe would best serve them in their lives, what would that message be?

Walking Between the Worlds: The Science of Compassion, is my answer.

The story that follows has been nearly 42 years in the making, and it continues. *Walking Between the Worlds* embodies what I believe to be the single most compelling message that I may offer to you at this time in our lives. Embodying hope, clarity and remembrance, this message may very well represent the greatest story of compassion ever demonstrated in our ancient future memory.

Through workshops and seminars, I have seen the direct effect of this offering upon others. Some have found these stories to be powerful catalysts within their own lives, moving them to redefine the meaning of hurt, pain and fear as well as the joy and ecstasy of past relationships. Others have discovered a timely context and validation for themselves, as well as loved ones with whom they share, in the mystery of life. With that validation has come the impetus to move forward in life's offering, embracing each challenge as an opportunity to demonstrate mastery, rather than another "test" from the school of life. The question that you are asked to address through the living of your life has been stated many times by many teachers:

Walking Between the Worlds

Are you a physical being having spiritual experiences, or are you a being of spirit having physical experiences?[1]

The manner in which you view this question determines, for you alone, the manner in which you will view the events of your life as they unfold before you.

SCIENCE AND OUR PROMISE

In the traditional sense of the word, science is hypothesis and verification. We apply science as prediction followed by test after test until a result or response is demonstrated to be reliable and consistent. Within the replicability lies the demonstration of truth. "If" these things happen in precisely this way, "then" such-and-such outcome may be expected, and it is so. Herein rests the truth of the science. Through rigid parameters of sampling, control and verification, the scientific method proves the validity of the process.

Almost daily, research is bearing witness, re-validating, truths offered through many ancient texts. These truths include evidence of previous high technologies of great sophistication, indications of a many-dimensional world and a fundamental force that provides the underlying fabric of creation,[2] a direct link between feeling, thought, emotion and the quality of our health and well being.[3]

Before reading further, please be clear of my intent and perspective in offering this material, in this way, at this time. From the deepest part of my being I feel that the shifts unfolding within each of our bodies, our lives and our world are part of an on-going process that began over 200,000 years ago. While I do not see the change as cyclic, ancient texts offer the view of a "Grand Cycle" of experience, of which we are very near completion. I believe that the earth shifts of seismic patterns and weather systems, the human shifts in family, social, political, economic and military systems and body shifts of new genetics, illness, disease and bacteria are healthy and natural examples of shifting patterns of energy.

We call those shifts *change*.

The laws of creation assure us that to the degree change is judged and discouraged, to that degree is change experienced in life as challenge. Though change is occurring within our families, societies, planet and relationships, there is nothing wrong or broken in these systems of energy. They are simply in change. Many ancient texts have revealed that change is precisely what this time in earth and human history is all about. Almost universally ancient calendars, written codices and verbal prophecies point to now, these days as being a time of unprecedented change in human and earth history referenced as The Shift of the Ages.[4] Additionally, we are told that the changes yield a world within our earthly reality that mirrors a familiar place in our collective memory; a time before time began.

> *"...the earth, and all that dwells therein, is but a reflection of the Kingdom of the Heavenly Father..."*
>
> ADAPTED FROM THE ESSENE GOSPEL OF PEACE[5]

The very nature of this shift requires change on every level of our lives from the way we eat, drink and breathe to the way we grow food, where we live and how we love. Change is our catalyst of growth, the trigger catapulting you and I to new ways of viewing ourselves, through our lens of feelings, emotions and relationships. We are asking ourselves to move beyond the limits that we have imposed upon ourselves, and upon one another, in the past. You and I, individually and collectively, are determining in this moment how humanity as a whole is to respond to change. Will we choose grace and ease or illness and disease? The change is happening now. It is occurring within your city, within your family, within your body, your emotions and your patterns of sleep.

The same texts that speak to you of the change also speak of a promise. That promise takes the form of a manner of life conduct that will carry you gracefully through this time of "purification" with ease. The promise was left to us through the texts and words of those who have come before us. In its simplicity the words are sometimes dismissed as irrelevant in this day and our age of technology. The promise states that while you are not your experience, you must know yourself through your experience to master life's extremes.

You must know your extremes to find your balance.

You are not your success, your failures, your careers or your poverty. You are not your joy, ecstasy, fear or pain. These are the elements of your experiences that allow you the opportunity to know yourself in all ways, so that those ways may be mastered. You are in this world and not of this world.

The promise describes a manner of conduct leading to the demonstration of personal mastery. Without exception, each event, every relationship, every love, each job, friendship, romance and betrayal that you have ever experienced has provided you key emotions and feelings leading to your mastery. How you perceive those emotions and feelings, how you define them in your life, is your way of training and teaching yourself, reminding yourself of the promise of compassion. Your mastery of compassion as a state of being is achieved as the culmination of two paths that may be lived individually, as well as collectively.

EXTERNAL TECHNOLOGY: THE FIRST PATH

I sense that this time in our lives represents a crossroads in conscious memory. We are being asked by virtue of our very experience to choose between one of two paths. Each path is valid in its own right, neither necessarily right nor wrong. Each path is complete with its unique choices and consequences, each leading to the same destination within different time frames. The *First Path* may be viewed as the dominant paradigm that has been, a path of external technology engineered outside of our bodies as extensions of ourselves interacting with the world around us. This path represents our cultural response to the challenges of life. Causes of life events are found "out there" in a world that is perceived as separate and distinct from our bodies. Therefore solutions are engineered "out there," discounting the interplay between us and our world. Illness, disease, deficiencies and conditions are viewed as originating and cured through things that we "do." Examples are vaccines, dietary supplements, antibiotics and gadgets that make "out there" better. Clearly, these are powerful and beneficial technologies. I bless these technologies and give thanks for their offering, for this has been our path.

External technology is us, remembering through our machines, the same principles that we demonstrate as life in our bodies. These principles include capacitance, resistance, transmission, receiving and storage of scalar and vector quantities of energy. In my years of service in the earth, space and computer sciences, I have yet to witness a technology developed outside of the human body that is not reflected as the body itself.

External technology is us remembering ourselves by building models of ourselves, outside of ourselves, and applying the models back to ourselves.

The First Path has brought you and me to the point where we are today, keeping us alive and strong, prolonging our opportunity to choose another way. The scientific method has been the way that we have chosen to demonstrate these "truths" to ourselves. Through science we have re-validated our inner nature as outer technology for the last two thousand years or so. Certainly this path has proven itself, and its reliability to a point, representing one possibility for experience. There is another path.

INTERNAL TECHNOLOGY: THE SECOND PATH

The Second Path is the path of internal technology. Remembered, rather than engineered, internal technology is expressed within you and me simply through the way we live life. This path remembers the human body as the sacred union between the atomic expression of "mother earth" and the electrical and magnetic expression of "father heaven." The ancient Essene sciences emphasize this idea as the basis of their earliest teachings.

> *"For the spirit of the Son of Man was created from the spirit of the Heavenly Father, and his body from the body of the Earthly Mother."*
> ADAPTED FROM THE ESSENE GOSPEL OF PEACE[6]

The path of internal technology remembers that each cell of our bodies is approximately 1.17 volts of electrical potential. Statistics indicate that the average body is composed of approximately 1 quadrillion cells. One quadrillion cells times 1.17 volts of potential for each cell equals approximately 1.17 quadrillion volts of bio-electrical potential per person. Each cell exhibits properties of capacitance, resistance, storage, transmission and receiving, and it does so at will, through intention.

Look at the potential that you live as your body! Do you know, do you remember, what you may do with your potential? Is any wonder that legitimate healers are able to do what they do? What virus, what bacteria, what condition can stand up to 1.17 quadrillion volts of force? How, you ask, is this force activated and regulated? The answer to this question is the essence, the very focus, of so many ancient texts, as well as Walking Between the Worlds. The answer is this:

The force of potential within you is activated and regulated through the manner in which you choose to conduct your life.

What do you choose as nourishment for your body each day? Where do you choose to live and grow with those that you hold most dear? How have you chosen to express your unique gift of life to this world? How do you choose to speak to others, and allow yourself to be spoken to? These questions represent opportunities of conscious and responsible conduct in each of our lives. The Second Path of inner technology illustrates a path of opportunity in personal expression. The opportunity is for you and I to demonstrate personal mastery through addressing the following question:

IF
we are truly who and what we say we are:
powerful and masterful beings of wisdom and compassion,
living just a few short years from
The Shift of the Ages
AND
we have remembered that peace is a higher choice to non-peace in a world of polarity
expressed as thought, feeling, emotion and conduct
AND
that responsibility for our lives, our vitality and well being,
originates from within us
Then
why create temporary solutions to our health and well being as technologies outside
of ourselves?

Why do we demand of scientists that "they" find a cure "out there" for AIDS, Cancer, Ebola, Hantavirus, Polio, Mad Cow Disease or any of the twenty or so viruses and bacteria that were not present only thirty years ago? Why do we demand of law enforcement agencies and global police that they maintain peace throughout our world? Why do we choose to shun the personal responsibility that is our birthright in determining how we respond to these powerful agents of change?

In his recent work, *The Sound Beings,* Joseph Rael[7] of the Tewa People explains our choice of medicines, vaccines and antibiotics as our way of becoming "unstuck" from a pattern of life. From the Tewa perspective, life is viewed as "two slices of light," each of a different quality, each moving always forward. When we become "stuck" in a belief, thought or pattern, the light cannot move through us. We experience "being stuck" as illness. Medicine is our choice, our path of engineering something "out there" to "unstick" us so that we may have motion once again.

While medicine certainly is valid, is it in our best interest to rely solely on our externally engineered solutions. Further, how permanent are the solutions, really? How many of the viruses that we believed were "cured" are reappearing now, thirty years later, as new, mutated and virulent strains that we have no medicines for?

Rather than *engineer* the technology out there to address these and other consequences of our past condition, why not accept the gift of our engineered solutions while we *become* the technology? Why not feel the feelings, emote the emotions and think the thoughts that allow us to shift to a state of being where bacteria, virus, change and even death are of little consequence? The cures are simply patterns of vibration engineered through our models of ourselves "out there." Why not *become* the models, why not *become* the vibrations from within?

Is it possible that viruses, bacteria, immune breakdowns, social and political upheaval and other conditions viewed as "horrors" are actually powerful agents of change? Is it possible that these experiences are catalysts that you and I have consented to in an effort to propel us collectively into a higher choice of being? If you believe that we are holographic in nature, then you must ask yourself, "Do I believe that my conduct in daily life has any effect upon others as a whole?"

I have often heard individuals respond to this question by answering that they do not know what to "do." The ancients say to us that compassion is not something that is done or accomplished. Rather, compassion is that which you allow yourself to become. Doing is a hallmark of the paradigm that has been. You have grown beyond the doing. This unique time in earth, as well as human history, is the time of becoming. Put simply, to become is the very essence of the powerful and ancient message that was left to you and me through many texts and traditions of those who have come before us.

The message is this:

"Those conditions that you most choose to have in your life, you must first become as your life."

Deceptively simple, this eloquent phrase is a summation of all of the work performed by all of the masters, all of the saints, scientists, technicians and families, each of your spiritual forbearers, preparing you for this very time in earth and human history. Those that claim to choose peace in their world must first become peace in themselves. Those that claim to choose prosperity, health and vitality for their loved ones must first become those very attributes themselves. Those that choose compassion for their loved ones and for those who look upon others with judgment and hate, must become that very compassion. The message of "becoming" is the essence of the most sacred of the ancient texts.

From this perspective, the time of our outer technology is obsolete. You and I have grown beyond the time of being served by the First Path. We have outgrown the requirement to build ourselves outside of ourselves.Within this moment lives the opportunity to choose the memory of ourselves in our truest nature. The machines, tools and gadgets are a collection of artifacts representing a technology that has been; it is our collective past demonstrated as a technology outside of our bodies. Today you have the opportunity to bless the technology of the First Path for all that it has offered, for the time it has afforded, the ease of life it has offered and all that it has meant to you.

Bless the technology and move forward in the Second Path. Far more sophisticated than any machines ever built by the most brilliant of our kind, the Second Path represents a tremendous upgrade of conduct and our very standard of living. We now have the opportunity to become the healing of the medicines, to become permanent and eternal health, to become the peace of the peacemakers, to become the compassion of the religions and vibrant companions of life, and to do so gracefully.

I invite you to reconsider the teachings that speak of a potent force of life that courses "through" your body. Therein lives the separation.

Beyond moving through you, that potent force is you!

There is no separation between you and that force. It is you who determines your response to the bacteria, viruses and ultraviolet rays from a depleting ozone, even the flu bug that circulates through your office. It is you that determines your threshold of anger, hate and rage at events that you have masterfully created in your life.

We are determining our outcome at this time in history by determining our response to this time in history. In our totality, we have something far greater to offer to ourselves and those that we hold most dear, than we will ever find in a machine that is designed and implemented "out there."

COMPASSION'S GIFT

The time of our outer temples, outer networks, outer grids and external guidance is nearing completion. For many, what has come as an inner knowing was stated clearly through the language of the time two thousand years ago, and even before. Our knowing reminds us that we live as an expression of a highly sophisticated union, a *sacred marriage*, between the elements of this earth and a directive non-physical force. We call that force "Spirit." Perhaps the most astounding of the ancient references restating its validity today is the link between feeling, thought and their relationship to human physiology.

> *"Three are the dwellings of the Son of Man, and no one may come before the face of the (One) who knows not the angel of peace in each of the three. These are body, thoughts and feelings."* (parentheses are author's)
>
> ADAPTED FROM THE ESSENE GOSPEL OF PEACE[8]

The peace that we seek in our world and in our body is the same peace of this Essene reference. Compassion is defined as a quality of thought, feeling and emotion. Compassion may be demonstrated as a quality of conduct in our daily lives. The vitality of our body, the quality of our blood and breath, our choice of relationships and emotion, even our ability to reproduce appears to be directly linked to our ability to embrace the force of compassion in our life.

To the degree that you embrace compassion in your life, change passes gracefully, with ease. For those who require proof, that proof is now available. For others, simply knowing that there is a direct relationship between emotion and DNA comes as welcome validation for an inner knowing that has driven the course of their lives for years.

THE SCIENCE OF COMPASSION

Following our definition of a science, if you do these things, then such-and-such will happen, clearly the ancients left to us a path. Today their path may be viewed as a science chosen to carry us gracefully through the Shift of the Ages. *Walk-*

Walking Between the Worlds

ing Between the Worlds is my offering of that science to you, the science of compassion. Our word for a sometimes nebulous state-of-being, compassion is feeling, thought and emotion within you allowing the 1.17 volt liquid crystal circuitry of each cell to align with the seven layered liquid crystal oscillator within your chest that we call "heart." Compassion, the result of coherent thought, feeling and emotion, is the program that you encode, determining your body's life giving response to the reference of earth's heartbeat.

Beyond simply feeling, compassion is the merging of feeling with emotion and directed thought made manifest as your body!

Offered to you within the context of twentieth century language, experience and relationships, *Walking Between the Worlds* is the rekindling of an ancient wisdom living within you. Compassion is the kernel of your very nature. The science is offered as a program of language and understanding as follows:

IF
you allow life to show you yourself in new ways
so that you may know yourself in those ways
AND
you reconcile within yourself that which life has
shown you
THEN
you become compassion.

It is within the very reconciliation, the coming to terms with whatever you have invited as life, that you become compassion. Deceptively simple, the understanding of life's mysteries has been the subject of controversy and debate for centuries. To what extremes have you taken yourself to know of the darkest of the dark and the lightest of the light? Clearly, the ancients tell you two things:

• That the events of your life serve you by allowing the opportunity of feeling and emotion through a broad range of experience: all of the "good" and all of the "bad."
• Further, there is a pattern to the order within which you will recognize the experiences: there is a sequence and a progression to the experiences.

The keys to compassion, then, lay in your ability to embrace all experience as part of the One without judgment. To live solely in the "light," shunning, ignoring, working against and judging anything other than light is to defeat the very purpose of your life in a world of polarity! It is easy to live in the light, if the light is all there is. You, however, have come to a world where light exists in union with its opposite.

Have you fallen into the ancient trap of deception where you may:
• see one aspect of polarity as better than another?

- believe that one aspect of our world of polarity is of something other than the creator?

I often hear of individuals who view themselves as spiritual warriors fighting the battle of light and dark, drawing the spiritual lines of war. This perspective is a path. Each path carries its consequence. Inherent in the perspective of battle lines lay judgment, the very hallmark of polarity.

There can be no battle without judgment.

In a world where we have come to experience and know ourselves in all ways, how can there be a "right" and "wrong" in the experience itself? It is the assignment of good, bad, light and dark as judgment that implodes unity into polarity. Is it possible that darkness is a powerful catalyst in our lives, similar to the viruses discussed earlier, catapulting us beyond polarity into an even greater technology born of compassion? Healing our sense of separation, *Walking Between the Worlds,* is the path of compassion. Again and again the ancient Essenes admonished us to remember the most sacred of all messages.

> *"...and this message was for the ears of man alone, they who Walk Between the Worlds of earth and heaven."*
> ADAPTED FROM THE ESSENE GOSPEL OF PEACE[9]

All too often, past discussions of the Shift of the Ages have focused upon the reality of the times prior to, and including, the day of the Shift. Quite possibly, you and I are the last generation to reach maturity before that day; the Shift of the Ages. I invite you to consider the implications. If true, then you and I are also the first generation to awaken on the other side of the Shift, in a world that has completed the purification as proclaimed in the indigenous and ancient traditions. With a clean slate of memory and consciousness, what becomes the foundation for our future memory? The state of being that you and I attain now, in these days, becomes the seed, the building block upon which we, and those who follow, will know themselves.

Do we love enough to change the cycles of polarity, rising above the judgment of light and dark to a place where all experience is viewed as creation knowing itself, experiencing the consequences of its own choice. Do we love enough to lay the foundation of compassionate wisdom, while still living in a world that has expressed polarity as hate, fear and judgment? Through compassion, you and I are offered guidelines for the manner in which we may conduct ourselves in response to life's daily offering. To follow in the footsteps of that path is a choice made consciously and intentionally. It is through compassion that we find within ourselves coherent emotion. This place is known as an experience of thought, feeling and time when our physical body *becomes* the peace, vitality and immunity that we have only imagined in the past.

The definition of a science has been offered above. The demonstration of the science may never be seen, due to a single factor-our element of time. If the ancient calendars are correct, if the momentum of the change and inertia of the effects remain intact, then we simply do not have the years to test and re-test, again and again, demonstrating to ourselves that their suggested course of action is in our best interest. Ironically, however, through the language of our own science we see the scenario unfolding precisely as it was mapped out for us, over six thousand years ago. Is it necessary to have a Shift of the Ages to nudge us into a lifetime of compassion?

PLEASE NOTE: As the resonant meaning of *Walking Between the Worlds* becomes a part of you, skillfully and masterfully you will create situations that ask you to demonstrate to yourself the level of that meaning in your life. Once you have read the words on these pages, you cannot un-read them. Once you have heard whatever the words mean to you through the filters of your life experience, you cannot un-hear.

Walking Between the Worlds offers a context and framework of order within which each moment of each day plays a powerful role toward preparing you to gracefully accept tremendous and accelerated change in your life. During this lifetime of Bodhisattva, in service to life through the eyes of compassion, your world can never look the same to you again. That difference is your gift to yourself and those that you love as you, with grace and intent, remember the Second Path and walk between the worlds of heaven and earth.

CHAPTER ONE

MYSTERY OF THE FORGOTTEN
OUR POWER OF FEELING

Plate II: *Bonsai Pine Tree*
Tibetan script represents Root, Beginning, Power

"A sudden gust of wind hit me at that instant and made my eyes burn. I stared toward the area in question. There was absolutely nothing out of the ordinary.

I can't see a thing," I said.

"You just felt it," he replied.

"What? The wind?"

"Not just the wind," he said.

"It may seem to be wind to you, because wind is all you know."

ADAPTED FROM *JOURNEY TO IXTLAN*
THE LESSONS OF DON JUAN, BY CARLOS CASTANEDA[1]

M EMORY IS A CURIOUS THING. SOMETIMES, THE DETAILS OF what seem like the most significant events of life fade within days. Often the events themselves are soon lost and forgotten within a few short years. I remember sitting on the shore of a river in the fall with my mother. The air was crisp and I was bundled in blankets and "big clothes." My mother and I were watching groups of young men rowing long narrow boats quickly through the water. The rhythm was so perfect, the motion so smooth, almost without a ripple in the water. I remember bouncing up and down on my father's shoulders as he walked down the winding staircase from our tiny apartment. There was a parakeet living in a cage on one of the staircase landings, just outside of Mrs. Wilkinson's apartment. She would watch me on days when my father was in school and mom had to work. As I recounted these early memories of childhood to my mother, she looked at me in disbelief.

"You could not possibly remember those days" she said in amazement. "Your father had just completed his service in the military and we had moved to Providence, Rhode Island where he was enrolled at Brown University. I would take you down to the river to watch the University Crew Team practice in the fall. You could not possibly remember that time, you were only a year and a half old!"

Memory is a curious thing for me because I do not remember many things following that time until nearly three and a half years later. At that time, within a few short weeks, two events would transpire that would forever change the course of my life. I don't remember the details leading up to that day. I don't recall thinking to myself,

On this day, I will create an experience for myself with such power that I may not survive. If I do survive, my life will never be the same.

On some level though, I must have known. If there was a knowing, it certainly was not a conscious knowing.

REMEMBER THIS FEELING

Two weeks earlier, on June 28, 1959, I had received a birthday gift; a battery operated train set. It was one of those Lionel™ specials, the whole train looked like a single engine. Electric power was fed to the train through a remote handset attached to the engine by about three feet of wire. I don't remember what I was thinking as I took the scissors from the kitchen drawer. They were mom's best; the big chrome plated kind that look as though they will cut through anything - even the wire attached to my new train set. As I severed the connection, I noticed in the cross section bared copper wire embedded securely in the rubber insulation. Again I took the scissors and began to trim the insulation from the wires. Once started, the process was easy. Within minutes I had two lengths of shiny copper wire in my hand. I was ready.

I placed the scissors neatly back in the kitchen drawer, believing that their role in the destruction of my new train set would remain my secret. Opening the screen door that led from our living room onto the front porch, I went directly to the power outlet that was situated just behind the door. What happened next I do remember, with a degree of clarity that amazes me to this day. Twisting the two wires together into one, I forced the stiff length of copper into one of the two openings in the outlet. Nothing happened. I immediately forced the other end of the length of copper into the second opening, pushing it back into the wall as far as it would go. Immediately, an array of flaming orange sparks sprayed from the outlet, showering my hands, arms and face with a searing heat. I did not feel any pain at first. For just a fraction of a second I could see the sparks in slow motion, each one scorching a little round point in the gray enamel that covered the deck. Then there was a light, a brilliant flash that seemed to come from inside of me, *inside of my head*. The flash was so bright that it blocked everything else. During that time, there was no sight, no thought, no memory and no feeling. The only sensation that I was aware of was the sound, an intense vibration that commanded my body, causing it to jerk and spasm uncontrollably. I could not let go of the wire!

Suddenly I found myself in what felt like another world. It was like the times when I would go to bed at night and begin to have the "feeling." Always a familiar feeling, it would begin with a tingling just before I would actually drift off in sleep. I would feel myself becoming small inside of my body. It was as if all of my awareness was being drawn from each cell of my body, recalled from all of the extremities, shrinking into a single point focused within my chest. Then, as that single compressed point of awareness, I would begin my dream without memory of transition. Expanding, I would become vast until I was everywhere and nowhere at once. I would wake up within this dream, losing all awareness of "me" in exchange for a sense of just being. The feeling was so familiar and felt so good that I would look forward to sleep each night to my time of waking up inside of my dreams.

I could no longer feel the vibration. In that moment, there was nothing. There was no sense of time or non time. There was no sense of "me" as a being, no awareness of myself as "I." There was no image of my hands being burned in the sparks, no feeling of the current shooting through my body. There was nothing, absolutely nothing. In the stillness of that moment a voice broke the silence, a voice that I would come to know and trust many times with my life, from that moment forward. The voice was neither male nor female and seemed to come from everywhere at once. Calmly and reassuringly the voice explained to me that the life that I had known within those first five years was "a gift of love," given freely and without expectation. For me to continue my life from that moment forward, however, would be a choice. In that moment, I was being asked to make that choice, the choice of "life" in this world or continuing the transition that I had begun to another world. The voice stated clearly, and calmly, "Do you choose life?" Without having to think I responded with a phrase that comes to me often, even to this day, nearly four decades later. From somewhere within me, another voice, my voice, cried out with all of the power that I could find. From inside of my mind, I screamed

"Life!"

"I choose life!"

Just as suddenly as it had begun, something grabbed me, a force that threw my small body backward away from the outlet. My back slammed into the protective rail bordering the porch. The sparks stopped as the copper wire dropped to the scorched deck. A searing pain shot through my body and I shook, uncontrollably, gasping. I could not think. I could not find a rhythm to my breath.

Looking back on that day, I know that the entire experience could not have lasted longer than a few seconds at most. At the time, it felt like the duration of forever and the quickness of a heartbeat, all in the same moment. I don't know how much time elapsed while I regained an awareness of myself. As I formed the cry for help in my mind, at first the words would not come out of my mouth; my mouth was open but my voice seemed paralyzed from the shock. I continued to scream in my mind until a sound began to emanate from my body. The sounds were definitely me, but something was different; they did not sound like me. From deep within my body each sound began to coalesce. Each sound was primitive and honest. Sheer will brought me to my feet as my body, and my screams, found the one person that I knew would be there for me. My mother looked at me, at my hands and arms, and in desperation pleaded over and over, "What's wrong?" "What has happened?" All that would come from my mouth were the screams. The entire event had lasted only seconds in the early afternoon.

A short while later, as I lay awake in my small bed reeling from the experience, I remember looking out of the window at the deep blue sky. A plane had entered my window view and disappeared from sight against the opposing pane. I remember thinking "Sky King," noticing that the engines sounded similar to those of the popular television program of that time. I also remember thinking to myself, "How strange that the sky should seem so blue!" Skies in the midwest typically held high amounts of moisture, creating a dull white haze, appearing slightly overcast, even on the clearest of days. My bed was nestled into one corner of the room. I had always felt safe there with one wall to my side and another behind my head.

Suddenly, without warning, I felt my head cradled gently in open hands. I knew that there was no one in the room. Tilting my head backward, my eyes rolled across the ceiling above me and down the wall behind to see a figure, a person, standing at the point where my headboard met the wall. The figure was coming from within the wall! Faint at first, as my eyes adjusted the image became clearer, though never solid. As the image moved behind my head, I could still see the wall. I was looking at the wall through this being. Several lengths of a deep maroon cloth were draped over the body, allowing only the hands to be exposed as the presence continued to cradle my head.

Without warning, a second figure appeared from the same place and moved from behind my head into the room next to me. Neither appeared distinctly male or female. At first, neither spoke. They began to touch my body in all of the places where I had been burned. I watched as their hands moved over my hands, then my arms. I noticed that my head and feet were to become the focus of the process, whatever the process was. As I lay between the two faintly visible beings, I opened and closed my eyes several times, squinting to clear and re-focus my vision. In doing so, the searing pain of my burns overwhelmed me and I began to cry. Opening my eyes once again, I noticed that the deep blue tint of the sky through my window had faded to the familiar milky white of midwestern overcast. At the same time, I could no longer see the beings at my head and feet, though I could still feel their bodies as they touched mine. In the words of a five year old, through the pain of the experience, I simply asked

How can I stop hurting?

How can I see you again?

For the first time, what was to become a familiar voice replied, reminding me, "Remember this feeling."

Hearing the words, immediately something within my body changed. From simply hearing the words something inside of me shifted. In that moment, my body no longer hurt. Through that shift, I could once again see the two beings whose voice would be there for me at crucial moments for the rest of my life. That day I learned something that would later become a pivotal experience in my life, allowing me to touch the lives of others. That something is this: Simply through shifting my feelings, I could shift the way that I saw the world around me!

I turned my face to look through the bedroom window. Once again the sky was deep blue, intense and clear. Something began to come over me. I became drowsy as the room faded from view. I closed my eyes again and began to slip into a dream, oblivious to the two beings that were comforting my body after the experience of just an hour or so before.

Our house was small and drafty. Mother used to call it a "Cracker Jack" house, a reference to the caramelized popcorn and peanut treats that used to come with a prize in each small, rectangular box. The house was one of a kind, situated in the center of a mobile home park that had grown around it in Raytown Missouri, a suburb of Kansas City. There was a swimming pool available for the tenants and guests of the mobile home park, and because we lived in the park, it was available to us also. With temperatures in the nineties and humidity levels usually not far behind, the swimming pool was a popular place for everyone, adults and children alike, during the summer months. Again, my memory is a curious thing. I do not remember much in the few short weeks between the experience with the copper wire and the events leading up to this day. My mother was with "the ladies," other women approximately her age at the pool side near the shallow end of the water. Many of the women had children and they, along with myself, would enjoy the cool, shallow water of the pool as their parents relaxed on the pool deck.

I do not remember thinking to myself that this was to be another day of adventure. I was stocky as a child, an emotionally painful condition for me that my parents playfully referred to as "husky." It was as a result of this degree of obesity that my body would experience an odd buoyancy in water. My thick little arms pulled my body from the shallow end of the pool up onto the hot concrete deck. I walked unnoticed to the far end of the pool, the forbidden deep end, and gazed at the bottom. The water appeared turquoise, although it must have been clear as I could see all the way to the bottom. I noticed the thick black lines indicating depth as they converged on the drain at the deepest part of the pool. Quietly I slipped into the water, without a splash, and as I let go of the pool's edge the momentum of my body weight in motion carried me quickly below the surface.

I do not remember thinking about holding my breath, the fact that the water was nine feet deeper that I could stand in and still touch bottom, or the fact that I could not even swim! I just slipped into the water, letting go of the side and continued, feet first, down into the depths of the pool. I opened my eyes and watched as my body slowed its descent. My feet began to rise behind me, until they were nearly level with my head. With my arms outstretched at my sides, I was floating just a few feet above the bottom of the pool when, without changing my position I began to rise, slowly, toward the surface. The entire experience had lasted only a few seconds until this point. I was in awe of the feeling. I had never experienced such physical freedom before. Slowly, my body stopped its drift upward. My buoyancy had brought me to resting place, just below the surface, hovering above the bottom. As I lay there motionless, arms and legs outstretched, staring at the dark lines below, I began to feel the familiar feeling. It was the feeling that I had experienced, just a few weeks before, as I had placed the copper wire into the power outlet and began the dream.

Having taken no breath since my body had slipped beneath the surface, strangely I did not feel the urge to breathe. I could not sense the cold around me or the chlorinated water that was filling my nose and lungs. I sensed nothing. Slipping into the feeling of my body becoming small, I closed my eyes and gave in to the urge to dream. Surrendering, in complete trust, I gave in to the experience and became drowsy.

In the darkness there was nothing, no feeling of having to be anywhere or do anything. There were no thoughts of what others at the pool were doing or what they would say or think if they saw me this way. There was no feeling of "me" as an individual. For the first time in my young life, I simply let go. As I drifted in this state of suspension, time became irrelevant. Seconds became minutes. What I was later told was approximately ten minutes, felt to me like the eternity of all there is.

The darkness of my closed eyes began to fade. Suddenly there was a brilliant flash and all that remained was light that I had seen just weeks before. From somewhere in that light, in the nothing, I heard a now familiar voice. It was the same voice that had been with me on the gray enamel porch to the house. The voice simply said

"Remember this feeling."

Upon hearing the voice, I began to shout, in my mind,

Life!

I choose life!

Suddenly, I felt hands grabbing me, pulling me by my legs and arms. Abruptly, I was jerked from the peace of the dream and thrust into the sunny world of a hot August day in Missouri. Arms embraced me, people were shouting. My chest and nose burned from the sting of chlorine and water. Someone had rolled me onto my side, forcing water from my mouth and nose. Amid my tears and the shock of what had happened, I coughed and sneezed at the same time. The force of water moving the wrong way made the abrasive water and chlorine in my sinuses worse. Opening my eyes, the first face that I saw was mom, there for me as she had always been. Everyone was asking questions; "Are you all right?" "What were you doing?" "What were you thinking?" "Are you all right?" Mom said nothing. She just stared at me, also with tears in her eyes, with that combined look of wonder and relief, glad that I was OK.

How can you explain an experience like this to someone who has never had the same experience? How can they relate to a voice that they have never heard? Knowing that I would not be able to share what had just happened, knowing that I was not completely certain myself, I wiped the tears from my eyes and apologized. This was only August. I wondered how many more adventures mom and I would experience before the end of summer.

FEELING: OUR FORGOTTEN PATH

It would not be until years later that I would completely realize the interrelated nature and true significance, of the two experiences in 1959. Within just a few short weeks in the summer of that year I had demonstrated to myself two keys that were to play a crucial role in my ability to experience, as well as convey, the body of information that would become my life and follow as this text. Each of the two experiences provided a reminder, a reference point, that was available and accessible at any time.

- The electrical experience had literally shocked me into a different reality; a world of clarity that allowed me to "see" that which is not often apparent in daily life. The experience had provided me with a feeling. In that feeling I could see those who had become present to care for me. In that feeling I could move beyond the physical pain of the electrical current shooting through my body and burning my hands and arms.
- The water experience had shown me clearly what it feels like to simply "let go." The experience had provided me once again with a feeling. This feeling was the feeling of utterly and completely surrendering to the

experience in complete trust without any thought of "when to get back" or "what will happen to me now."

Through each experience, I had demonstrated to myself that by simply feeling, intentionally feeling, I could shift my awareness to a very familiar place that provided astonishing clarity, comfort and guidance. In this place, I knew that I could trust what I heard, trust what I felt, and that information would come quickly; information that was to guide me on a path that was often clouded in my own emotion and the fear of those around me.

PLEASE NOTE: I am not suggesting that the experiences of electrocution and drowning are necessary to discover these feelings within yourself. Quite the contrary, my intent in offering these very personal experiences is to demonstrate that it is through the gift of emotion, the science of emotion, you have the ability to shift your focus in this world. Through emotion, you may tune your awareness to your world "within," as well as your external world of day to day. As you will discover in later chapters, emotion is the switch that triggers specific DNA codes within your body. These are the same codes that allow you the freedom to live without illness, disease and deterioration as you progress through linear time of your life. Inherent within your gift of life is the power that you have to regulate your body and the manner in which you express your life. That power is simply the power of emotion.

Looking back to July of 1959, I believe that the events of that summer were less of a teaching and more of a wake up call, a remembering. My experience has shown me that most individuals have a similar memory of feelings that propel them into clearer states of awareness. Their experiences may be remembered as feelings that have been compromised in the past, as a trade off for family acceptance or emotional survival. It is the experience of life itself that calls to us, asking us to remember.

CHAPTER TWO

THE BRIGHTEST OF THE BRIGHT

Two Becomes One

Plate III: *Mountains*
I Ching symbol represents The Darkening of the Light

*"Darkness and Light
are both of one nature,
different only in seeming,
for each arose
from the source of all."*

EXCERPT FROM
THE EMERALD TABLETS OF THOTH[1]

For years as a child I had questioned my conditioning in the concepts of dark and light, and what each of the forces meant in my life. I knew what I had been taught through school, church and family of the polarities between the two forces. I was taught to recognize the forces of light and dark in the outcome of an event and the effects of that event upon the lives of myself and those around me. Things that hurt were of the darkness and the joy of feeling good was born of the light. I felt that what I had been taught made little sense, as it did not apply to life as I had witnessed life. The teachings did not match my experience.

Inherent in the conditioning of darkness, for example, had always been the implied fear that *something is out there,* something horrible representing an extreme example of our most polarized memory. That "something" was so powerful that its very nature rivaled that of the opposite extreme, the light. If that were true, it meant that something out there, some force, had power over us, power over me.

Consistent in the teachings was the idea that this force was lurking, waiting for just the right time, just the right moment when, in a moment of weakness, all of the good that I had ever achieved could be taken away, negated from my life. I knew that I would have to reconcile myself within the context of that force at some point in my life.

JOURNEY TO LOST LAKE

My life had reached a point of convergence. It was one of those magical times where it appears as if all that you have ever known or held as true comes crashing down at once. I often refer to these times of focused shift as the Bulldozer of Change. The Bulldozer clears a path through life, flattening anything in its way, then backs up and comes through again, just to make sure that nothing is left standing. With little grace or finesse, the Bulldozer of Change cleared my diversions of school, romance, income and friendship, collapsing them within just a few weeks of one another into what appeared as the darkest moments that I had known at that time in my life. Within me was a suspicion that all of the events unfolding within my life were inseparably related to my choice to know, to feel, the relationship between good and evil. All that was occurring in my life was seen through my interpretation of these forces. And so it began...

I was attending college and working in Ft. Collins, Colorado at the time, struggling with a delicate balance between an overload of nineteen core level classes and three jobs to cover the expense of out-of-state tuition. Grades were plummeting, the jobs were exhausting, friendships became transparent and the most stable romantic relationship that I had known until that time in my life ended. I explained to all of my college professors and each of my employers, that I needed some down time to collect my life. Not to my surprise, neither the professors, nor employers shared my sense of urgency. I gave notice to the university and each of my employers, with an agreement to transition out of the positions over the next few weeks.

Packing what I felt that I needed for fall in the Rocky Mountains, I began driving West through one of the best kept secrets in Northern Colorado, the Cache la Poudre Canyon. Named after an outpost from the French explorers, the mouth of Poudre Canyon had served as a supply depot, complete with gunpowder (poudre) for those venturing West over the Rockies two hundred years earlier. Driving higher and higher, I eventually found myself in a small town ninety miles from Ft. Collins, Walden, Colorado. After talking with locals at the neighborhood market and service station, I was directed to a dirt and gravel turnoff leading into a wilderness area of glacial lakes and pine forests. This was a perfect place of seclusion for whatever was to happen over the next few days.

I found myself at one particularly beautiful lake, Lost Lake, as the sun had already begun to drop behind the snow capped peaks to the West. I set up my tent in the shadows on the soft pine needle floor of the forest, just a few feet from the banks of the lake. This was one of my favorite times of year, with the skies deep and intensely blue. Occasionally, massive and well defined clouds slid between me and the sun, throwing the entire lake into shadows for much of the time. I had chosen this particular area for the isolation and the privacy that it offered. At ten thousand feet in elevation, I packed in a tent, minimal food supplies, and water to last for one week. I had planned to supplement my supplies with wild food available in the area. I soon discovered that it was not the best plan.

I knew that to reconcile the forces of light, fear and darkness, I would first have to know each force for myself as my own experience, rather than those reported to me by someone else. As night fell on the first day, I built a fire for warmth and cooking. It was fall and the evening temperatures dipped well into the teens. Little did I know that the same fire I had built for heat would become the window for the experiences to follow. The first two days were spent settling in. I prayed, meditated, thought and prepared. I did not know what the outcome of the experience was to be. At the same time I was certain that something had to change. I could not continue my life with the prospect of a dark force of "undoing" lingering over each choice and every experience.

THE DREAM FIRE

On the third evening, the sun had set and the evening temperatures had begun to drop. The wind had stilled and there was an unusual calm that fell over my portion of the lake and the camp. Sitting on the upended stump of a log that I had placed next to the fire, I began my prayers. For each of the previous evenings, I had closed my eyes, meditating and praying as my training in my family and the martial arts had taught me. On this third evening, for some reason, I did something different. With my eyes wide open, I stared directly into the fire in front of me. The tip of each flame tapered to a point. From yellows and oranges into blues and violets, each flame eventually faded into the air above, the colors lost in the night's darkness as they moved away from the fire. The coals themselves throbbed in the heat with patterns of glowing blotches moving across the dark mass beneath them. Unknown to me at the time, I later learned that the indigenous peoples of the world often use fire to induce an altered state of awareness, an open eyed dream, with the coals providing a point of focus.

As I stared into the flames, something began to happen to my body. Waves of emotion began to ripple through me, from within me. The waves pulsed outward toward my extremities as I quickly recognized what was happening. Each wave carried with it a feeling, a familiar feeling that I had known many times throughout my life. These were the feelings that came from "letting go," the same feelings that had been demonstrated to me earlier in my life as a near death experience. In their familiarity, I was able to follow the feelings, without question, into a state of deep trust and surrender. I knew that moment had come to me as an opportunity. In that knowing, I posed the question that best encapsulated the purpose of my quest to Lost Lake. In the traditions of the ancient and forgotten ones, those who have come before us, I had often asked for a sign or guidance from the forces of the earthly mother and the heavenly father. On this night I simply began with a question.

Father, I ask for the wisdom to understand the relationship between light and dark and the role that each plays in my life. I stared into the flames, waiting. Nothing appeared to be happening. Again I asked the question. Suddenly, quite unexpectedly, a voice that came to me, from within me, a familiar voice asking me a question.

"How are you to understand the *relationship* between these two forces without knowing the *nature* of the forces themselves?"

In asking a question of this nature, I had expected an answer, not another question posed back to me. As the words reverberated throughout my body, it dawned on me, possibly for the first time, that I really had no first hand knowledge of the force that I had been conditioned to call "darkness." My concepts of this elusive power were the composite images of all that I had been taught, told, shown and conditioned to have.

Staring into the flames of the fire I drew upon that conditioning, calling to me in that moment every form that I could imagine representing the power of darkness. In the eye of my mind I could see the forms of hideous, grotesque and disfigured bodies. I saw my childhood Bible depicting layers of reality, defining the boundary line between the domain of darkness below and the world of above and all that is held as light in our world. I could see the images from churches, museums and galleries of cracked and faded paintings showing evil consuming all within its grasp and looking for more. I continued until I had conjured up, what for me in that moment represented the epitome of darkness embodied as the single form of one individual. I had been taught that the form I was seeing, the embodiment of all of those concepts, could only exist as the image of one who was called Lucifer, as well as a myriad of other names, each representing the polarity of darkness.

To be clear at this point, I am not suggesting to you that this image was a true reality to be reconciled in your life. I am simply describing to you one reality of my experience, a lens that was meaningful to me at one point in my life. My choice to look through the lens led me to a point of remembering a great truth that I believe lives within us all.

Though the memories were forming within the eye of my mind, something began to happen in the fire as well. As I stared without focus in my open eyed dream a form began to appear, suspended, floating in the tips of the flames themselves. Nebulous at first, the form began to solidify, to crystallize, in front of me. I turned my face away in disbelief. Blinking my eyes, I looked back into the fire. The image remained and grew clearer. There, floating in the tips of the flames, was the physical manifestation of the figure that had coalesced in my mind, a result of my request to know the nature of darkness! The face hovered and, fortunately, did not look directly at me. Rather, it stared into the sky to my right, as if either unaware of me or not acknowledging my presence. Even so, I could not look directly at the image and considered leaving the fire, quickly. I did not leave, however, and as I became accustomed to the figure, I did look at it directly. There the head and chest of a being lingered in the flames of the fire, allowing me to study the creases and the texture of the loose flesh that covered the face. I was fascinated by the opaque quality of the image, while at the same time, in awe of the experience. Throughout the entire time, my feelings were more akin to curiosity rather than a sense of fear. I felt no threat.

Suddenly, the head began to move, turning until the face stared directly at me. For the first time our eyes met. Hovering in the flames before me was a very real, conscious and intentional presence. The presence was definitely there and it was definitely focused on me. As I stared into the eyes of this being, the epitome of all of the evil that I could conjure up for myself in the moment, something even more unexpected began to happen. The expression of the face began to shift. The change was subtle at first, becoming more and more pronounced. The hideous creases and gross texture were softening before my eyes. The face grew rounder and younger as the creases fell away. The entire image began to change from the discolored, creased and loose flesh of, what for me, was the image of Lucifer into something very different. Within the space of a few seconds, hovering in front of me within the flames was another face, the face of a very young child. Neither male nor female, the innocence of the face was betrayed by a power of wisdom, a power that can only come from "knowing." I sensed a longing, almost a plea, for me to understand.

The child looked at me, directly into my eyes. I stared, motionless watching in disbelief as something magical began to happen, something that I feel to this day each time that I share this story.

The child in the flames began to cry.

Huge tears rolled from its eyes, down the curve of the cheeks and I found myself in tears also. An unexplained sadness swept over me and I felt a strange sense of kinship with the child in the flames. Without the words to justify my emotions, I knew that this experience, and this being, had touched an ancient memory from somewhere deep inside of me. I also felt, that somehow this experience would be key in my choice to heal the separation that I had known, that we have felt for so long. The image began to fade from view and I knew that I was waking up from the open eyed dream. I glanced around my camp, across the darkness of the lake in front of me and at the cloudless sky above. According to my watch, nearly thirty minutes had passed. Everything around me looked the same. I knew from that night on, however, that my life could never be the same. I remember that night often, and refer to it as the night that I saw Lucifer cry.

REVELATION IN PERU

It was not until eighteen years later that the final portion of this experience would occur and I would fully understand the gift of that night on Lost Lake. At last, nearly thirty five years after my near death experiences, the message would be complete. Apparently, for myself and the way that my life has unfolded, the years and experiences between 1959 and 1994 were necessary to position the building blocks that I was shown into a meaningful framework. Following the completion of each life initiation, the very act of resolution signaled to creation that I was available for the next experience. Deep in the experience, trapped within the emotion, it is not always easy to see how each relationship, every feeling and thought has led to a particular situation. I believe that our lives work in that way if we have the wisdom to see the continuity of experience over long periods of time. For me, it took thirty five years of experience before I was able to recognize, and yet another year before I could even begin to express what follows.

It was in the Spring of 1994, that my experience of Lost Lake found completion. The month of June signaled the beginning of what the locals call the "dry season" in the high Andes Mountains of Peru. During the third day of a four day trek, my group of twenty two hikers, five Peruvian guides doubling as cooks and twenty two porters, would cover approximately seven and one half Peruvian mountain miles. Crossing over three mountain peaks above twelve thousand feet, we would descend from each pass into the lush, green cloud forests three thousand nine hundred feet below in preparation for the ascent on the next pass. The evenings had been well below freezing and my goal was to get each of the trekkers into camp and warm, dry clothes before the temperatures dropped dangerously low. We had just become aware that during the same time one year previously, two of the porters supporting a similar trek had died after the second day, having frozen to death sometime during the night. Wet clothes and sub-freezing temperatures are ideal components for hypothermia, a condition in which the body loses heat faster than it is able to generate heat.

Though we had acclimated for five days, illness and altitude had weakened some of the hikers. Our group has essentially split into two groups, separated by several miles, each being led by expertly prepared Peruvian guides and porters into a camp with warm tents, hot meals and tea awaiting them. Hiking through the morning hours with the lead group, we arrived at a temporary lunch camp with freshly prepared meals of fresh bread, avocados and tomatoes. Following a light meal, I chose to double back, checking on the distance and conditions of the second group. They had been joined by a Peruvian holy man who, along with our guides, would accompany them into camp. Satisfied that they were together and in good hands, I headed back toward the first group, already well on their way into the evening camp.

As I climbed the steep, rocky trail I looked toward the summit of the pass above, and glanced down the talus slope behind me. Suddenly, I realized that for the first time since we had left Miami six days earlier, I was alone; absolutely and completely alone. As I neared the pass, I paused briefly to immerse myself in the sheer beauty of this land. Although there were still several hours before dusk, the sun was already dipping behind the peaks towering over the valley below. We would all be hiking in shadows soon. Directly below me was a glacial lake that I had not noticed before, like a perfect crystalline mirror, reflecting the high peaks that surrounded me. The rich and intense colors surrounded me in all directions. Deep emerald green jungles below supported the snow capped peaks jutting into that intense, blue and crystal clear sky that we always thought photographers somehow doctored up for the magazines. A gentle breeze brushed my face, welcome relief from the howling winds that had ripped through the valleys just hours before.

Silently, I gave thanks for the opportunity to experience such raw beauty as I completed the short distance to the saddle of the pass. With the top just a few feet away, I paused sitting on a smooth rock that looked like it was made for just that very moment. I had carried a wooden Native American flute from New Mexico to accompany our group prayers and meditations. This pass felt like a perfect opportunity to offer a melody of thanks. I pulled the flute from its protective cover and offered long, slow notes. Quickly, each flowed into the deep, resonant tone of a melody coming from somewhere within me. It was a melody that I had never heard before. The notes echoed from the rocks in front of me as the wind carried them away. I remember wondering if the others could hear my song. They later said that they did not. I began to breathe deeply, inhaling the sensations of one of the purest places on earth.

Suddenly, quite unexpectedly, I felt tremendous waves of emotion surging through my body, pulsing from my chest outward. The pulses grew stronger and the waves more intense. Tears welled up in my eyes and I found myself crying uncontrollably in long, deep sobs of appreciation for this moment of sheer beauty. As I wept in the experience, I noticed a shift in my body. Once again, it was the *feeling,* surrounding me, engulfing me in the warmth of surrender and allowing. This was the feeling, the familiar feeling, from Lost Lake seventeen years earlier. Though I had often created the feeling willingly, this feeling was simply happening, quite spontaneously.

One of the reasons for offering this four day trek as part of the Sacred Journey to Peru, is for the pure physicality of the experience. The effort exerted to complete this journey takes so much energy, that there is nothing left to stand between each participant and his or her emotions. There is nothing left to hold the "walls" of distance, distraction and indifference in place. The trekkers are supposed to get in touch with themselves through a direct and intimate experience with creation. Now, the very experience that I had intended for the other hikers was happening to me, there on a thirteen thousand foot pass, unplanned and un-orchestrated.

As the familiar feeling surged through my body I closed my eyes and experienced the connection, the absolute and complete resonance with the creative forces that have always been there for me. In the days prior to leaving for Peru, and throughout the journey, there had been a question that I had chosen to resolve. The question embodied a core understanding vital to the very process of my life. In the space of this acceptance and loving resonance, once again I asked the question.

Father, I ask for the wisdom to know of the relationship between the forces of light and dark. Please guide me to understand the role of these forces within my life so that I may know of their resolution.

The wind picked up and began to dry the tears that had fallen into my beard. As I wiped the salt from my eyes, I perceived a voice, a familiar voice that I had heard many times before. Again, the voice was neither male nor female, was from nowhere specifically and everywhere at once, and began with a single question, to me.

"Do you believe in me?"

Without thinking, my body responded with a mental yes. The voiced asked again.

"Do you believe that I am the source of all that you know and all that is your experience?"

There was no need to think or ponder the answer. I had affirmed many times before in prayer my belief in the single source of creation, the fundamental vibration, the seed tone of the standing wave that allows the hologram of life's patterns. Without thinking, once again my body responded with a mental yes. The voice echoed its reply.

"If you believe in me, and you believe that I am the source of all that is, then how can you believe, at the same time, that anything of your experience is other than me?"

Upon hearing the words, a tremendous sense of resolution filled my body. Though a part of me had always known what the words had just offered, for the first time, I felt the wisdom of that truth. My body actually felt the knowing. Of course there were still the words of light and dark in my vocabulary. Those words would never mean the same thing to me again. Specifically, the conditioned belief that darkness is a force, unto itself, a fundamental power, in opposition to and separate from all that is good, no longer held any truth.

Each of us is asked to reconcile the force of darkness each day of our lives through the direct experience of one of darkness' many derivatives. Fear, anger, rage, hate jealousy, depression, control issues, violation are each expressions of darkness playing out in our modern lives. In that moment, through the tool of my own logic, I was offered the opportunity to recognize darkness for what it is rather than what my conditioning had taught me. I was able to see darkness as a portion of the whole, a part of the source of all that is, rather than a fundamental force to contend with.

"If you believe in me, and you believe that I am the source of all that is, then how can you believe, at the same time, that anything of your experience (including darkness) is other than me?"

Through our perceived polarity of darkness and light, we have the opportunity to view ourselves from a different perspective, a necessary perspective, if we are to know and master ourselves in all ways.

The entire event had occurred in less that fifteen minutes. In less time than it would normally take to eat a meal, at an elevation of thirteen thousand feet in the Peruvian Andes, I had felt an experience that would forever change the way in which I approached the collective perceptions of light and darkness. This mountain top experience demonstrated to me, through my own logic, that darkness and light are not two distinct and separate forces at odds with one another. Rather, each represent a portion of *precisely the same whole,* the same source of all that is. Darkness as well as light, must be embraced without judgment as a part of creation, rather than a rival and renegade power outside of the One of all that is.

This subtle yet powerful realization propelled me into a dizzying chain of "if-thens." I recalled all of the times that I was taught, asked to hate the darkness. I remembered just months earlier listening intently as a minister in Southern California asked his congregation to hate the powers of darkness and Lucifer. I will ask you the same question that I then asked myself.

IF
darkness, and the family of darkness are a part of the One,
THEN
How can a being of compassion hate a part of the One?

As I stood up on the rock, there was still no one behind me as yet. Moving up over the pass I began the long trek down into the valley below. I could see no one in front of me. I was still alone. Though I was in the shadows, the temperatures were unusually warm. They had not yet begun to drop. I immersed myself in the solitude and followed the loose rocks on the trail that would lead me into camp. We would all be hiking in the dark that night.

THE FORGOTTEN ACT OF COMPASSION

What follows, previously has been offered in the privacy of a workshop or seminar, in an environment where I am able to look into the eyes of each participant and find the words that are meaningful in that room, in that moment. I can feel their feelings to know if they have heard what I offered, rather than the words that their past may have conditioned them to hear. Through these pages, I can not look into your eyes. I can not feel you as you read the word patterns that I am about to offer. For what follows I trust in the process of group memory, our memory, as it unfolds between us. From you, I ask for patience if my words are not your words. By their very nature, the words of our language are limiting, serving as approximations of the message behind the words. Please search within yourself for the message and intent underlying the words that follow.

You may find what I offer next to be in direct opposition to all that you have been conditioned to understand about light and dark in Western traditions. You may also discover that the words stir something deep inside of you, an ancient knowing that feels right, safe and good to remember. It may well be that each experience, of every lifetime, the lessons of all of your spiritual forbearers has paved the way to the moment of this understanding. This may be your opportunity to heal your sense of separation!

I will begin with a question to you. In your many years and many modes of education, who have you been told that Lucifer, the holder of all evil was and is?

When I ask this question in the seminars, though the answers vary in wording, each usually expresses a common theme. We are taught, primarily through the Biblical texts, that Lucifer was originally an angel. The answers then become even more specific. He was not just any angel. He was an *Archangel*, the Brightest of the Bright and the highest of the high. A being of such brilliance, wisdom, love and power that he sat at the "hand of god," unequaled and without peership. My next question demonstrates where the confusion begins.

What happened to Lucifer? What caused this most powerful and brilliant of beings, The Brightest of the Bright, to change his position from the highest of high and end up as the lowest of low?

To answer this question is to understand the power and the role that fear has played within each of our lives throughout this evolutionary cycle of experience. Within many western traditions today, the name of Lucifer is synonymous with that of the Devil and Satan. The modern Biblical text uses these names nearly interchangeably in the discussions of the beings of power that became "lost," falling from the graces of heaven in the eyes of our creator. Prior to this time, however, the name of Lucifer, from the Hebrew name of "light giver," is not associated with the concept of "fallen angels" or Satan at all!

Interestingly, this connection was not made until the twelfth century A.D. It was at this time, through what I see as a well intentioned error in translation that Lucifer and Satan were treated as one in the same. Detailed by Andrew Collins in the book, *Templar Legacy & Masonic Inheritance within Rosslyn Chapel,* the error may have come from an interpretation of the Biblical book of Isaiah.

"How art thou fallen from heaven, O Lucifer, son of the morning"[2]

According to Collins, Biblical scholars are in agreement that this is a reference to the king of Babylon at the time, Nebuchadnezzar, known as "The Morning Star." Collins goes on to say that the term "Lucifer" is believed to have been a name given both to the king as well as the Morning Star, Venus. Prior to this time there was a powerful distinction between the two in origin, purpose and mode of earthly expression. According to the pre-twelfth century texts, Satan also had been an angel, although not an archangel of the highest order. Through an obscure series of events, Satan and a band of followers, became lost in the experience of physicality, carnal knowledge and density, straying from the position of "light holder" to something of an anomalous renegade. He was banished from the "highest places" and would spend the remainder of his days in the experiences that he tampered with through his misguided deeds.

This is not the case with Lucifer. Herein lives a powerful distinction.

Within the context of a world in polarity, the ancient texts tell us that the stage for our cycle of existence was set as the anchoring of two extremes, two polarized extremes of precisely the same whole. Those extremes are represented as the lightest of the light and the darkest of the dark, both as aspects of the same One. Historically, there is agreement as to who the force is that anchored the light. The texts say that a powerful representative of the light, also sitting at "the hand of the One," Archangel Michael offered to hold the patterns of light for the duration of this cycle of human experience. He chose this task as a visible demonstration of his love for the earth, and those whose courage would bring them to this earth. He, along with his legions, remains with us today as a force anchoring the lightest of the light, serving as a mirror reflecting to us whatever light we choose to offer this world through our lives. He anchors the greatest possibilities of light so that we may know ourselves in light and in that knowing, see ourselves in all ways.

The "light" is one polar extreme, one of the two binary possibilities of this earthly experience. Who anchors the opposite extreme? Perhaps even a better question is "Who would want to?" What being could be so powerful as to anchor the darkest of the dark as the other end of the polar spectrum? What being has the power, tempered with wisdom, love and compassion to hold that anchor without the legions of others, offering himself to this task of "love made visible," for nearly 200,000 years? What being of strength could possibly hope to survive in the polarity of darkness for the duration of this earthly cycle? Cut off from all those that he had known, loved and cherished, what being would have a prayer of surviving without becoming lost in the experience?

With these questions in mind, lets return to my experience of Lost Lake, and the mountain pass in Peru. What happened in those experiences? Why are they so important today? Following is what I believe I was offered as a single experience drawn out over a period of seventeen years. I believe that in my asking, I was shown an ancient truth regarding the worlds of light, dark, good, evil and life.

- I saw that the force of darkness, Lucifer, is here as the result of an intentional choice, rather than the result of an accidental "fall" from a previous state of grace.
- That the Archangel Lucifer has lived among us for nearly 200,000 years, for the sole purpose of "anchoring" the extreme polarity of darkness, because you and I have asked for that polarity to find our strength.
- Using the power attained by becoming the highest of the high and the Brightest of the Bright, Lucifer holds our mirror of dark experience so that you and I may know ourselves in darkness, as well as in light. In the knowing, we find the power within ourselves as our truest nature of compassion. Where is the challenge of living compassionately in the

light, when all that exists is light? It is light, referenced to dark, that draws from us our truest nature for our very survival.

Is it possible that the Archangel Lucifer, in perhaps one of the greatest acts of compassion ever witnessed in our ancient memory, willingly gave and continues to give of himself as our personal mirror of darkness *because he loves us that much?* To find our balance we must know our extremes. Who holds those extremes? Is possible that, in his unconditional love for us, Lucifer has immersed himself into the very opposite of all the light that he had attained, to hold that possibility for us so that we may know ourselves in all ways? Could Archangel Lucifer love us that much?

This is precisely the scenario that I believe we are living. Somewhere in the murky depths of our group ancient memory, we remember the love of a being, a friend with a power beyond our knowing. We remember a being of such compassion that he willingly and intentionally left us and the form that we had always known him in. In his choice to serve us, through a love never before demonstrated, he immersed himself among us as that part of our consciousness that we would shun, judge, hate and kill for. Some force had to do it. Some power had to anchor the opposite of all that we would ever know as light so that you and I could find our power in a world where we choose our course of action in each moment. Those choices are where we find our greatest strength. In those moments of choice you and I remember our truest nature.

What I will say next I feel with equal portions of certainty and clarity. In my vision beside Lost Lake in 1977, I saw the face of Lucifer transform into the face of a very young child. As I looked into the eyes of that child, I saw the child cry and felt a tremendous sadness fill my body. I believe that the sadness was the remnant of a memory from Lucifer as well as myself. I believe that my memory is a portion of a greater group memory. Lucifer showed me his truest nature, the purity and innocence in which he, as well as you and I, began our earthly experience over 200,000 years ago. In the very nature of the experience itself, each of us has innocently given huge portions of ourselves away, loosing ourselves to the callousness and hardness that has resulted from our "hurts" upon earth. Now, our lives are asking that we call those fragments to us so that we may once again know ourselves in wholeness.

Lucifer showed me himself, trusting me to see and remember his innocence. As I saw him cry, I felt his loneliness. I sensed his loss and the separateness that he has endured for over 200,000 years. I believe that he is pleased to see our cycle nearly complete. I believe that he is tired and wants to come home. I sense that we all feel his longing for home to some degree. Lucifer's home and our home are one and the same! It is our quest to find our home that asks us to fill the perceived void of separation. Filling that void drives us to seek wholeness in one another as we recognize reflections of ourselves through our relationships. Each time we are "left" or abandoned in a relationship, loss of a job or someone that we hold dear, our ancient sadness of separation is mirrored once again.

Lucifer and darkness are not out to "get" you, lurking at every turn of life choice. Rather Lucifer is committed in service to you, through your growth, as you experience the consequence of choices that take you from life giving and light giving experience.

Darkness is just as much a part of us as light. Lucifer is just as much a part of us as Michael, and we are all part of the same creator that brought us here eons ago so that we may know our strength as compassionate beings of non-judgment. Archangel Lucifer, Archangel Michael, our creator and you and I are all part of One, nothing is separate. They trusted that we would remember.

From this perspective, Lucifer as the Archangel is a benevolent power in service to you as the great mirror of your own darkness, just as Michael mirrors your personal quest into your own light. It may very well be that Lucifer, as well as Michael, in the very act of offering themselves to us for 200,000 years, demonstrated the primal acts of compassion that would became the living bridge for each being that would ever choose to follow.

How does this feel to you?

How does it feel when you read the words suggesting that the Master of darkness, Archangel Lucifer, *loves you?*

Will you allow yourself to believe that darkness is an aspect of love? An ally of your growth? For some, the words are so foreign to their frame of reference that they immediately dispute the offering, citing all of the ills, wars, disease and horrors of the world and Lucifer's darkness as the cause. Certainly these things exist. To ignore them is to shun a reality that faces each of us in each moment. This is precisely the point. Darkness, and each of its derivatives, are a part of our experience. Fear, anger, hate, incest, jealousy, depression, control, judgment, suspicion, denial, pain, death, illness, disease and the myriad descriptors of the very things most would least choose to experience in life are rooted in our perception of darkness. Is it possible that our perception of darkness, and its many and varied expressions, are rooted in obsolete assumptions based in poor translations of an ancient text seven hundred years ago?

This is the scenario that I believe we are experiencing now, in these days, in this lifetime. There certainly may have been a time in our history when it served us to view evil as a grotesque devil with saggy skin, scaly arms and legs and an appetite for the human flesh of those who have strayed from the path. This viewpoint, in its simplicity, may have served us for those hundreds of years, providing a yardstick by which to measure the qualities, deeds and actions of others. In the measuring we would know how best to relate to them.

It may have served us so well that we are now at the point where we are asking ourselves to move beyond the very conditioning that has carried us here.

I believe that we have moved beyond our conditioning. We have created a society of externally based technology; machines that mimic the very processes of life. Through this external mirroring, we are reminded of our physical nature. Society asks that we reconcile this tremendously sophisticated life view with a "light" and "dark" scenario that originated hundreds of years ago from what quite possibly was an inaccurate assumption to begin with. Is it any wonder that the worlds of external and internal technology appear mutually exclusive? Now we seek to develop an internal, spiritually based technology mirroring the reality of light and dark. We are asked, by virtue of our lives, to redefine what "dark" and "light" mean to us and live that new truth.

ALLOW FOR THE POSSIBILITY

We have spent countless lifetimes, and years within this one, driving darkness from our lives, killing the darkness that surrounds us, with little success. Creation's law of energy explains why.

Energy follows attention.

Those who hate darkness focus their attention on the war, disease and illness, for example, and they see the energy of conflict, disease and illness everywhere. Is that a surprise?

The question is, "Where do these things come from?" Where does the technology to create tools of war, viruses of control and the torturous methods of fear-based control come from?

The answer often elicits a shocking silence resulting from the truth of a deep inner knowing. We have created these things. Perhaps not you and I personally. Rather the consciousness that we are part of. We are part of the horrors, as well as the joys of this world and we must own that responsibility. There is no one else "out there." There is no "them"!

The way to avoid the power of darkness is by making choices in life that do not require the service of darkness. Stating this to the positive, we may say "To embrace a life of light, choose light, while allowing for the possibility of light's polarity." Choosing light, while compassionately allowing for light's opposite expression is key toward our mastery of compassion. In the choice lay a level of responsibility, reclaiming the personal power of trust while living in the polarity. This distinction is deceptively subtle, yet powerful.

To experience light in your life, allow for the possibility of darkness, as well as light.

It is through our darkness that we know of our light. To deny the existence of darkness and the role of dark forces in service to the One is to perpetuate the very thinking that has veiled us in our myth of separation! In your allowing, make choices that will not require the services of the dark forces. This is not to say that you will not be witness to other's expressions of darkness. Their darkness does not have to become your experience. Hating Lucifer and blaming others for fear and dark experience provides just the opposite effect to that intended. Throughout history, our true Christs and reference beings have never asked us to hate anything as a way of life.

Rather, we have each been given the opportunity to hate, complete with the wisdom to transcend our hate, becoming something greater in the completion than we are in the polarity of the experience. That wisdom is the science of compassion.

To the degree that you "give in" to the urge to polarize an experience, to judge it as good or evil, to that degree do you perpetuate the illusion of separation! This choice is no longer a question of right or wrong. Now you make the choice of wholeness or separation.

The holographic mirror assures that you will experience that which you judge, that which you have a charge on. We have been conditioned to view the world, and life, through the eyes that mirror separation; right, wrong, light, dark, good and evil.

How may you reach wholeness in separateness?

Allowing darkness is not a condoning of what darkness offers. Allowing darkness is not agreeing with the effects of dark forces or an invitation of non action in the face of atrocity and injustice. Allowing darkness does not mean that you have chosen darkness in your life.

At this point in our discussion, allowing simply indicates that we acknowledge the existence of darkness as a force in service to us. Darkness, anchored by the Archangel Lucifer, is there in service to those who choose, knowingly or unknowingly, to have its experience. The allowing signals your willingness to rise above the illusion of separation as a being of compassion.

What happens if we change our obsolete conditioning? What happens if we remember to view the events of life for what they are, catalysts moving us into new experiences of ourselves, without good or bad, right or wrong? What happens if darkness is re-defined as a powerful form of love, compassionately gifted to us in a way that has not been clear, in the past? What happens if you are able to sit with your children and those that you love, watching the six o'clock news, and you begin to "see" through new eyes?

What happens is this: It is impossible to hate and fear if you allow for love in darkness.

During the *Zero Point* workshops, the discussions of Lucifer, Michael, good and evil generally finish sometime Sunday morning before lunch. Many hotels in large cities use ballroom or conference facilities to host the Sunday services from local churches or religious organizations. These services are complete with choirs, sermons and after service brunches. One particular Sunday at a hotel in Southern California, our workshop shared a common wall with such a service offered by an inner city congregation. Having just completed the stories of my open eyed dream at Lost Lake and the trek in Peru, our group was ready for a short break. I had just asked them to consider the possibility that the power of Lucifer was a benevolent power that loved them, rather than a vengeful power that wanted them.

Leaving our conference room, I passed the adjacent congregation and noticed that their door was ajar. I stopped to listen to the message of the minister to his people and was in awe, though not surprised by what I heard. Just as I was listening, the minister said to his people,

"If anyone tells you that Lucifer loves you, turn and run, for that is the work of the devil and the devil hates you!"

As I had not listened to the entire sermon, there is a good chance that what I heard was out of context. Even so, I was amazed at the synchronicity. There in that hotel, separated by approximately six inches of sheet rock, wood and insulation were two groups of people discussing the same concepts from two polarized viewpoints. I remember thinking to myself,

Somewhere in heaven, the powers that be are sitting at the big table in the sky, watching us this morning and rolling with laughter.

A few minutes later I found myself standing next to the minister of the congregation in the mens room and spoke with him briefly. If only those white, porcelain urinals could talk! From this brief encounter, I honestly believe that the words he offered to his congregation were heartfelt and what he believed would best serve "his people" in their offering. Living in the inner city, they very well may have been precisely the words necessary for each of those people at that point in their lives to keep them alive long enough to consider other viewpoints.

I also know, from a very deep place within myself, that what I had offered in our workshop was heartfelt and precisely what I believed would best serve our participants in the days and months to come in their lives. Two views, neither right nor wrong, separated by a six inch wall and two rooms full of very well intentioned people. These are the times that we live in; dwindling polarities of a closing cycle.

In our choice to know ourselves in all ways, we have explored all possibilities of extremes, taking our experience to the depths of darkness as well as the heights of lightness. Lucifer has simply held the mirror in place, anchoring the most extreme possibilities so that you and I could know ourselves as we approached his extremes. He serves us by holding the mirror, reflecting back to us that which we choose to explore in our lives. If you choose to have "no darkness" in your life, then do not become darkness. Without the charge, there is nothing to attract darkness to you.

You have the opportunity to transcend the polarities of light and dark by embracing them as equal expressions of the force that brought you here. You are asked to transcend light and dark while you still live within light and dark! Compassion is the key that was left to you to accomplish your task.

Will you remember? Will you call to you the fragments of your awareness, possibly shattered in your innocence through the very act of life itself? Will you allow yourself, as the sum total of all of your fragments of belief, feeling and emotion, to once again express from the compassion that brought you to this world? This is the opportunity that you behold at this crossroads of your life. Do you choose the living path of internal technology expressed as compassion?

I experienced childhood in the midwest with what I would consider to be relatively traditional western values. These values included nebulous concepts of light, dark, good and evil. I believe that these values were offered to me as well intentioned guidelines for my response to whatever life held in store for me. Additionally, I felt then and now understand that many of the traditional concepts, having served each of us for thousands of years may no longer serve us.

Through direct life experience I have witnessed individuals cling relentlessly to outdated concepts of darkness and light. In doing so they remain entrenched in the very experiences that they so long to overcome. Their hearts cry for love, nurturing, compassion and oneness, while their belief-driven actions are born of judgment, hate, and separation. These qualities of emotion are the hallmarks of a dark polarity. Oddly, when faced with applying their view of life to their own experiences, they will tell you that their belief systems no longer make sense. Perhaps even more odd, is that they have forgotten that their choice of feeling and action is their living demonstration of life's mastery. Without knowing precisely why, these individuals create life experiences that remind them that energy follows attention.

In the redefinition of darkness and its many forms, lives the opportunity to remove the charge from the patterns that we least choose to experience. The significance of compassion and the role that compassion may play at this time in our history becomes clear. You, the last generation to mature before the time that the ancients called the Shift of the Ages, you with the power to create through thought and emotion   you are asked to call upon your power and do something that has been the goal of every generation of spiritual forbearers until this time.

I find it interesting how something that has served so well at one point in life, may no longer serve in the same capacity at another time within the same life. I believe with all of my heartfelt being, that we are living precisely this scenario; old beliefs of polarity are no longer serving us. As I witness the events unfolding about each of us, on a daily basis, I see lifetimes of expansion and exploration struggling to know themselves within the confines of an ancient belief system that no longer fits. From the perspective of consciousness, you and I were children 3,500 years ago, longing to know ourselves. The rules and guidelines of that time served us well, allowing us to live long enough to reach this point in history, today, where we may transcend the rules and guidelines. As we know, we lose our innocence in exchange for the wisdom of experience.

Our group wisdom beckons to us to rise above the old conditioning that has asked us to hate and kill that which does not conform. Our group wisdom is asking us to become something greater in our totality than we have been as splinters and fragments of a lesser truth. We have outgrown the images, myths and concepts of a paradigm that is giving way to something vast, whole and all encompassing. While I suspect that you feel this truth somewhere within your being, seeing it written is a powerful catalyst that validates your feeling, allowing you to move forward in life's offering.

In workshop and seminar situations I have witnessed the impact of the previous stories upon the lives of those who have trusted enough to listen. I invite you to follow in their paths, allowing yourself to become a living bridge to those that you love the most and hold most dear. If these stories are meaningful to you in any way, fear and its derivatives of anger, hate, jealousy and judgment in your life can never mean the same thing to you again.

Are you willing to do something new?

Will you allow yourself to change the old cycles, redefine obsolete conditioning and create a new paradigm in the process? If you are living in these days, then not only are you willing, very probably this is your purpose as you remember the compassion that allows you to gracefully *Walk Between the Worlds*. Please join me in an experiment with the written word, as the resonant patterns of this writing awaken within you one of our most ancient group memories, the memory of the part of us that we call Brightest of the Bright.

CHAPTER THREE

THE SCIENCE OF COMPASSION
Our Second Path

Plate IV: *Bamboo*
Sanskrit symbol represents Jewel of the Lotus Descends Into the Heart
Spoken as the Mantra of Compassion, OM Mani Padme Hum

"... the most difficult [task] of all

Is to think the thoughts of the angels,

To speak the words of the angels,

And to do as angels do."

THE ESSENE GOSPEL OF PEACE[1]

As individuals, and as a nation, we have been asked to reconcile violence and hatred within our families and neighborhoods, as well as that of other nations as they define their limits of respect for human life. In 1994 for example, possibly during the six o'clock news over an evening meal, we had the opportunity to witness approximately ten thousand indigenous people lying dead along the rural roadsides of Rwanda, the victims of repressed forces making themselves heard. Our only view of this event was through the bias of the media that brought us the pictures. We may never know what really transpired in Rwanda during that time.

ANCIENT PROMISE: MODERN SCIENCE

More recently, we watched with horror the tragedy of TWA flight 800, the outbreaks of the deadly Hantavirus and AIDS viruses, the bombing of a Federal Building in Oklahoma, a U.S. Marine base in Saudi Arabia, and numerous instances of terrorist, group and individual acts of violence for no apparent reason. Beyond the differences of expression, there is a common "thread" that runs through each of these occurrences. In each instance, many people have lost their lives and we are asked to make sense of the loss within the context of our lives. How may you and I deal with the horrors that we experience? How can we reconcile the shock that our instant information technology brings directly into our living rooms? Inherent in the answer to this question is the opportunity of this lifetime. In witnessing events that push our beliefs and senses to the edge of who we believe that we are, we are offered the opportunity to awaken the strength of our truest nature, gracefully leading us to the memory of ourselves.

Within the hearts of the children of forever lives the seed
that each planted for themselves long ago;
a gift of truth;
sleeping...

> Awakened, that seed rekindles the ancient promise
> of those who have come before us;
> the promise that each soul survives the "darkest" moments of life,
> to return home once again, intact and with grace.
> That Promise is the seed of truth that we, today, have named compassion.
> You are the children of forever.

Within you lives a seed kernel of memory, intact, whole and as new as the day of your birth. This kernel has remained untouched by any experience, any feeling or emotion, of any lifetime. Safe, nestled within protective layers of awareness your promise has been with you always, patiently awaiting the moment that you would remember and call it forth in service to you once again. Your memory kernel will not be revealed to you as a physical expression of muscle and tissue. Deep within you, "X" and "Y" coordinates will never betray the location of your seed to the scrutiny of a scientist or an engineer.

Beyond technologies based in space and time, you may consider your seed as a place in thought without time. Your seed is accessed by the power inherent within you that carries you through the portals of creation. You knew that you would find this seed inside of yourself someday. Perhaps you have felt it lingering, stirring "in there," calling to you as flashes during moments of insight. This seed is the gift that you were to keep as a reminder of yourself. Living within your seed is the promise of all that you would grow to embody in this lifetime. Each sacred journey of relationship, every experience regardless of its outcome, is leading you back to the truth of your seed.

The *promise* that guided you to this world has become the *science* that will carry you home. You know that science as compassion.

COMPASSION DEFINED

In modern times, compassion is defined as "..a feeling of pity that makes one want to help, or show mercy."[2] Through this view, compassion is regarded as a verb describing something that is done, an act that is offered to others.

Ancient texts, through the language of their time, offer insights into a perspective wherein the outcome of an event is less significant than what one becomes through the experience. For example, one hallmark of compassion is the ability to witness an event in the absence of judgment. This quality of witnessing may only be known through the eyes of compassion as all is viewed equally. Through the Essene texts of both the Nag Hammadi Library, as well as the Scrolls of Qumran, the symmetry of experience is illustrated clearly.

> *...If I ascend up into heaven, thou art there; If I make my bed in hell, behold, thou art there...for the darkness and the light are both alike to thee...*
>
> THE ESSENE GOSPEL OF PEACE[3]

...When you make the two one, and when you make the inside like the outside and the outside like the inside, and the above like the below, and when you make the male and the female one and the same...then will you enter the Kingdom of my Father...

THE NAG HAMMADI LIBRARY⁴

From a perspective of equality in all expressions of life, we are extended the invitation to view life as consequences of choices rather than "shoulds," "should nots" and tests within our hearts and minds. The examples of compassion left to us in these texts depict a state of being far beyond the outward expression of merely doing. What language could have been chosen 2,500 years ago to express concepts of "being" rather than doing? What words do I choose today? Through the eyes of our ancient memory, compassion is our birthright, a collective inheritance of our truest nature. Compassion is the living reminder of our promise of life.

Routinely, we give blood to others, thinking little about the gift. In life and in death, we donate organs, fluids and tissues to others so that they may live. We give of our time, offer our labor, share our bodies, our most intimate thoughts and deepest emotions with others. We even create life through one another and still the question remains.

Beyond the donations of offering, sharing and giving, do we love enough to become the very things that we most desire for ourselves and others? Do we love enough to become the nurturing, compassion, love and understanding that we pray for in our caring for others? Do we love ourselves enough to become the health, vitality and peace that we hold sacred and pray for in others? The very idea of compassion as something that we become asks us for clarity in our daily conduct of life. Inherent in every experience and each relationship, on a daily basis you ask yourself this question:

Do I love enough to move beyond *doing* in my life? Do I love enough to *become* my truest nature and express that nature as my life? Perhaps more specifically, the question may be stated, Do I love myself enough to remember my most precious gifts, and embody those gifts as compassion in my life?

There can be no single definition for compassion. As our truest nature, compassion is expressed through each individual as unique responses to life choices. Reflecting varied and individual memories of life purpose, every person expresses his or her version of compassion in degrees, simply through their choice of conduct in each moment. Compassion may, perhaps, be the purest, most intact portion of yourself remaining in this space and time experience of earth. Subtle and wholly intact, it may not have made much sense to access this relic of yourself at any point within any other lifetime. In its subtle nature lay an awesome power, the alchemical marriage of emotion and DNA. That marriage may be seen in the science of thought, feeling and light. For the purposes of our work here, please consider compassion to be defined as specific qualities of thought, emotion and feeling.

Thought without attachment to the outcome of the event. This quality of thought mirrors your ability, and willingness, to trust in the very process of life itself as it unfolds before you. Your level of mastery allowing this expression of thought is attained through the resolution of your universal fear of trust, and all of its derivations such as judgment, criticism, suspicion, jealousy, anger, rage and hate for example.

Emotion without the charge of polarity. A hallmark of compassion is emotion without the charge of judgment and bias. Your level of mastery allowing this expression of emotion is attained through the resolution of your universal fears of trust, self worth, separation, abandonment and all of their related expressions, detailed above.

Feeling without the distortion of bias and conditioning. Your feelings are indicators of your quality of thought and emotion. What you think and how you emote determine, for you only, the way that you feel. The unique way that life has taught you to combine thought and emotion, determine your level of feeling mastery. If you are often or easily hurt, look to your thoughts about life, and your emotions of life, to recover the joy of life.

Each component will be developed fully as a foundation to the "science" of compassion.

YOU AS THE LIVING BRIDGE

You and I are holographic in nature. We are cells of a body that encompasses our whole. Your parents are part of the body, as are your friends, your husband or wife, your children. Our lives mirror patterns of experience embedded within patterns of experience, embedded within patterns of experience. Each pattern is whole and complete unto itself. Each pattern provides a vital key to a much larger whole.

For example, there is a high probability that the sadness you feel during a movie while witnessing the loss of a powerful relationship has little to do with what you have just seen in the movie. There is a good chance that, within the space of minutes, the movie images have triggered within you, your emotions of every time you have lost something that you hold dear or every time something has ever been taken from you. All of those feelings, over all those years, probably have less to do with relationships actually lost and more to do with that portion of yourself that you have lost to survive the experience that life has shown you. Not knowing or remembering these signals of memory, you may react to triggers such as movies, to remind yourself of your truest nature.

Our lives work in this way, holographic mirrors as each cell reflects complete patterns of itself, while serving as a vital portion of something much larger. An ancient law of Hermetic Science, the forerunner of modern Homeopathy, beautifully illustrates this concept in the simple code, "as above, so below."

Our holographic model may be viewed as a single pattern repeating itself over and over again as varying magnitudes of expression from micro to macro. For example, sub-atomic particles are part of atoms, atoms are part of molecules, molecules are part of cells, cells are part of bodies, bodies are part of the Gaia organism and so on. This is the nature of our hologram. Each cell functions within its own space while, knowingly or not, is in service to the entire body. It does not take many individuals to anchor a new seed of thinking, feeling or emotion into present patterns of our whole. By becoming the desired outcome, a relatively few individuals may introduce change regardless of how long the old patterns have existed.

By their nature, life-discouraging patterns collapse upon themselves, consuming themselves in their completion. Life-giving patterns perpetuate themselves, spawning new life in their expression.

Imagine the implications!

What happens if one person chooses to respond to "violated trust" for example, as something other than hurt or anger? What happens if one person chooses to watch the six o'clock news and does not feel the need to seek revenge upon those who have wronged others? What happens if one person allows for the possibility that perhaps, just perhaps, illnesses such as cancers and AIDS are powerful agents of change that we have consented to in our world to nudge us into another way of viewing life and our role as life?

What happens is this: that one person who allows for a new possibility becomes a living bridge, both a pioneer and midwife, for every other person who will have the courage to choose the same path. Each time another individual makes the same choice that choice becomes easier, then easier for the next and easier for the next.

What if one person chooses to see beyond hate for those who oppress, while still living among those who oppress? This does not mean that they condone, agree with or would ever choose to have oppression in their lives. It simply means that one person has chosen to become more than the circumstances that they find themselves immersed within, breaking the cycle of response that has been, becoming the higher choice. Within this example lay two key, life-affirming patterns:

- the choice to see beyond hate originated from within the very system that spawned the hate, rather than being imposed or levied upon the system from an outside authority.
- the individuals making the choice to respond in a higher manner become the living bridge for those that they love the most. This is where they will find their power, in the choice to express their truest nature within a world that may not support that expression.

Your expression of life as anything less than your truest nature of compassion, is you expressing as a fraction of your possibility. I often hear from those who choose compassion that to become compassion is work. Why would we choose so much work? In response to this question, I reference Gibran's statement that "work is love made visible."[5] I believe with all of my being that any effort expended through our bodies in this world is our opportunity to show our love for this world, "our love made visible." From this perspective, the tremendous work involved in becoming compassion may be viewed as a tremendous and visible expression of your love made manifest. The mirror of compassion may be seen in the benefits of the choice. As compassion, your body is tuned beyond the range of physical parameters that discourage your fullest potential. Illness, aging and deterioration, your body's response to viruses, bacteria, longevity and vitality take on new meaning within the context of becoming compassion. Recent research demonstrates the direct benefits of compassion upon physical health such as cardiovascular, respiratory, immune and reproductive systems.

As compassion:

- Fear, and all of fear's derivatives, are redefined:
  Anger, rage, hurt, pain, illness, disease, even death, become a choice of response rather than a reflex of habit. While you still have the experiences that may have produced these patterns in the past, they are embraced as powerful, masterfully created agents of change, indicators of pinpoint accuracy detailing opportunities to modify your expression and interpretation of life.
- Your body need not deteriorate with time.
  While your body may experience time in a linear sense as the passing of sequential events, the cells of the body do not break down in response to the passing of that time. Through coherent emotion, feeling and thought, (such as love) your body's pH levels remain healthfully alkaline, DHEA levels remain constant, and cellular frequencies allow an increased immune response.
- You become genetically biased toward immunity as DNA responds to compassion. Furthermore, research indicates that specific qualities of emotion program DNA.[6] Your state of emotion actually determines your state of physical being!

As compassion, disease and illness born of viruses and bacteria do not have the same meaning to your body, though your body encounters them in the world. Compassion elevates the base cellular response into a range where there is a low degree of resonance between the wave form of the disease and the wave form of your cells. Your body may still create its own illness in response to a belief system. Compassion does not judge the illness. Rather, the illness is viewed as a response to a given belief, a pointer to know of the validity of the belief and its healing.

While there are obvious physiological implications, compassion is not to be considered as a shortcut to healing, clearing fear or staying young. Compassion is a path through which you may choose, from the love and respect for the gift of your body, to express your appreciation and give thanks for your gift. Compassion is not something that you do. Rather, compassion is a state of awareness, a way of being, that you choose to become.

PIONEERS OF THE WHOLE

The model of a holographic consciousness provides for a single element of change anywhere in the system to be reflected throughout the rest of the system. For each shift in perception, each time one person chooses a higher option of emotion to a life challenge, to some degree everyone in the system benefits.

We live within the same system. Consciousness is driven by inertia and momentum. When you choose to think, feel or express emotion in a new way, to some degree every other person in our system benefits. Your choice anchors the new possibility, the vibration of that feeling, seeding that possibility into the grids of consciousness. Each time someone else opens up enough to recognize that they have a choice in how they respond to life, your choice of compassion assures that they have another possibility to select from. You are one person from a population of approximately six and one half billion and still you have an effect! Herein lies the beauty of the hologram. Change in relatively few people has a tremendous effect upon the whole. To plant the seeds of change, those few must simply embody the change. They must become the change in their bodies that they have consented to experiencing in their world.

Representing a technology hundreds of years ahead of vector coordinates and super conducting circuits, compassion is the part of your memory that does not have to think to accomplish. This is the part of you that recognizes the truth of each experience, in each moment, seeing into the whole beyond the fragments of pain and joy, while still experiencing pain and joy.

Someone must do it first. Someone must take the initiative to move beyond the cycle of old choices and responses and recognize the opportunity of a higher response to life's offering. Even though our choices may not be supported by others, it is within the choice to change that we find our gift.

Consider the tremendous personal power required to accomplish such a task! An individual must have a great enough power to see beyond the world that has been, while at the same time holding their focus within that world, without becoming lost in the experience of that world. If this description has a chord of familiarity to it, I am not surprised. What I have described in the preceding sentence is precisely what you are asking yourself to accomplish daily, through each moment of your life. Each day your life asks you to see something greater in life's offering, while maintaining a focus in your experience of life. You are asked to live life without becoming lost in the experience of life. Without exception, each emotion, feeling and/or thought is your opportunity to see beyond the experience at hand and recognize what your life has just revealed to you.

COMPASSION APPLIED

With increasing frequency, I meet individuals today who claim to have dealt with events of tragedy by simply avoiding reports carrying the information. They turn off the television, shy away from public discussions and stop reading newspapers and news magazines. In the avoidance they no longer force themselves to deal with the events of the world as they unfold. While avoidance may be considered a valid path, it is a temporary path of survival rather than a conscious path of mastery. In avoidance, the events that cause the discomfort are simply deferred. Experiences that are found difficult to master are set aside for another time, or possibly never. Your strength, your mastery, comes from your ability to view the events of life directly, through eyes that have chosen to view the events from a new perspective.

Soon after the tragedy of Rwanda, I met with friends who chose to deal with the horror of what they had seen by rationalizing the events through logic. "It was their path," one woman spoke as we began the discussions. I looked into her eyes and felt little emotion as I heard the words leave her mouth. "They knew on some level that they would die in that way," another gentleman spoke as the discussion moved toward karma and balance. While karma and balance certainly come into play with each life on a very intimate level, I felt clearly that these paths of discussion were unconscious diversions, moving us away from the shock of what we had just been asked to make sense of on our televisions. I suspected that what was happening with my friends was a subtle trap between the path of loving detachment and the defense mechanism of denial. The instance of Rwanda may provide clarification as to the differences. How do you know when you are in the detachment and denial trap? Following are guidelines designed to help you recognize compassion and denial in your life.

DENIAL

If you view ten thousand Rwandans laying along the roadside and feel nothing, there is a good possibility that you may be emotionally numb or in denial. This has been a common defense mechanism to survive something that is so painful in its horror, that you remove yourself from the reality through justifications and reasons. You are speaking "about" the event rather than addressing the event itself. Any emotion, if present, may be displaced as anger in defense of your logic or justification. In the loss of life, any life, you will feel something. Whatever has died is a part of you that you will no longer know or experience. For my friends, they had just seen a part of themselves laying lifeless on the rural Rwandan roadside; they felt the hurt.

POLARITY

If you view the images of Rwanda, choosing feelings of anger, outrage and thoughts of revenge, retaliation and getting even, there is a good possibility that you are living in the polarity of un-tempered logic. Expressed as thoughts of right, wrong, good, bad, light and dark, it is polarity that will assure that you remain in separation. While anger may be a socially acceptable way of responding to an event of horror, ask yourself, "Does my anger serve me in this moment?" Does the situation warrant your response of emotional contraction, physiological depression and the compromise of your immune system, each an expression of anger?

COMPASSION

If you are able to view the above scene and feel for the people that have had the experience and their survivors, without anger, revenge and the need to "get even" with those responsible for the pain, you have made the choice of a higher form of emotion. To the degree that you are able to view the events with thoughts such as the following, you are viewing life in feeling, removed from the polarity of the rightness or wrongness of that which has transpired.

"I grieve for their suffering and pain."

"I will miss those people, their customs, the uniqueness that each had to offer our world."

"It didn't have to happen."

These are powerful choices of feeling that place you in a powerful position in your life. Your choice allows you the opportunity to experience in your power rather than allowing the experience to make you feel. You are remembering the science of compassion, without anger, fear, rage or revenge. This level of mastery is one example of transcending polarity while still living in polarity.

Perhaps two examples may aid in clarifying these nebulous and sometimes abstract concepts. I will offer these examples to you in much the same way as they were offered to me in life. First I was presented with the experience, then the opportunity to exploring what the experience meant to me. Following these examples, I will offer the tools, the science of compassion so that they may be applied back to the experience at hand.

Within the course of this lifetime some of my most compelling relationships, and most powerful teachers, have been those of the animal kingdom. During the summer of 1992, I was conducting a combination workshop and retreat in a small inn near Mt. Shasta in Northern California. It was during this time that a tiny black kitten wandered down the hallways that were off limits to him and found my room and the beginning of a powerful relationship that lives within me to this day. This kitten had been born approximately five weeks earlier to a young female that had never birthed before. For unknown reasons, the mother was unable to nurse. The employees at the inn believed that the entire litter had died. Days later, however, the mother emerged carrying a tiny heap of bones and fur that had survived those days with no food. Immediately the staff at the inn began to nurse the kitten back to health. Acknowledging the magic in his sheer will to survive, the staff named this "all black with not a spot of anything else on him" kitten, Merlin. During his convalescence, Merlin had the run of the property with the exception of the rooms themselves, which were supposed to be off limits.

Finding my room that evening, Merlin purred and meowed until I gave in to my desire to care for every animal on the planet and let him in. During the week of the workshop, Merlin slept with me each night and sat with me during my in room breakfasts in the morning. He would watch me shave from the edge of the bathroom sink and walk across my slides as I prepared them at night. Each morning he would stand on the edge of the tub as I showered catching tiny droplets of water in his mouth as they bounced off of my body in the spray. Before the end of the week I found myself very attached to this gentle creature with such a powerful will to live. Following our retreat, I left Merlin in Mt. Shasta and traveled for an additional month of workshops and engagements, thinking of the friendship that I had developed with him, certain that such a beautiful animal would find a home quickly with residents of the inn or passing boarders.

One month later, I found myself back in Mt. Shasta for a second week long intensive. To my surprise, Merlin was still there and remembered me. Once again we slept together each night and he "helped" me with my routines each day. The inn was unable to provide a home for Merlin, as they had their quota of animals on the property. At the end of the seminar, I agreed to adopt Merlin and on that day began a powerful relationship that was to last for two years, almost to the day. He and I journeyed from Mt. Shasta to Los Angeles, then West to New Mexico. He was with me each evening as I prepared dinner. He sat on my lap as I read and cat-napped beside the tiny Apple computer while I wrote the Awakening to Zero Point book. Merlin became my family in New Mexico and his presence was very much a part of each day.

In July of 1994 during the week that the comet was impacting Jupiter, Merlin went outside one evening and I never saw him again. At first believing that he had gone for a kitty "walk-about," though unusual for him, I was hopeful for the first two days. When I did not see him after two days, the search began. I took no phone calls, returned no correspondence, did absolutely no business for nearly a week as I walked the fields and scoured the high desert valley near Questa, New Mexico searching for Merlin. Was he trapped or caught in an old building, trying to get out? Did he become ensnared in one of the traps that the ranchers set for wild predators endangering their sheep? I looked in every coyote den that I could find. I searched the owl's nests and looked in badger burrows near the property, at first attempting to rescue Merlin. Following three days of fruitless searching my strategy changed. Instead of looking for Merlin, I began to look for a trace of Merlin, perhaps some fur or his collar. Nothing was found, absolutely nothing.

One morning as I was laying in bed just before sunrise, I closed my eyes in a half dream and half awakened state and simply asked for a sign to provide me with an indication as to Merlin's condition. My prayer began.

Father, I ask for the wisdom to know what has happened to my friend Merlin. Is he alive? Is he trapped, waiting for me to find and free him? Is he no longer with us? "Please," I asked, "show me some kind of sign."

Before the prayer was finished, immediately something happened that I had never seen before, nor heard again, to this day. From the loft of my home I began to hear a sound coming from outside, then another, then another. Within seconds, emanating from every direction, completely encircling the property I heard the cry of coyotes. In that moment I heard more coyotes than I had ever heard the entire time that I had lived on my property. They yipped, cried and yelled for what seemed like minutes, until, just as suddenly as they had begun, they stopped. I had tears in my eyes as I said out loud,

I don't think that Merlin is with me any longer.

In that moment I was shown what had happened to my little friend. I knew that I would never see him again.

Later the same day, I began to see coyotes all around our property. Certainly I had seen may coyotes throughout the years, usually just after sunset or just before dawn. Today, they were everywhere and it was broad daylight! Single ones, two or three, young pups and families, casually walking through our fields.

Here is the reason that I offer this story. Each time I caught a glimpse of a coyote, I had an opportunity. With each sighting came the opportunity to hate. I hurt from the loss of my friend. In my hurt lay my opportunity. I knew that I had a choice, and that anger was a path. I could have killed each coyote that I saw, not knowing if it was "the one" that had taken my friend away or not. I could have been so angry that I wanted to kill each coyote in the valley to assure that I would never lose another family pet to these wild dogs. I could have stood watch high up on a farm building with a rifle, sniping at each coyote, taking their lives one by one to avenge the loss of my friend.

I could have, and I did not.

At that point in my life, to hate was not my nature. Though I hurt, I simply did not feel the anger. I missed my friend. I missed his personality, the little mannerisms that were unique to him. I missed his companionship and the funny sounds that he would make as he stalked "big game," like the moths on the screen door at night. I missed the way that he would look at me while lying upside down on the cool tile floors in the summer time and his attempt to cover up the remains of each meal with anything laying on the floor within a radius of several feet. I did miss him! I missed him, however, without the anger of wanting revenge on the forces that took him away. The emotion of missing without the anger of revenge allows the path of compassion.

Perhaps this is an insignificant example. In light of the injustice and inequities that we have witnessed toward one another, alone and as a culture, the loss of a pet may seem slight. I offer this example because of the principle involved. I believe that this principle may be universally applied to any situation that offers itself to you to be reconciled in your life. Whether we are discussing the massacre of approximately ten thousand Rwandans in their own land by their own people, the attempt to take the lives of entire populations of religion, race or ethnic origin or the loss of a single life that we hold dear, the principle remains. We are asked to reconcile within ourselves the emotion of the experience.

As an aside, I honestly believe that there is an agreement in the animal kingdom regarding the hunter and the hunted. I believe that no animal necessarily chooses to be killed for food. However, if they are cornered or trapped, I also believe that they surrender to the situation and slip their bodies easily. I have seen it happen too many times to doubt. That is why rabbits, mice, birds and yes even cats, die so quickly. They do not appear to fight for the last breath of life in the inevitable situation of death. They simply let go.

INTENTIONAL COMPASSION

Ancient texts detail the path of compassion as a science. Described as guidelines of parable and story illustrating the equality of all life, the science is left to us inherent in our very life experience. Our technologically based culture asks us to access the same wisdom through the eyes of logic. Our culture seeks an equation, a logical sequence of thoughts and concepts allowing for the demonstration, as well as the definition of compassion in our lives. While accurate in its offering, the use of logic alone is, very probably, incomplete. Herein may be found the mystery as to why the idea of compassion in our culture has been so nebulous in the past.

Indigenous peoples of the world have offered a similar idea for compassion based in logic, though with a greater degree of completeness. From their perspective, the logic of the mind alone is not enough. Mental logic must be tempered with a greater wisdom, the wisdom of the heart. Viewed as the conscious program of life, thought becomes the navigator of emotional energy originating from within the body. Thought directs the power of emotion. The quality of that energy is determined by the nature of the emotion. From an engineering perspective, we say that the oscillations of the seven layered liquid crystal matrix of the heart are directed by wave forms of conscious and intentional thought. For the purposes of these discussions, I offer the following:

Compassion may be defined as specific qualities of thought, feeling and emotion. Thought without attachment to the outcome of the event. Feeling without the distortion of bias and conditioning. Emotion without the charge of polarity.

Compassion may be demonstrated as the allowing within another individual possibilities of thought, feeling and emotion that you may not allow in yourself. At the same time, you take whatever action you are led to take without attachment to the outcome, distorted feeling or charged emotion.

The question:

How are you and I to consciously reconcile the events of our world, with the feelings and emotions that the events create within our bodies? Herein lay the very seed of the concept of mastery. Mastery is less about forcing change upon the world around you and more about re-defining what your world means to you.

Through the mastery of intentional compassion, you determine how you feel, what emotions you perceive and the quality of your thoughts, regarding a given situation. Ancient texts detail the significance of thought, feeling and body-based emotion, as well as the role that each plays in our lives. An earlier reference to the Essene texts reminds us that man lives in the realms of body, thought and feeling. To know peace in our world we must find "the angel of peace" in each of these three realms. In the Gnostic texts, the "Angel" or energy of Peace is further described as a key in the aligning of the body with feeling.

"...if the two (thought and feeling) make peace with each other in this one house (the body). they will say to the mountain, 'Move away,' and it will move away." (parentheses are author's)

ADAPTED FROM THE NAG HAMMADI LIBRARY[7]

Why has something that you have heard or witnessed made you feel the way that you feel? Why have you allowed something beyond you to determine the expression of being that is you, in a given moment? Stated another way, Why have you given your power away to an experience outside of your body? You are reminded, through a variety of ancient texts, that peace and compassion are your truest nature.

You know from experience that life's offering may provide an opportunity for you to become something other than your truest nature. Your greatest challenge may be to fully immerse yourself in the experience of life, without losing the integrity of your truest nature to life.

In the traditions of the Tewa people, Joseph Rael describes this very challenge as an integral part of the life journey. From the Tewa perspective we come into this world following one or some combination of five sounds, each with its unique quality of resonance and life experience. The qualities are those of Purity, Placement, Awareness, Innocence and Carrying. As Joseph so beautifully relates through his teachings, the key to life's mastery, then is to

"...remove ourselves from the purity, placement, awareness, innocence and carrying by being present in the experience without attachment. By being in the world and not of the world."[8]

As individuals, groups of family, culture and society we have consented among ourselves to deviate from our truest nature to survive the extremes of life's offering. Unknowingly, in our innocence, little by little over time, we have agreed to respond to the challenges of life through actions that do not truly reflect our highest expression of being. Patterns that we have named anger, hate, rage jealousy and greed have become socially acceptable mechanisms of giving our power away to experience. We have even agreed among ourselves to have mass occurrences of giving our power away to conditions such as depression, viruses and cancers.

How you respond to the challenges of your life is a very personal choice made by you and you alone. You as anything other than compassion, is you expressing as less than your true nature. Responding in fear, or any of fear's derivatives, perpetuates the very cycles of polarity that you have come o this world to transcend. You as anything other than your truest nature is you as a fragment of the promise that you made to yourself by virtue of being in this world.

Imagine the power inherent within the ability to determine whether you respond to life through anger, allowing or joy! More than any time in recorded human history, this is a time of responsibility, personal responsibility. You determining your response to your world is perhaps the greatest expression of personal mastery.

As a being of compassion:
- you have an opportunity to see beyond the right, wrong, good or bad of an event. Through compassion, the actions of others and the events of life will be viewed in the purity of their offering, rather than the judgments of your experience and conditioning.
- what you "do" is of less significance than what you "become" in the doing. Compassion is your choice of response, born of action rather than re-action.
- only you may determine the highest response, appropriate for yourself, in a given situation in a given moment. Compassion is uniquely ex-

pressed through you, as you. There are no "shoulds" and "should nots" or "better thans" in compassion. How may something be viewed as less than compassion until it is compared to something else? In our uniqueness, what may serve as our standard of reference?

PLEASE NOTE: compassion is not an invitation to non-action or complacency. Compassion is not a license to sit idly, viewing the events of life from a perspective of non-involvement, numbness or denial. Becoming compassion is your invitation to immerse yourself fully into the experience of life, whatever the offering, from a place of non-judgment. Serving simultaneously as the path that you may become, as well as the gift that you offer to others, compassion is only possible in the healing of polarity. Perhaps your greatest task in this lifetime, as well as the greatest gift that you may offer to yourself and others, is to transcend your personal polarity, while remaining in this world of polarity.

It is often easy to allow the degree of injustice to determine the degree of response. For example, we may find the drive-by shooting and instant death of a youth in a bustling population center easier to reconcile than a planned assault upon another youth that results in a slow and agonizing death. The result of each experience is identical. In each case a precious life is lost. Only the path to the result differs, yet the agonizing death has evoked more anger in the past. Why? To what degree must we carry ourselves to know of our extremes? How far must we push the individual and collective limits of who we believe we are before we remember that the outcome is the same?

Life is precious!

Whether it is one life or hundreds of lives, whether each dies quickly or suffers, the outcome varies only in degree. Life is a gift to each of us. We are asked to act accordingly, on behalf of all life, regardless of the degree of injustice or violation shown to that life.

THE PATH OF COMPASSION

With these guidelines let us return to our previous example of the massacre in Rwanda, examining how the concepts of compassion relate to what you and I were asked to reconcile for ourselves in the offering. Of all the horrors that we were shown during those days in 1994, our logic and emotion were asked to find resolution between themselves, to become the union that is compassion. Viewing yourself from the perspective of a program of soft processors, moving patterns of information through bio-electric circuits of your body, then compassion may be approached as a sub-program of instruction introduced into your operating system of life. The key element in this analogy is that you and I use sub-programs, codes of instruction, each time we choose our response to life's offering. Do we continue to use existing programs that have served us in the past, even though they may not serve us in the present?

The Second Path offers an alternative. Through our memory of the Second Path a new sub-program allowing a new outcome is introduced to our soft processor. From the perspective of this analogy, the coding of a new sub-program is your opportunity each time you make a new choice in life. Your software of consciousness is accessed as a combination of left and right brain instructions. These instructions are sequences of your thought and emotion! Following is an example of how the sequences may be applied in your life. When life asks you to reconcile an event of shock, horror or tragedy:

Step 1. Determine your Mode of expression
This determination identifies the lens through which you will view what life has shown to you. Having witnessed or experienced an event, honestly assess for yourself your response. Choose from the three discussed previously as:
- numbness or denial expressed as the rationalization and logic of what has just occurred.
- polarity expressed as anger, rage or the desire for retribution , or to get even.
- Compassion expressed as sadness and grieving for the loss without judgment of the "wrongness" or "rightness" of the experience.

Having acknowledged your response, the next step in creating your new code is to consent to the possibility of whatever you have felt, regardless of how inappropriate your past conditioning may dictate. This is you honoring your past. If you *feel*, then you feel. How can your feelings be good or bad? In the consenting to the possibility of your feelings, *any feelings*, you open the door for exploring new and higher modes of expressing your feelings.

If your response from above was anything less than compassion, why? Are you numb in the horror of your experience? Are you outraged at the conditions of what you have witnessed? What are the codes of your belief system that have kept you in numbness or polarity? Having served you well in the past, do they serve you now, in this moment?

Step 2. Through the use of your left and right brain, logic and emotion, you build new programs of feeling. Viewing compassion as a program of emotional and logical circuitry within your body, the following codes are offered as paths of access to your program. Following is the equation to the "science" in the science of compassion.

IF
you become these things,
THEN
you become compassion.

Ancient texts tell us that we must come to terms with each code to find peace in our lives. The coded equation for accessing your program of compassion is to reconcile, for yourself, the following statements.

If You:
Acknowledge

that there is a single source of all that is or may ever be. Do you acknowledge that every life event, without exception, is part of the One.

Trust

in the process of life as it is shown to you. Trust in divine timing with no accidents.

Believe

that each and every experience drawn to you, without exception, is your opportunity to demonstrate your mastery of life.

Believe

that your life mirrors your quest to know yourself in all ways. Believe that in knowing your extremes you find your balance.

Truly believe

that your life essence is eternal and that your body may enjoy the same experience of eternity.

Then:

How can you, at the same time, judge yourself, a life event, the choice or action of another person as right, wrong, good, bad or as anything other than an expression of the One?

These five simple statements serve as powerful agents of change, providing the code, determining for the rest of your body, the response to a given situation. Note: The use of the word "believe" rather than "know" is intentional and done for purposes of clarity. "Knowing" may only result from direct experience. Believing allows for the possibility of something in your life, though you may not, as yet, have had the direct experience of knowing. Unless you have consciously experienced life as constant and eternal for example, you probably believe that it is so. Until you pass beyond life, you may believe that life is eternal. Specific meditations and the near death experience are examples of the knowing of the eternal nature of life essence.

Using the thoughts (directional system) of your
left and right brain,
driven through your emotion (power system),
your ability to resolve
your feeling world (union of thought and emotion) regarding each statement,
is you re-patterning the code
that determines how you see your world.

The words in each of the five statements serve as triggers within you. Each statement asks you for clarity regarding your feeling about the statement. Do you agree or disagree? Does the statement push a button within you, if so, why? To come to terms with the events of life as they are shown to you, you must come to terms with these statements.

IF
you question or do not believe in the essence of even one of these statements,
THEN
you have just defined your next step in your path toward balance and mastery.

Subtle and perhaps deceptively simple, to answer each of these statements for yourself is to bring to a focus the basic tenets of the way you feel and perceive life and your place in this world. Let us examine each in greater detail.

Are you able to Acknowledge that there is a single source of all that is, or may ever be? Is there a place within you that allows for the possibility that each and every event shown to you by life, regardless of its expression, is and always has been a part of the One that created life, whatever the One means to you? Can you allow for the possibility that the darkest moments in human history, the darkest moments in your life, as well as the greatest joys are a part of, and not separate from, the source of all life in our world?

If the answer is "No," then you have just acknowledged a separation between your perception of the One and everything other than the One. Life will allow your perception of separation, demonstrating to you your expectation in relationships and experience. As you are led to a point in life where the separation no longer makes sense to you, life will allow your perception of the healing, mirroring to you your allowing of Oneness in relationships and experience.

Do you Trust in the process of life as it is shown to you? Do you trust that the intelligence that led each and every soul to the experience of this world remains with them as they journey through this world? Do you trust that there are no accidents, although the reasons and causes of life events may not always be clear in the moment? Can you allow for the possibility that you have come to a safe world, where there are no forces "out there" at odds with your life plan?

If the answer is "No," then you have just acknowledged a charge on the issue of trust. Life will allow your perception of "No Trust," demonstrating to you, your expectations regarding trust in relationships and experience. As you are led to a point in life where, "No Trust" no longer makes sense to you, life will allow your perception of the healing, mirroring to you your allowing of Trust in relationships and experience.

Do you Believe that each and every life experience, without exception, is an opportunity for you to demonstrate your mastery of that experience? Can you allow for the possibility that, in ways that may not be known in the moment, each experience that has ever crossed your path, from the joyous to the tragic, has responded to an energetic opportunity for you to demonstrate your truest nature? What is your life saying to you? What is your life asking you to recognize?

If your answer to this question is "No," then you will see life as an opponent and the events of life as tests to determine your strength or ability to take what life has offered and endure suffering. Herein lies the fallacy. Suffering is simply the feedback mechanism of life choices. Suffering is not the purpose of life itself. To recognize the indicator is to remember your truest nature of compassion and joy. To accept suffering as a way of life becomes a path through which you will always feel tested. Life will allow your perception of being tested demonstrating to you, your expectation of tests in relationships, friendships, partnerships and experience. As you are led to a place in life where, your perception of the tests no longer makes sense to you, life will allow your perception of the healing. Mirroring your allowing of opportunities, the tests of life become welcomed experiences. In my experience of life I have never seen anyone tested. I have often seen opportunities to demonstrate mastery.

Do you Believe that life mirrors your quest to know yourself in all ways? Do you believe that you must know and accept the rage, anger and darkness within yourself to accept the rage, anger and darkness in others? How else may you know yourself in aloneness until those that you love have left you alone? Do you believe that you seek balance in life and to find your point of balance, you must know your extremes?

If your answer to these questions is "No," then you will see life as a string of unpredictable random events that occur for "no reason" and without warning. You may believe that "bad things happen to good people." To accept the mirrors of life and recognize what the mirrors are saying is to remember our promise of reminding one another that we act out of love, and that love has many masks. Viewing life as a series of non-related, random and unpredictable experiences will allow your perception to be shown to you in relationships, friendships, partnerships and experience. As you are led to a place in life where you see continuity, order, reason and opportunity in each life experience, life will allow your perception of the healing. Mirroring your allowing in relationships and experience, the events are viewed as portions of the whole, no matter how outrageous. Each is an integral portion of a mirrored reality.

Do you Truly believe that you are eternal? Do you believe that there is a part of you that may not be created or destroyed? Can you find a place within you that allows for the possibility that you are as new and intact as the day that you burst forth from the heart thought mind of your creator. Do you believe that no earthly experience has ever tainted the shininess of your soul? As much as you honor the gift of your body and the experience of life, can you allow for the possibility that the charge of pain, hurt and death are the very magnets that draw these experiences to you for resolution?

If your answer to these questions is "No," then you will see life as dangerous opportunities to lose this finite quality of life. Each choice that crosses your path will be viewed as a risk through which all that you have ever loved may be lost, rather than an opportunity to know yourself and, in the knowing, experience your highest gain. Life will prove to you your expectations of risks, finality and loss until, in the contraction, there is nothing left. Only then, from a place of having lost all that you have ever held dear, will you find the eternal nature of you! It does not have to happen this way. The path of loss is a path of choice. I invite you to recognize the gifts at hand. You were never lost in the first place. Life has simply reminded you that "you" are "you," no matter where you are, no matter what the experience, no matter how long or how short the time; you are always you, intact, whole and shiny. As you are led to a place in life where, you recognize your eternal nature and the impermanence of the world that you have created, where you see each experience is an opportunity rather than a risk, then life will allow your perception of the healing. You will mirror your expectation of life in life-giving relationships and life-affirming experience.

To truly come to terms with these program statements is to master the codes within your body that determine your life experience. These are the codes responsible for your vitality, immune response, ability to form close and intimate relationships, be present for others and live your life consciously with intent. The feeling that you have as you resolve these tenets within your body is the marriage of your left brain, right brain and emotional bodies finding their balance.

What you sense as your *feeling* is the physical expression of pH balances shifting within your cells, amino acid sequences locating new coding sites along the double stranded ladder of your DNA and body chemistry shifting in response to new commands. You write the programs as logical thoughts directing wave forms of emotion. This is you shifting the Sacred Code of your operating system from within yourself.

Please do not be deceived by the simplicity of this process. In its simplicity lies the elegance. You answering these five guidelines will prompt you to reconcile within yourself the very essence of the life force that pulses as your body. Addressing each of these questions prompts your "inner programmer" to shift and adjust the patterns of energy that are your body, fitting the patterns that you have opened in the asking. If your answer to any of these questions is uncertain, then your path has been shown to you. You must reconcile for yourself, in your own words, through the experience of your own life, your life's meaning and your opportunity of this lifetime.

THE GIFT OF BLESSING

A gift is left to you, as codes of story and parable through the 2,500 year old records of the Essenes and other texts of High Wisdom. The key in these records is a common thread that runs throughout the Tibetan, Buddhist and oral traditions of indigenous peoples throughout the world. We are asked to remember the codes as the mystery of the blessing, demonstrated through life-giving relationships. As compassion is your program of reconciliation, blessing is your code of opportunity that makes reconciliation possible.

Rooted deep in the science of compassion is the opportunity to zero out the charge created as an event is viewed, judged and labeled through the eyes of polarity.

As you view life's offering without the ancient charges, the values of your judgment reflect your neutral charge.

PLEASE NOTE: Just as compassion is not an invitation of complacency or inaction, blessing is not an excuse or condoning of an event of tragedy or injustice.

The events of life that we are asked to reconcile within ourselves have already transpired. You are not asked to reverse time and change what has occurred. Rather, you ask of yourself to *heal your perception* of events that have occurred within time. This healing allows you to make sense of the senseless and find reason for the tragic.

As a being of compassion and blessing, you are offered the opportunity to transcend polarity while still living within the polarity. The seeds of compassion and blessing are rooted within your nature, laying dormant until the time that their value may be recognized; their memory awakened. Perhaps that time is now.

BLESSING DEFINED

Your gift of blessing is a modern expression of the promise that was given to you so long ago. This ancient promise given by those who have come before, remind us that each soul survives the darkest moments of life, to return home once again, intact and with grace.

Blessing may be defined as a quality of thought, emotion and feeling that allows you to acknowledge the holy and divine nature of an action, release any emotional charge surrounding that action, and move forward with life.

The gift of blessing lay in the power of thought and the spoken word. Mirroring the thoughts, feelings and emotions underlying the word, blessing induces a biochemical shift within your body. This is you healing your fear, anger and judgment and moving on with life.

Viewed as a bodily re-alignment, key parameters such as cell pH, and the formation of vital amino acids serve as biological feedback mechanisms demonstrating to us that, indeed, a shift has occurred. The code words allow for the release of the electrical charge held within the body as patterns of memory attached to an emotion or event. Within recent years, new research sheds light on ancient and key phrases such as

"Through our words we shall heal, and be healed."

Words are the audible and vibratory equivalent of the pattern behind the words. Inherent in the blessing of an event is the acknowledgment of the holy and sacred nature of the event. Blessing an action does not consent or signal agreement with an event that has transpired. Blessing an event does not even mean that we like what has happened. You exercising your gift, your right of blessing, simply acknowledges the divine nature of the event, allowing you to move forward with life.

Blessing an action simply indicates that you allow for the possibility of the event within the overall expression of the One. A state of being far beyond the outward expression of "doing," the gift of blessing is accomplished through the intentional and conscious consent to compassion. Once again, the question that you ask of yourself, in the heat of charged emotion is, "Will I allow myself to remember my gift of blessing and live that memory as my life?"

BLESSING APPLIED

With these ideas in mind, how are we to apply blessing in the daily occurrence of lives? Let us return to our previous example of Rwanda. Through the eyes of compassion and blessing, what is the message offered in viewing this tragedy. When I first saw the images that were shown to our media, I reacted with horror, outrage and anger. Those reactions were me, responding to pain through the way I had known myself, in the past. Through new eyes of compassion and blessing, what would have been a higher choice of response? How else may I have dealt with my feelings and thoughts at the time?

I recently had the opportunity to apply these codes to a series of events that unfolded during the last weeks of July and the first weeks of August, 1996. Perhaps overshadowed by the headlines of TWA flight 800 in the Atlantic, the 1996 Olympic bombing and the bombing of a U.S. Marine base in Saudi Arabia, an incident very similar to Rwanda, on a lesser scale, had occurred. On July 20th of 1996, approximately three hundred thirty civilians were massacred in the country of Burundi, just south of Rwanda. Time magazine reported,

"Images of women and children with their heads split open, of babies stacked in heaps, of limp corpses sprawled in doorways have become almost routine in this part of the world in the past two years." — TIME MAGAZINE, AUGUST 5, 1996

As I saw the articles, my initial thought was *Not again! How can this happen, in the same part of the world, to the same people, again?* How are we to deal with this tragedy? What role do the lives of these people that we never knew, from halfway around the world, play within the context of our lives, here and now? As I designed this portion of the book, I asked myself, *Is it a service to offer the process that I am about to lead you through?* What became clear to me was that it was a disservice not to. It is a disservice not to offer these ancient keys to a mechanism of releasing charge, allowing the next step, whatever that step is, to come from a place of peace within your body.

Following is a description of the personal process that I experienced as it applied to Burundi. I have used the same process to come to terms with other "injustices," past and recent. Examples include the invasion of North America nearly five hundred years ago, Hitler's invasion of Europe nearly sixty years ago and the loss of human life in Bosnia, Ireland and England. Also included is the group violence that permeates the streets of our cities today and the loss of each life as it is made know to me, including the recent rash of airplane "incidents." In each example, though the scale and magnitude may vary, the net result is the same. Human life is lost.

In return for the gift of my life and whatever role my life is to play each day as this world unfolds, my commitment is to come to terms with whatever it is that life shows to me. The alternative is to lose myself in the hurt from loss in my own life, giving myself away to numbness, anger, retribution and bitterness. None of these is my truest nature. My choice is to address these events from a place of personal peace, becoming change, moving forward with concise and definitive action rather than the crippling patterns of anger and hate. Following is an accounting of my process with Burundi.

I began by acknowledging the initial feeling, the gut reaction of
Oh no, not again!

Quickly I noticed that the familiar anger surrounding the Rwandan massacres a few years earlier was replaced by a wave of sadness and grief. In a strange sense, the anger at those responsible for the atrocities, even the atrocities themselves, seemed less significant to me this time. What was significant was that lives were needlessly gone forever. For what purpose? Why were they gone?

My process began.

Step 1 What was my mode of expression?

As I viewed the reports of Burundi without anger, outrage or the desire to "get even," I knew that I was not in a response of polarity. I also knew that I was not numb or in denial at the atrocities. If I had felt the once familiar feelings of anger or outrage at the images that I had just seen, then my path would have been to ask myself the question,

Is this path of anger, that has served me so well in the past, serving me now, in this moment?

I did, and still do, feel a deep sense of grief and sadness that these events had happened at all, in my lifetime, in this way. The lack of polarities, such as anger or hate, coupled with the absence of numbness signaled an opening to compassion.

Step 2 Could I reconcile, for myself, the codes of my body's program of compassion ? I asked myself the following:

Do I Acknowledge that there is a single source of all that is or may ever be. Do I acknowledge that every life event, including what has happened in Burundi, is part of the One?
Do I Trust in the process of life as it has been shown to me in Burundi?
Do I Believe that each and every experience drawn to every individual in this African city, without exception, is an opportunity for each to demonstrate their mastery in life?
Do I Believe that life mirrors our quest to know ourselves in all ways?
Do I Truly believe that our life essence, the life essence of each of the villagers of Burundi, is eternal and that each and every body may have the same experience of eternalness?

An answer of "No" to any one of these questions, in all probability, would discourage my ability to find that point of convergence within myself where each answer bears witness to a universal purpose.

Answering each question to the best of my ability with a resounding "Yes," I continued.

With respect to Burundi,

How can I say "yes" to the questions above while, at the same time, judging this event as right, wrong, good, bad or anything other than an expression of the One?

How can our creator be "wrong"?

How can I believe that the events of Burundi are outside of, or anything other than, the One? There can be no "them." These events in Burundi are a part of us. That is a part of me, laying on the roadside in Burundi!

If I believe in what I have just consented to, then I must acknowledge that all has been part of something much greater than the taking of a life on a rural African roadside...and...still lives were lost! Still it did not have to happen! Still, I feel a sadness for all who gave themselves so that we may know ourselves.

What do I do with the feelings? How do I move beyond the lump in my soul for the part of me that has just died?

Step 3 The gift of the blessing is that it takes no sides and sees no right or wrong. Without condoning, agreeing with or encouraging an action, blessing an event or individual simply acknowledges the divine nature of the action that has occurred. The question then becomes a question to myself. *Can I move beyond my gut reaction of an old paradigm based in polarity, to a place within me that recognizes the sacred nature of that which has played itself out in Burundi? Have I arrived at a point in my life where I can move beyond the polarity that allows such tragedy?*

If the answer to these questions is "yes," then this is the time to accept the ancient gift of blessing. If I truly believe what I have offered to others, then the power of the blessing is there for me as well, my personal key to release the charge of what I have witnessed. So I began:

I Bless these acts of choice that have allowed the people of Burundi to know themselves in this way.

I Bless the soldiers that have taken each life in Burundi, so that they may know themselves in the taking of life.

I Bless those who died in this village. I Bless those who loved enough to give their lives so that they may know themselves in the giving of their lives.

I Bless myself in the witnessing of this event, so that I may know myself in the witnessing.

I continued, again and again. I continued until I felt the "feeling" within my body, the familiar feeling of peace that can only be present when there is truly a balancing of charge. Sometimes accompanied by tears and sometimes not, this feeling is referenced in ancient texts as a "state of being" achieved as the result of coming to terms with life experience. In the Egyptian texts for example, the master Thoth actually refers to the feeling as a "wave of vibration" that begins in the brain.

"...when unto thee there comes a 'feeling' drawing thee nearer to the Dark Gate (fear, anger, hate, etc), examine thine heart to know if the feeling thou hast, has come from within...send through the body a wave of vibration, irregular at first,

and regular second, repeating time after time until free. Start the wave force in
thy brain center, direct in waves from thine head to thy foot..." (parentheses are author's)
ADAPTED FROM THE EMERALD TABLETS OF THOTH[9]

Thoth's "vibration" is the feeling of compassion. In this strange place of peace, I know that everything is somehow all right. It is from this place that I remember life, and the many and varied expressions of life, have never betrayed my trust in life. It is in this place that I truly "know" that this scenario did not have to happen. And it has. It is from this place that I AM.

I AM my power. Whatever action that I now take surrounding this experience, results from clear, intentional and conscious choice. I know what I feel, why I feel it and what the feelings are saying to me.

I AM peace. I feel no tension or contraction in my body surrounding the events in question. I recognize each individual involved as a powerful and masterful being of experience.

I AM compassion. From my place of compassion I may address this and similar tragedies, anywhere in the world, from any time in history, taking the steps that I choose to avert or prevent similar loss of life again.

I AM because I have reconciled the event from within my own mind and body. No One Else May Do This For Me. No One Else Can Do This For You! You must come to terms with whatever life has offered and find that place of peace within your own body to move on unencumbered, clear, whole and complete, toward your healing. Herein lay the opportunity of the gift of blessing.

Possibly beyond the capability of words on this page, possibly mirroring my inability to convey feeling through the written word, I ask you now to see beyond these limitations to the peace that awaits you as you as the gift of blessing. Through the workshops and seminars, I have seen this peace within the eyes of participants, time and time again. I sometimes show a brief film clip of the movie, "Dances With Wolves,"[10] a scene in which Kevin Costner is watching helplessly as soldiers take the life of his beloved companion, the wolf that he has named "Two Socks." As we watch the images together, there is a tactile charge that settles over our group. The room becomes thick with emotion at the injustice of what we have just viewed. When I ask for responses, the replies are varied. Some would like to "take out" the soldiers who have not only killed the wolf, but have beaten Kevin Costner as well. Some feel that to kill the soldiers is too easy. These people would like for the wolf to kill the soldiers. Some simply "wish" that the wolf were still alive, without getting even with the soldiers. Regardless of the expression, nearly all who see the images are "charged" with a powerful and unsettled emotion.

Leading the entire room through the same process that we have just completed with Burundi, something begins to happen. The root of the charge comes from those who have not resolved one, or some combination of the program codes offered previously. Though I am not surprised, I am always in awe at what happens next. Even if all five of the codes have not been resolved within each individual completely, the willingness to resolve creates an energetic opening. It is this opening, the willingness to allow for the possibilities, that paves the way for new possibilities, new actions and a higher response to life's offering. The willingness to move forward allows for the possibility of the gift of blessing.

As the entire room Blesses the images, each man, woman and child discovers for themselves the peace that is the Gift. Saying the blessing out loud enhances its effect, making it more real to the individual. Quietly at first, then louder, the entire room begins:

I Bless these acts of choice that have allowed us to know ourselves in this way.

I Bless the soldiers that have taken the life of this wolf so that they may know themselves in the taking of his life.

I Bless this wolf who has loved enough to give his life, so that he may know himself in the giving of life.

I Bless myself in the witnessing of this act, may I know myself in the witnessing.

The words may vary each time and still the outcome is the same. Shortly after we start the blessing, it begins with sniffs, coughs, shifting body postures and reddened eyes. Soon after, accompanied by an occasional sob, I see tears well up in the eyes of attorneys, health care professionals, career military, technical engineers and law enforcement officers alike. Though each person is having a unique experience of the gift of blessing, all in their own way feel the familiarity of the peace that comes with the resolution; the relief of experiencing another response. In summary, in their own way, each person has:

- Acknowledged any thought, feeling or emotion to be present, knowing where the feeling comes from and why they feel as they do.
- Allowed for the possibility that whatever they feel has served them well enough in the past to bring them to this very moment of life, when they may choose a path that better serves them.
- Resolved for themselves the five equations of compassion's code. Resolving these five questions has enhanced their body's chemistry allowing them to address the emotion at hand.
- Invited the gift of blessing into their lives by acknowledging the divine nature of life's offering without condoning the expression of the event.

Suddenly, for some individuals quite unexpectedly, the room becomes "light" and there is a general sense of joy that may only present through the wisdom of personal peace. Laughter breaks out as some look into the tearful eyes of others sitting close by, acknowledging what they have just remembered. The feeling of lightness and relief is the shift of body chemistry in response to a higher choice of emotion. The choice is each person exercising the power inherent within them to "become" rather than "do." A greater code has been chosen. Each has remembered their truest nature. This is the ancient gift of blessing as compassion and the Second Path.

CHAPTER FOUR

THE FORGOTTEN LINK
RESONANCE AND OUR SEVENTH SENSE

Plate V: *Water Lily*
Tibetan symbol represents Everything, All, Total

"Give love to all things,
plants, rocks and mountains;
for the spirit is one,
if the Catsinas are many."

MEDITATIONS WITH THE HOPI[1]

For thousands of years the indigenous people of our world have asked us to love our home. Through their songs, ceremonies and prayers we are reminded of our relationship to our earth home. Throughout history, those who have come before us set aside special days to celebrate their sacred relationship with the earth. They knew that their bodies, their lives and all that they saw as their world were intimately connected. The "link" was held in place through forces with descriptions ranging from the beauty of angels, to an array of mysterious and unseen spirits. Varying from the privacy of quiet observance in the home to elaborate ceremonies involving hundreds of people, the earth's sacredness, and our relationship to that sacredness has long provided the foundation for entire belief systems based in honoring our planetary home.

Collectively, as well as individually, our observations and ceremonies serve to remind us of a principle that was instilled into the culture and lives of our ancestors thousands of years ago.

Simply, that principle states that without exception you and I are a part of, and intimately enmeshed within, all that we see as our world.

Somehow, through unseen "threads" and immeasurable "cords," we are a part of each expression of life. All rock, each tree and mountain, every river and ocean is a part of each of us. Perhaps most importantly, you and I are reminded that we are a part of one another.

The ancient Essene Mystery Schools offered a similar memory nearly 2,500 years ago. From the perspective of the Essene masters, our bodies are living beings, complete and distinct from the consciousness that inhabits our bodies. From this perspective, your body is an agreement of sacred union between the forces that make up this world. Those forces willingly unite, as a marriage of the Angels of our Heavenly father and Earthly Mother allowing you and me our opportunity of life in this world.

"I tell you in very truth, Man is of the Earthly Mother, and from her did the Son of Man receive his whole body, even as the body of a newborn comes from the womb of his mother. I tell you truly, you are one with the Earthly Mother; she is in you and you in her."

ADAPTED FROM THE ESSENE GOSPEL OF PEACE[2]

"For the spirit of the Son of Man was created from the spirit of the Heavenly Father, and his body from the body of the Earthly Mother." "...the Angels of the Earthly Mother number seven." "...the Angel of Sun...the Angel of Water...the Angel of Air...the Angel of Earth...the Angel of Life...the Angel of Joy...the Angel of our Earthly Mother, She who sends forth her Angels..."

ADAPTED FROM THE ESSENE GOSPEL OF PEACE[3]

In the modern idiom, those angels are our electrical and magnetic forces of masculine and feminine energy, "slow light" moving as patterns of energy through our awareness. The angels of this world love us so much that they have agreed to offer themselves to us, honoring their promise of union for the duration of the time that our will consents to hold that vibration in place. We live the privilege of occupying the life form of our bodies, symbiotically sharing our experience until the agreement completes or is dishonored.

Your body can only exist as a combination of the very same elements that make up the world that you experience your body within. Through the process that we call life you have projected the awareness of who you believe yourself to be into the template of a shell composed of the same materials that form the world around you. Through the ancient wisdom of the sacred circuit, the connection as well as the mystery, goes even deeper. A universal and ancient tenet underscores this perspective with clarity. Simply stated, this belief reminds us that our body is our mirror, reflecting our quality of thought, feeling and emotion.

TEARS OF THE EARTH

Growing up during the 1950's and 1960's in the midwest provided a first hand opportunity to see the attitudes of friends and neighbors, with regard to their home, the earth. I remember watching the family television during the years of the Cold War, the war of words between the ideals of Communist East and the Democratic West. Frequently as part of the commercials and paid advertisements horrifying images were flashed on the screen that would haunt me into the evening hours and throughout the next day. Often these flashes were the all too familiar images of a nuclear explosion. Even though the films were in black and white the fury of the explosions was clear. Wood frame structures blew apart and tremendous winds swept everything clear of the countryside. For anything unfortunate enough to be within a critical distance of "ground zero" there was nothing left as the objects, human or otherwise, were vaporized in the intense heat. Looking at the aftermath of such an event, a very real threat implied through the Cold War at the time, I remember thinking to myself as I witnessed the explosion,

How could they?

How could they do such a thing to the earth?

There is an odd, if little known, correlation between the nuclear detonations of the post war era and weather patterns of the same time. Observed by scientists immediately following an atomic blast, there is often a tremendous thunderstorm. These storms are complete with high winds and a downpour of rain, drawn to the area of the blast. As I watched the image of the mushroom cloud streaking into the atmosphere above the earth, I remember feeling a sense of pain, a sickening feeling inside of my body. Earth had just been injured. Upon learning of the rains following the explosions, a voice from within, a familiar voice, simply said,

Rain, tears of the earth.

I remember those times and think of them often.

I also remember driving with my family across vast expanses of paved roadways, the new Interstate Highway System in Northern Missouri. Originally designed for quick mobilization of military resources anywhere in the country, the highways quickly became an industry unto themselves. Within a few short years there were roadside mechanics and drive in garages. Soon hotels became motels and, of course, the advent of roadside fast food. There was a new kind of restaurant being birthed during those years, the fast food "drive in" restaurants, such as McDonalds and Smacks. It became possible for the entire family to peruse a menu, order a meal, pay the cashier and be back on the road in minutes, without ever leaving the car.

Quite clearly, I recall driving along the freeways and looking out from the backseat window of our Plymouth station wagon at the medians and islands along the roadside. For miles and miles, the shoulders and medians were littered with trash, every kind of trash that I could imagine. Abandoned automobiles, old washing machines and car parts, plumbing and building supplies, discarded tires, Coke bottles, cigarette and gum wrappers and, of course, food wrappers were commonplace. As entire carloads of people would eat their meals from bags, sandwich wrappers, french fry bags, drink cups, plastic straws, napkins, packets of catsup, mustard, salt and pepper all were disposed of in what seemed at the time the most logical place, right out the window. Where did all of that trash go? What could we have been thinking?

There was an unspoken belief in our country that earth was so vast it could absorb all of that trash. The idea was that through some, as yet undocumented process of breakdown, the garbage would magically "take care of itself." The belief applied not only to the land masses but to the oceans as well. For decades, industrial waste from factories of many kinds, paper, steel, copper, dye and textile mills, chemical and petroleum plants, as well as residential waste, was disposed of in the largest and least expensive disposal sites available at the time, in our oceans.

Ignoring the warnings of scientists and those labeled "environmentalists," our dumping continued until the late 1970's when the unthinkable began to happen. One day the waste began to wash back upon the shores of popular beaches and resorts along the coastal areas of the U.S. This was not just any waste. Toxic materials from medical laboratories and hospitals and pharmaceutical corporations re-appeared on public beaches. Large areas of coastline in the northeast were suddenly littered with hypodermic needles, surgical supplies, packets of discarded organ and tissue. The problem could no longer be ignored. Since that time in this country, measures have been initiated to regulate the disposal of waste. What about other countries?

When I lead groups on Sacred Journeys into Peru, we usually fly into Lima and spend at least one night in an upscale portion of this huge city, the Miraflores District. Here, the beautiful haciendas and plush compounds of some of the country's most elite and prosperous are situated within a few blocks of the Lima's ocean and beaches. Participants in our groups are in awe of a sight that is now routine to the residents of these beautiful areas. Early in the morning and just before sunset each day, it is not uncommon to see hundreds of sea gulls circling high over the shores, as dump truck after dump truck line up along the cliffs overlooking the ocean and beaches several hundred feet below. The trucks are disposing of raw garbage. Trash that has been collected throughout the city is dumped directly into the ocean! Apparently the practice is sanctioned as the city is so large, approximately six and one half million people, and generates so much refuse there is nowhere to store it. It is often a challenge for those in the groups to witness without being in judgment of the process of our neighbors learning the same lessons that we learned, just twenty five years ago.

The point of this discussion is that almost universally, for reasons ranging from ignorance to total disregard, there has been a lack of respect for the role that our planet plays in our lives and very survival. This lack of respect is not noted here for purposes of judging the acts as right or wrong. The indiscriminate dumping of our past has been our path, our First Path, and the path has served us well. With each path there is a consequence. It is the consequence of recursive garbage, our trash "resurrecting" upon us that has led us to a place where we have learned another way. We have chosen a higher option of honoring our home, replacing the indiscriminate dumping. As a species we are remembering once again a lesson that the ancient and forgotten peoples of the earth have offered for hundreds of years. Time after time they have admonished us to love our home, love our earth, and our earth will provide for us. Why now?

Why is it that we now feel the sense of caring, nurturing, stewardship and guardianship for the earth? What is the mysterious connection that we have experienced since antiquity as an honoring of our home?

OUR SEVENTH SENSE

Most everyone agrees, or at least suspects, that our planet is important to us, that it somehow plays a role in how we live our lives. In the past, that role has often been unclear, nebulous at best. Precisely what is the role that earth plays in our lives? To understand that role is to understand one of the most ancient of mysteries. That mystery allows you not only to be a part of your world, but to intercede on your own behalf toward the desired outcome of the quality of your world.

The memory of your relationship with earth is your memory of one of the great mysteries of the ancients. This is the mystery of the sacred circuit.

Modern studies of the life sciences have taught us that the brain is our master organ, regulating the function and performance of each cell of our bodies. Directing minute electrical pulses along biological circuits of nerve fiber, our brain conveys vital information to our muscles and glands. Each serves as an electrical substation within our body. Additionally, this line of reasoning has demonstrated that the brain actually controls each function, within every cell, of the human body. Each cell's ability to regenerate, the processes of aging and deterioration, triggers of chemical and hormonal secretion, even the immune system itself, is directed by signals from the brain. This concept is the primary reasoning behind many of our models of physical, as well as mental, health today.

While these functions of our brain have certainly been demonstrated, ancient texts remind us, and modern scientists suspect, that the model may be incomplete. Until very recently, a mystery surrounding our brain's function has puzzled life scientists.

The mystery is this. Acknowledging that rhythmic impulses from the brain regulate the systems of the human body, where does the brain receive the information necessary to perform these functions? Where do the brain's signals come from?

Recent research has now confirmed what the indigenous people of the world have offered through their sciences, for thousands of years. Data from western researchers has digitally proven a connection that the ancient texts have offered through tradition and lore for so long. Our brain is directly linked to another vital organ in our body. *Our brain is tuned to our heart.* While continued studies may indicate other connections, the link referred to here is a non-physical, though digitally measurable connection. This connection my be considered as a tuned and resonant circuit. It is the vibratory connection between our heart and brain that provides the pulsed, neural pathway that bathes our brain in fields of information.

Generating signals of reference, it is our heart that provides the opportunity for our brain to function optimally. The term used to describe this relationship is that of "entrainment." As we build our concept of the sacred circuit it may be said that our heart entrains the brain and our brain in turn entrains each cell of our body. I emphasize that the reference signals of entrainment represent an *opportunity* of entrainment only. Choices in lifestyle and belief system play an important role in our earth heart circuit.

Almost immediately, researchers asked the next question, "If our heart entrains our brain, and our brain entrains each cell of our body, then where does our heart receive its signals from? Precisely what is our heart tuned to?"

Looking to the teachings of our planetary elders, we find a subtle, yet powerful clue. For uncounted generations we have been asked to love our world. We have been told that those who do so may expect to live a long, healthy and fruitful life, having learned to gracefully allow the changes of that life. This loving of the earth is not necessarily an invitation to ceremonies of worship and ritual, though there are those who have chosen to symbolize their love in such a manner. Rather, this request, at times almost a plea, to honor the world that provides for the very opportunity of life, is a literal acknowledgment of yet another component of our sacred circuit. Could it be that there is more to the ancient urging than meets the eye?

Looking to nature for the clue, researchers recognized a similarity between the low frequency ranges that the heart appears to respond to, and their similarity to a well known series of frequencies that were first measured less than one hundred years ago, the harmonic frequencies of earth resonance. Historically hovering around 7.83 cycles per second, or 7.83 Hertz, there appeared to be at least the possibility of a connection, a "resonant link," between the base pulse of the earth, earth's magnetic fields and the signals of optimum function for the human heart. Documented in 1992 as a paper entitled "Testing the Effects of Heart Coherence on DNA, and Immune Function,"[4] researcher Dan Winter commented on early-stage research performed at the Heart-Math Institute in Northern California. In this particular report, electrodes strategically placed on selected individuals, as well as within the earth herself, recorded the electromagnetic pulse, the vibratory response, to changes within the earth human system, on both sides of the system. As the monitors traced the electromagnetic rhythms of both the earth and the human participant, an amazing set of patterns became clear. There was a direct correlation between the peaks and valleys of the human heart with the peaks and valleys of the earth, in that location at that moment.

In a second paper titled "Can the Human Heart Directly Affect The Coherence of The Earth's Magnetic Field?" Winter comments on further data from HeartMath regarding EKG measurements from the human heart and ELF (extremely low frequency) resonance of the earth.

"Our data shows that where the earth grid phase locks the human heart is particularly at the very lowest frequency longest wave end of biology's most intense resonator."[5] As a resonance, the two-way exchange of electrical information, was established between earth and the subject's heart, each began to entrain the other. This entrainment reflected the degree of harmony between the participant and the earth. These results, while not surprising in light of the ancient texts, are an astounding validation of the message in many of those texts, reminding us of our relationship with our world. Now possibly for the first time our sacred circuit was identified, as well as digitally measured. The studies demonstrated that not only is the human heart "tuned" to this signal from the earth, additionally the earth appears to respond to changes in the human heart! Now, an exciting view of our relationship to the earth begins to unfold. Beyond the flesh, bones, hair and organs of a life form walking upon this world, we have direct knowledge of a resonant link, a relationship based upon our ability to tune to the patterns offered to us by our nearest signal of reference, our earth home.

Viewing our hearts as layered liquid crystal resonators, the heart becomes our master organ shifting its resonance to match that offered by the earth. Our brain, as a secondary resonator, lives in harmonic resonance with the reference signal that the heart has to offer, regardless of the signal's quality or completeness. As the master organ regulating the function of other organs and metabolic functions, it is our brain that distributes this sacred vibration throughout the systems of our bodies. This understanding in and of itself provides a greater and more complete context for the ancient references of the "song of the earth" and the importance of our ability to "learn" that song as an integral step toward our physical and emotional well being.

As if these correlations are not interesting enough, there is an added component to these studies. As researchers viewed the readout of the graphs, there were well-defined peaks and valleys that formed, indicating periods of greater or lesser resonance. When the subjects were feeling "in harmony" with the earth, the peak on the heart line would match with the peak on the earth line. As the subject moved away from feelings of harmony the peaks no longer matched up, shifting from one side or the other as the entrainment lessened.

The human participants discovered that they could change the correlation, having fewer and less pronounced peaks and valleys with the earth, simply by shifting their emotions. Volunteers in the experiments found that they could enhance or discourage the entrainment between their hearts and the earth, simply by having a feeling.

Could this be possible?

Could it be that by shifting the way that we feel, we not only affect, we determine, our tuning to the resonant circuit of creation? This circuit is responsible for the quality of the signal that feeds each cell within our body. This circuit determines the vitality and well being of each cell, and the organs that the cells create. Is it possible that a feeling may determine the quality of that signal?

The answer to this question may be "yes." Possibly for the first time, the indigenous peoples have a digital validation for the advice that they have offered for so long regarding the relationship between our heart, our earth and our bodies. They have simply asked us to love our earth and love our bodies. Our sense of this signal now becomes our *seventh sense,* our knowing of times that we are in "sync" with earth and when we are not. It is our seventh sense of harmony with our sacred circuit that provides the lens through which we view the events of life, labeling those events as desirable or undesirable.

The times that allowed the greatest harmony between earth and the participants occurred at moments of sympathetic vibratory resonance, a feeling that we call "love." Creating a negative or inharmonious feeling, such as hate or fear, though it was only for the purposes of the test, allowed the participants to move "out of phase" becoming less optimally tuned to the earth. The question is why?

The answer is that during expressions of fear, and any of fear's derivatives, our sacred circuit is incomplete.

LOVE, FEAR, PAIN AND INTENTIONAL EMOTION

Could it be that how we feel, the quality of our feeling, and to what degree we allow ourselves emotion, has some impact on the quality of "information" coursing between our earth heart brain cell connection? Intuitively, many individuals sense that the answer to this question is "yes." Lacking the digital validation to justify their sense, they will simply say that it feels right, as though there is a connection. There must be.

I believe that there is a place within each of us that remembers this sense, this inner technology, as a state of being.

Recent research now lends credibility to this belief, offering for the first time to those who are more comfortable with validation, a graphic and numeric basis for what our intuition says to us. *The American Journal of Cardiology* recently carried the results of studies between the relationship of human emotion and the human heart. The conclusion of a paper entitled, "The Effects of Emotions on Short-Term Power Spectrum Analysis of Heart Rate Variability" is summarized as follows.

"Results {of the study} suggest that positive emotions lead to alterations in HRV (heart rate variability), which may be beneficial in the treatment of hypertension and in reducing the likelihood of sudden death in patients with congestive heart failure and coronary artery disease."[6]

Original research conducted by William Tiller of Stanford University, along with Rollin McCraty and Mike Atkinson of the Institute of HeartMath, was published in the *Journal of Alternative Therapies* in January of 1996. The paper entitled "Head-Heart Entrainment: A Preliminary Survey," reported the findings of a study of the role of "mental and emotional self-management and heart rate variability." The report concluded with the following.

"The results of this work demonstrate that sincere feelings of appreciation produce a power spectral shift toward MF [medium frequency] and HF [high frequency] activity and support other studies indicating that: (1) the major centers of the body containing biological oscillators can act as coupled electrical oscillators, (2) these oscillators can be brought into synchronized modes of operation through mental and emotional self-control, and (3) the effects on the body of such synchronization are correlated with significant shifts in perception and cardiovascular function."[7]

Clearly, it appears that there is a connection, possibly a direct link, between our quality of emotion and the quality of our heart function and response to life. Is it any wonder that so much attention has been placed on the role of the heart in our relationships with others? The heart is where we feel the joy of love or the pain of fear mirrored to us as our relationships. Our joy and pain may now be considered from the perspective of the quality of the information, the resonant signal of our sacred circuit, as it pulses through the liquid crystal resonators of our heart and brain. From our brain the signal continues, regulating the interconnected systems of our bodies. Research now demonstrates what we have long suspected as common sense.

Our feelings and emotions do, in fact, influence the quality of our heart, vitality and life.

In this sacred circuit of earth heart brain cell, it is clear that any change, introduced anywhere into the system, must be accommodated throughout the rest of the system. Our own science has demonstrated that earth is changing. New magnetics and new frequency are redefining the expression of earth as interrelated systems of energy.

IF

earth is changing,

AND
each cell of every human is "tuned" to the earth,
THEN
we must shift within our bodies to accommodate the change in our world.

We live the sacred circuit. In the research referenced previously, an interesting phenomenon appeared in the studies. Though there does appear to be a direct and resonant link between the human heart, brain and earth, the degree of tuning varied from individual to individual. In other words, the quality of the tuning was not constant for each person tested, shifting for individuals even during the time of the testing. The question is "Why?"

What shift, coming from within the individual, could possibly affect a circuit so universal? The answer to this question is the opportunity of the sacred circuit. Our earth heart brain cell connection is regulated, at least in part, by feeling and emotion. It was the quality of thought and the quality of emotion that determined the quality of the tuning for the individuals tested!

Could our feeling world direct the degree of that connection?

If so, we would expect to see the impact of feeling mirrored within the systems of the body, regulated as the sacred circuit. In the summer of 1995, Glen Rein, Ph.D., Mike Atkinson and Rollin McCraty, Ma., published a paper in the *Journal of Advancement in Medicine*. Titled "The Physiological and Psychological Effects of Compassion and Anger," the paper focused upon the study of salivary immunoglobulin A (S-IgA), an antibody found in mucus that is key in defending the upper respiratory tract, gastrointestinal tract and urinary tract from infection. In general it may be said that "higher levels of S-IgA are associated with decreased incidence of disease to upper respiratory infections." The abstract of the paper concluded that "Anger produced a significant increase in total mood level disturbance and heart rate, but not S-IgA levels. Positive emotions, on the other hand, produced a significant increase in S-IgA levels. Examining the effects of a six hour period we observed that anger, in contrast to care, produced a significant inhibition of S-IgA from one to five hours after the emotional experience."[8]

Additional studies have implicated emotion in occurrences of hypertension, congestive heart failure and coronary artery disease. Why would we expect anything less? If we are, in fact, tuned in resonance to all that we see as our world, why would we expect to be anything less that intimately connected to the functions of our world? More precisely, the following questions come to mind.

- If as the evidence indicates, this circuit tunes us to all that we see as our world, then why does the tuning vary with individuals?
- Why don't we always have the best possible connection between ourselves and our world?
- What could be the source of interference that prevents whole earth heart brain cell resonance?

The answer to each of these very good questions appears simple and complex all at once. Deceptively simple, the answer is the emotion that we call "fear." At this time fear is the single pattern of interference known to prevent whole earth heart brain cell resonance. Stated another way, fear is the emotion that keeps you separate from your world, from those that you love, from feeling good about yourself, from creation and ultimately, your creator.

Consider your body as a point of focus, a place in space and time, that allows the merging of multiple aspects of creation in one location. The shell of your body can be nothing more than the materials available to you in this world from which to build your shell. If you lived in another world, with other elements, those elements would then become the building blocks for your body. It is into the template of your body that you have skillfully merged your awareness. Through the formative years of your life you learn to maneuver the marriage of your awareness encased within the shell of your body. While experiencing the world of "time" you do not exist as time exclusively. While experiencing the world of "space" you do not live as space exclusively. While experiencing the worlds of matter and non-matter, you live within both, neither exclusively.

You are the resonator, the meeting place for the worlds of time, space, matter and non-matter. You determine the quality and duration of each component as you masterfully, direct the proportions of time, space and matter into the form that you call your life. Your tools, the codes that allow the meshing of these powerful states of creation lay in the subtle power of thought, emotion and feeling. It is through these elements of inner technology that we define the patterns that either enhance, or discourage, our forgotten link to all of creation. Now we remember our "lost link," our sacred circuit.

Used loosely, with varying definitions in many circles today, our ideas of memory, thought, feeling and emotion play a key role in coming to terms with our sacred circuit.

MEMORY

As we redefine the nature of earth to reflect new understandings of earth systems, we must redefine our own nature to accommodate those understandings. Perhaps among the first concepts that we are asked to address is that of an experience that we call "memory." Our present technology regards memory as a biochemical phenomenon that originates from within the brain itself. An oversimplified explanation of our present view basically states that it is within the cells of our brain that the bio-electric equivalent of our experiences reside.

Research into shared memory describes a collective experience referenced in ancient texts. Each suggests that it is not our brain that remembers! The experiences of our lives do not live as circuits encoded within our brain. Rather, our brain is a *resonator*, the liquid crystal oscillator that allows us to tune to the place in creation where the vibratory equivalent of our experience lives.

Through your life experience you build new pathways, neural circuits of resonance, that create the vibratory links between you and where your experience is stored. Your memory becomes a vibratory equivalent of the experience that provided the memory. As you remember, it is the filters through which you see your experience that determines how your memory appears to you. Someone else accessing the same vibratory memory may see a very different experience, as it is interpreted through the unique filters of their personal experience. You may think of this place of memory as your special niche within the standing wave patterns of our collective memory. This magnetic array of human memory is often called "Akasha" or "Akashic Records."

Our brain function is not unlike that of bookshelves in a library. In this analogy, the shelves represent the original wave patterns that provide the template of our consciousness. Into the shelves, our individual experience falls into place, the nature of each experience determining into what shelf it is placed. Your neural codes create your vibratory pathways, leading you to the resting place of your experience. Memory, then, may be defined as the act of tuning your neural pathways to the vibratory equivalent of an experience that has passed.

I remember reading a research article discussing the qualities of brain tissue that are suspected in cases of extraordinary memory. The article detailed a procedure that was performed on Albert Einstein's brain following his death. Over the years, his neural tissues were stored, tested and studied by various research groups. The hope was that they would discover some clue, an indication of some abnormality that would explain why Dr. Einstein was able to view the world as he did. Much to the surprise of the scientists, there appeared to be nothing different that would allow Einstein's brain to function more optimally than anyone else's. This is precisely what I would expect to find, in Albert Einstein's or anyone's brain. Following our new model of memory, our brain is simply the resonator, vibrationally accessing the information of our lives, rather than an immense reservoir that actually holds the information.

THOUGHT

Thought provides the guidance system, the direction, for where the energy of your attention may be directed. In its purest form, thought may be considered as potential with no energy driving it to fruition. Scientists call this potential a "scalar" quantity. In the absence of the power of emotion, your thought may be considered as a model or simulation an experience that has yet to occur. The idea of thought is closely associated with "imagination."

EMOTION

Emotion is the power that you pump into your thoughts to make them real. In and of itself, emotion may be considered as potential, a scalar quantity, with no energy driving it to fruition. It is not until the power of emotion is united with the direction of thought that a real of vector form of energy appears. You experience emotion as sensation flowing, directed, or lodged within the liquid crystalline form of your body. Emotion may be experienced spontaneously or as the result of a choice to "be." Closely aligned with desire, emotion provides the "will" to allow something to become so.

FEELING

As you experience love, hate or compassion, you are experiencing feeling. Feeling may be considered as the union of thought and emotion, a vector quantity of something "real" resulting from the union of "scalar" quantities of potential. Feeling is the sensation of emotion, coupled with the direction of thought regarding your experience in the moment. The liquid crystal resonator of the heart muscle is the focal point of feeling. It now becomes clear as to why your body responds so well to love and compassion. Through love and compassion your heart is optimally and openly tuned to the earth, allowing the circuit to express fully and completely.

From these possibly oversimplified definitions, it becomes apparent why it is impossible to "think away" fear and pain. Thought provides direction for your attention, emotion provides the fuel for your attention. Again, we are reminded of the ancient axiom stating that energy follows attention.

As you are *thinking away* that which you do not want in your life, in reality, the quality of your thought has placed a tremendous amount of attention on the very experience that you are choosing to avoid. In the "not wanting" you create a charge. Your charge promises you the opportunity to experience the same charge at some point in your life, to find its balance. Rather than place your attention on the negative of what you believe you do *not want,* a higher choice is found in identifying that which you do "choose" to have in your life.

The moment that this opportunity is recognized represents your choice to redefine the charge through compassion. Ancient texts speak to you directly, through the powerful message of compassion. Defined as specific qualities of thought, feeling and emotion, compassion represents the vibratory code of living without fear and experiencing without pain. Stated to the positive, we may say that this is living in trust and with joy. Earlier in this text, compassion was defined as thought without attachment to the outcome, feeling without distortion of past experiences tainting the feeling, and emotion without the charge of the emotion.

The code of compassion, answers the mystery of life without fear and pain. To live in the absence of fear and pain, you must allow for their possibility. That is it, simply allow for their very existence. In the "allowing" for the possibility, is found the removing of the charge. Please be clear regarding this subtle, yet powerful, chemobehavioral code. Allowing for the existence of something does not mean that you are choosing for something to happen. It does not mean that you condone it or like it. It does not mean that you would ever wish that something upon someone else. Allowing simply means that you acknowledge its existence and the role that the "something" plays within the overall context of life. That is all, no more and no less.

It is the very act of commanding, denying and resisting fear, pain, anger and rage, that a powerful charge is created. That charge becomes known to you as the place where your attention is focused. Can you see how in the *not wanting,* your attention (thought) and energy (emotion) are placed into the position of actually creating for yourself the very things that you say you would least choose in your life?

A brief example may help to clarify this powerful, yet nebulous, concept. I have met individuals within the last few years who are actively and professionally studying methods of promoting peace in the world. Unquestionably a great and worthy cause. In their studies, however, they have developed an aversion toward anything that does not fit the template of peace, as they have defined it. They "want" the weapons to go away, to stop being produced. Their office walls are covered with photographs and artist's renderings of the fruits of weapons. Non-peace, global oppression, inhumane treatment of political and war time prisoners, all examples of the very things that they work to eradicate. They pore over notebooks and files of articles, newspaper clippings and reports of violations of human and animal rights, violent sports and films, domestic, family and child abuse. They do not have to look far for examples of "non-peace." Each day is filled with opportunities to view life from a non-peaceful perspective. While we all see examples of what may be interrupted as an absence of peace, the key to change lives in how we feel about what we have seen.

In reacting with anger, rage or fear, consider the tremendous charge that is placed on the event. Seen through the eyes of anger, the "experts" see anger and rage surrounding them in their world. They identify with it through the charge they have placed upon it. Their lives may become unhappy as they attempt to impose their template of peace and balance upon a world that lives in polarity and extremes. As these individuals watch the events of our world unfolding, they see change through the eyes of their charge on peace. Their thoughts are expressed as "how do we *keep* them from doing this...?" and "how do we *make* them stop that...?"

Interestingly, studies have demonstrated that the private and home lives of many of these researchers is often experienced as anger, disharmony and abuse. Why? What is happening here? Energetically, these well intentioned individuals are placing so much attention on "not wanting" violence, anger, rage and imbalance to happen to them, that they have created a tremendous charge on that very experience. Their charge assures that they will have a similar experience in their lives. Though you will "see" all events as they unfold around you, you will primarily experience what it is that you identify with.

From an energetic perspective look at how different the "allowing" is from the fear and commanding not to happen. In the allowing, focus is removed, attention is shifted. What if the focus were redirected to the positive charge of what is chosen in life, rather than identifying that which is not wanted in life? What if the attention were placed upon new ways of helping communities work together, to helping families understand their emotion and feelings? In the shifting of the attention, the possibility of violence and abuse is allowed. It is always there as a possibility because it is one extreme of a polarized reality. In thoughts of peace, understanding and support, however, rage thoughts and violence thoughts make little sense. Though they are allowed, their power is dissipated.

The quality of our thought and the quality of our emotion determine the quality of our feeling. Is it any wonder that we feel in our heart? This sacred chamber of resonance, the place where we marry our thought and emotion, is our primary place of resonance between our body and our earth. From this perspective, fear, without the judgment of the "goodness" or "badness" of fear, simply represents a quality of thought and emotion that discourages our relationship to creation.

Through our understanding of the sacred circuit, we now have the language and the context to view fear from a new and meaningful perspective. It is this perspective that I believe to be one of the most powerful memories of our role in this world at this time. I will introduce that perspective through a discussion of one of the greatest mysteries of the life sciences.

OUR "FORGOTTEN" CODES

In the mid 1950's, James D. Watson identified the sequences of molecular codes that allow carbon-based life to exist as it does in our world. Describing the building blocks of biological life as specific combinations of carbon, oxygen, hydrogen and nitrogen we reference Watson's matrix of possibilities as the *genetic code*. Almost immediately, researchers identified a mystery regarding the code. This mystery has become the foundation of nearly 40 years of research and investigation. Of the 64 possible combinations allowed for in our genetic code, why aren't each of the combinations "enabled"? Why do some codes appear to be "ON," while others are "OFF"?

The implications of a variable matrix that determine the very expression of our lives are immense. For example, why do most other animals have the codes enabled that allow them to synthesize Vitamin "C" within their bodies, while ours appear to be disabled? Guinea pigs, apes, monkeys and certain bats are among the few animals that share this condition with humans. Why are some individuals more prone to susceptibility of certain viruses, disease and illness, while others are less prone to the same agents? The answer to each of these, and many additional questions, may be found in viewing the nature of our genetic code, within the context of emotion and our sacred circuit.

Within each cell of the human body are found what may be thought of as "micro antenna." These may be thought of as tiny molecular receptors, tuned to varying qualities of vibration by their very nature. Structurally, these antenna appear as relatively long and intertwined forms of a double helix, known as deoxyribose nucleic acids, our familiar DNA. Physical properties of the antenna, such as the length of each molecular bond, even the bond angle itself, determine the ability of that particular antenna to tune, or find resonance, with the reference signal of the brain.

In the terminology of molecular biologists, these receptors are expressed as sugars bonding to one of four possible structures designated by unique symbols as "A," "C," "G" or "U." The sequence of these bases along each strand of the DNA molecule determines the makeup of the familiar amino acids that are essential to carbon based life as we know it (*Table I*).

Within this matrix we find the mystery, and possibly the answer, to the relationship between human emotion and DNA. Of the sixty four combinations possible in our genetic code, why does it appear that only twenty of those combinations are "ON" at present? If each of the codes represents a unique antenna, allowing us to tune into and receive a unique quality of vibration, why have we had only twenty of those combinations enabled in the past? For example, consider rows three through eight of column one, enclosed within the box in Table I. The amino antenna of Leucine (LEU) is represented by the code UUA. This code represents a unique combination of the elements that make up this basic building block life. The next row, row four however, is another code representing a different combination of elements, UUG. However, UUG results in precisely the same compound as UUA, Leucine. Why?

	Col. 1	Amino	Col. 2	Amino	Col. 3	Amino	Col. 4	Amino
U	UUU	PHE	UCU	SER	UAU	TYR	UGU	CYS
U	UUC	PHE	UCC	SER	UAC	TYR	UGC	CYS
U	*UUA*	*LEU*	UCA	SER	UAA	BLANK	UGA	BLANK
U	*UUG*	*LEU*	UCG	SER	UAG	BLANK	UGG	TRP
C	*CUU*	*LEU*	CCU	PRO	CAU	HIS	CGU	ARG
C	*CUC*	*LEU*	CCC	PRO	CAC	HIS	CGC	ARG
C	*CUA*	*LEU*	CCA	PRO	CAA	GLN	CGA	ARG
C	*CUG*	*LEU*	CCG	PRO	CAG	GLN	CGG	ARG
A	AUU	ILE	ACU	THR	AAU	ASN	AGU	SER
A	AUC	ILE	ACC	THR	AAC	ASN	AGC	SER
A	AUA	ILE	ACA	THR	AAA	LYS	AGA	ARG
A	AUG	MET	ACG	THR	AAG	LYS	AGG	ARG
G	GUU	VAL	GCU	ALA	GAU	ASP	GGU	GLY
G	GUC	VAL	GCC	ALA	GAC	ASP	GGC	GLY
G	GUA	VAL	GCA	ALA	GAA	GLU	GGA	GLY
G	GUG	VAL	GCG	ALA	GAG	GLU	GGG	GLY

Table I

Matrix of the Human Genetic Code
Adapted from The Molecular Biology of the Gene, *by James D. Watson[9]*

In rows five through eight we see a similar phenomenon. Each code represents a unique expression of elements, however, they all yield the same compound; Leucine. Why? Another way to consider this mystery may be seen in Table II. The column to the right is a summary of all possible combinations of carbon (C), oxygen (O), hydrogen (H) and nitrogen (N) available as our genetic code. Each is represented by its unique three-letter symbol. To the left is the single amino acid that the combinations to the right resolve to. In this Table, our example of Leucine (LEU) may be seen in row two. Note the six coded combinations of C, O, H, and N, separated by commas. However, as different as they appear symbolically, each resolves to the same amino acid of Leucine.

Amino Sequence	Possible Codes					
PHE	UUU,	UUC				
LEU	UUG,	CUU,	UUA,	CUC,	CUG,	CUA
SER	UCU,	UCC,	UCG,	UCA,	AGU,	AGC
CYS	UGU,	UGC				
VAL	GUU,	GUC,	GUG,	GUA		
TRP	UGG					
TYR	UAU,	UAC				
PRO	CCU,	CCC,	CCG,	CCA		
ALA	GCU,	GCC,	GCG,	GCA		
ARG	CGU,	CGC,	CGG,	CGA,	AGG	
GLY	GGU,	GGC,	GGG,	GGA		
ILE	AUU,	AUC,	AUA			
BLANK	UGU,	UAG,	UAA			
MET	AUG					
HSI	CAU,	CAC				
ASP	GAU,	GAC				
THR	ACU,	ACC,	ACG,	ACA		
GLN	CAG,	CAA				
GLU	GAG,	GAA				
ASN	AAU,	AAC				
LYS	AAG,	AAA				

Table II
*Comparison of Possible Combinations of C, H, O, and N and the
Amino Acid that each Combination Resolves to. Original Research, Gregg Braden 1995*

Why do six of the sixty four different combinations code for precisely the same amino acid? Why is it that each code does not produce a unique amino acid (antenna)? We see this mystery repeated again and again throughout the matrix that defines our genetic expression; multiple and unique combinations of elements that code for less than unique compounds.

For clarity, three of the codes have no amino antenna associated with them. They are key sequences that tell the genetic processors when to "Start" and "Stop" reading the coded sequences. Taking these three codes into account with the twenty known antenna, forty one codes remain unaccounted for in our model of the human genetic map. Some researchers say that the codes have become generalized. For some unknown reason, somewhere in our ancient past, these codes have lost their ability to express uniquely.

What are these codes saying to us and how do we apply their meaning in our lives? What would our lives be like if we had access to the information enabled by these remaining codes? To answer these questions is to open the door to one of the greatest mysteries of our role, purpose and function in this life.

Our knowledge of the sacred circuit provides the context within which to view this mystery. An examination of the structure of the double helix, and the location of the "antenna" that form along the helix, provide a powerful clue as to the role of emotion, and our body as an expression of that emotion. Regarding our amino acid compounds as the micro antenna discussed earlier, we may say that

Each amino acid = one tuned, resonant, biological antenna.

Two questions arise immediately.
  1. What determines the location of each antenna along the structure of the double helix?
  2. What determines whether or not each antenna is "ON" or "OFF"?

Recent research by Dan Winter indicates the possibility of a direct relationship between emotion, the location of an antenna and whether or not the antenna is turned "ON" or "OFF." In a paper published in 1994, Winter describes the possibility that the "Long wave of emotion programs the short wave of DNA."[10] In his book, *Alphabet of the Heart,* Winter suggests that it is the resonant location of emotion's wave upon the double helix that determines the structural site of active or inactive genetic codes. Could it be that emotion's "touch" upon our DNA is what tells our bodies where to place the building blocks of life? The implications of this study alone are vast and profound as we view a possible link between DNA and emotion.

Our extremes of emotion, love as well as fear, may be viewed from the perspective of an electrical and magnetic field expressed as a wave. From this vantage point, fear is seen as a long and slow wave (*Figure 6-2*). Due to its length, relatively few complete waves are expressed per unit of DNA measured.

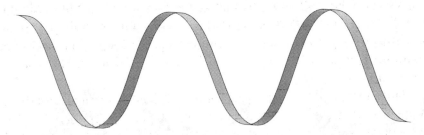

Figure 6-2 *Fear viewed graphically as a relatively long and slow wave of emotion.*

Love, on the other hand, may be viewed as a field of higher frequency. It appears as a shorter and faster wave with a greater number of complete waves expressed per unit of DNA measurement (*Figure 6-3*).

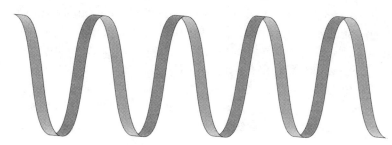

Figure 6-3 *Love graphically represented as a relatively short and fast wave of emotion.*

Superimposing the field of fear upon our double helix structure, we see that the length of the low frequency waves allow few opportunities for the helix and wave to touch (*Figure 6-4*). The very nature of the wave discourages access to the biological structure allowing its expression. This perspective illustrates the limiting and contracted nature of fear.

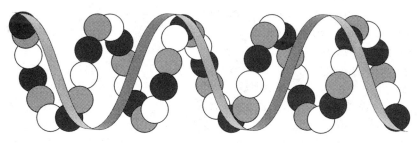

Figure 6-4 *Fear superimposed upon the double helix of DNA. Note the relatively few number of potential coding sites available due to the lack of intersection points.*

Similarly, superimposing the field of love upon the double helix, we see that the shorter length of high frequency waves allows more opportunities for the helix and wave to intersect (*Figure 6-5*). In this instance, the nature of the wave encourages access to the helix. From this perspective the emotion of love is seen as expansive.

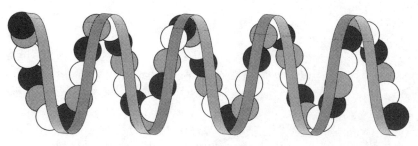

Figure 6-5 *Love superimposed upon the double helix of DNA. Note the relatively greater number of potential coding sites available due to the increased number of intersection points.*

Could this relationship between the non-measurable quantity of emotion and the measurable quantity of biological material represent our "forgotten" link to creation? Is the place where non-physical touches the physical, within the ancient reference to our Holy of Holies, the sacred space of each cell within our own bodies? Winter's studies suggest that it is, in fact, the physical intersection of emotion's wave form upon the structure of the double helix that provides the blueprint for possibilities of DNA coding sites. With this relationship in mind, note how many more opportunities there are in the sympathetic vibratory pattern that we call love, for the waves of emotion and DNA to touch.

These pictorial illustrations of the relationship between love, fear and our genetic code, may explain many of the phenomenon that we see in individuals whose lives express extended and lengthy patterns of fear. Case histories document that individuals with chronic depression often exhibit symptoms of a low vitality accompanied by a depressed immune system as well. From our model, this is precisely what we would expect from such a condition. The long, slow wave of fear, expressed as depression, has relatively few opportunities to touch the double helix and become potential sites of coding for the amino antenna that provide vitality and immunity.

Carrying our sacred circuit to the level of the basic building blocks of our body, DNA, the quality of our emotion appears to play a key role in the quality of our lives. Again, the magnitude of the implications open the door to new possibilities that researchers are just now daring to question.

Is our genetic code "fixed" as a set combination of patterns that originate at birth or are our codes variable, responding to our quality of thought, feeling and emotion? As recent studies suggest, is it possible to shift the codes of our genetic blueprint for life? Is it possible to think, feel and emote combinations of codes that we have believed inaccessible to us in the past? This is precisely the internal technology that I believe the ancients have attempted to convey to us, as the science of the second path.

With the relationship between DNA and emotion in mind, let us now return to our discussion of the sacred circuit and our ability to tune our bodies to the reference signals of our earth. This is where context becomes so important. Without the context of the Shift of the Ages, these discussions are reflections of interesting possibilities. Certainly ideas to entertain and research. Viewed as a phenomenon occurring within a few short years of the close of a grand cycle of experience, we must ask ourselves the question, *why are these phenomenon occurring now?* What role could our ability to change patterns of DNA possibly play in preparing us for the rare event of the Shift of the Ages? Within the last few years before the close of the grand cycle of experience, collectively and individually we are asked to accommodate greater change, within a more compressed period of time, than any other time in recorded human history. Our body, beliefs, immune system and emotions are challenged to unprecedented levels.

Could the opportunities that we perceive as the challenges of life be our way of nudging ourselves to the very edge of who we believe we are? Could our greatest challenges of health, relationship and survival be our way of coaxing ourselves right over that edge, to redefine the limits and boundaries that we imposed upon ourselves at some point in the mists of our history?

For example, could the twenty (plus) new, potentially fatal, and at present incurable viruses, unknown just thirty years ago, be our biological "nudge," pushing us to the memory of compassion that renders those viruses meaningless to our bodies? Recent reports in the open literature support the feelings of many who sense that there may be something amazing occurring right before our collective eyes. Individuals are surviving what were once believed to be life-threatening conditions, and they are doing so without medication, surgery, machines and gadgets. Clearly medication, machines, surgery and gadgets have a place in our healing as they are examples of us remembering ourselves "out there" and fixing ourselves "out there." Certainly a powerful and valid path.

These individuals have chosen another path, however, a second path that allows them the graceful transition from the potential loss of life, to affirming life. The technology of this path originates from within themselves. When asked how they do what they have accomplished, they simply say that they feel differently about themselves, that they believe differently and live that belief. These individuals may be the living bridges that remind us of our possibilities. Their lives may be the pointers to our potential.

The holographic nature of our consciousness not only allows for just this kind of experience, it prepares us for this kind of experience. We are treading on the fertile ground of a new wisdom. Each time we remember, that ground becomes ripe for the planting of new seeds. You and I have prepared that ground for ourselves.

Someone must live a new truth first. Someone must have the wisdom to recognize the possibility, the courage to become that possibility and the strength to live that possibility as a reality. The reality must be lived among us, in a world that may not always support that truth. That someone becomes the living bridge. By anchoring the possibility of a greater expression of life into our grids, that possibility becomes available for the next one with a similar desire to rise above the conditions of that which life has offered them, then for the next and the next and so on.

Do these people exist today? Are there those who are willing to live a possibility allowing us higher choices to life's offering? I believe that is the underlying theme of the events unfolding within our communities today. Clearly, the willingness may not always be conscious. The living bridges may not even know that they are living bridges. If we define "human" as we have within the context of our genetic code, with specific patterns expected as the twenty amino acids and specific expressions of genes and chromosomes, then I can say something to you that is both amazing and awesome all at once.

I can say to you, in all sincerity, that among "us," within our cities and families, possibly within your body, there is a new species of human that is being birthed! This new species demonstrates within themselves the potential living within each individual sharing our world today.

If we define ourselves genetically, this new species looks different in terms of specific DNA, though their bodies may appear as the familiar bodies of friends and loved ones. On a molecular level, beyond the seeing of the naked eye, they have allowed themselves to become genetic possibilities that were not available just a few short years ago. In the open literature there are reports of a phenomenon that scientists have named "spontaneous genetic mutation." They are called spontaneous because they appear to have developed during the course of an individual's lifetime in response to a life challenge, rather than appear as a new form of the code detected at birth. In these instances, the genetic code has "learned" to express itself in a new way that serves the individual's survival.

A study released in the August 17, 1996 issue of *Science News,* reports that about 1% of the population tested, now have developed genetic mutations that make them resistant to HIV infection![11] Research carried out at the Aaron Diamond AIDS Research Center in New York, led by Nathaniel R. Landau reported that, "The mutation is common in some human populations but rarer in others. These findings suggest a rather recent evolutionary origin of the mutation" concludes Landau's team.[12]

Additional reports from the Aaron Diamond Center include the work of William Paxton. Paxton and his colleagues have focused their efforts on individuals who appear to have a natural resistance to the HIV virus. Cells from these individuals were cultured in the laboratory, and then introduced to HIV. In these studies, a percentage of the cells remained resistant to the virus. In 2 instances the resistance continued with up to three thousand times the amount of HIV normally required to introduce the infection. According to Paxton, "...the resistance is probably the result of particular genes carried by a small minority of people."[13]

Studies carried out at the University of Alabama, Birmingham, by Richard Kaslow and his colleagues may shed additional light on the emerging phenomenon of HIV immunity. These studies have focused on genes that code for MHC (major histocompatibility complex glycoproteins), key elements in the HIV immune response. Kaslow has found that long-term survivors testing positive for HIV,

"...often possessed genes called B27, B57, B18, B51, A32 and A25."[14] Andrew McMichael of the Institute of Molecular Medicine in Oxford notes the possibility that the genes identified by Kaslow's team may be responsible for the cellular resistance found by Paxton's team. "They could be interrelated," he says.

Other studies regarding HIV and AIDS have reported children who were born HIV positive at birth, testing "clear" of the virus at age four or five. The virus is not lying dormant within the body opportunistically awaiting an external "cue" to become active, it is eradicated from the body! In the April 1995 issue of *Science News,* a study was reported that documented one case of this "disappearing" virus. A male who had been born HIV positive was monitored with the active virus for at least the first two months of his life. Tested as a kindergartner, the child was HIV-free; the virus was not present in his body. The article stated that,

"...researchers at the University of California, Los Angeles, School of Medicine report unambiguous evidence of a boy who tested positive for HIV twice- at 19 days of age and one month later. Yet, by every measure, this kindergartner appears to have been HIV-free for at least 4 years."[15] The study was reported by Yvonne J. Bryson and her colleagues in the March 30 {1996} *New England Journal of Medicine.*

In the not too distant past, researchers believed that the mortality rate for the HIV infection was one hundred percent. These studies, certainly open to interpretation, now demonstrate that something has changed; something is happening. What could that something be? Clearly, research is bearing witness to a powerful possibility of human experience offered, almost universally, in many ancient texts. Time and time again, we are asked to choose our conduct of daily life carefully. We are asked to become the union of our feeling and thinking worlds, as a key toward balancing the emotions of life. That balance we know today as compassion.

Why is it that a documented one percent of the human population tested is mutating to resist HIV? Why is it that a child, born HIV positive, is documented to be HIV free for four years following his birth? These are living examples of our potential. I believe that we are the new possibility now, among ourselves. In the not too distant future, I believe we will look back at this time and recognize that "now" is when the choice was made. In 1994 and 1995, "we" made the choice to become our greatest potential.

The ancient texts emphasized that there would be a powerful generation that would be born just before the Shift of the Ages. This generation would have a "force" living within them. Within this force would be a power beyond their knowing. To survive the world that they had created, as well as the challenges that life would offer to them, this last generation would have to reach deep within themselves, to choose the path of love, harmony and compassion. This is the path that would carry them gracefully through the times that the Hopi call the days of "purification," or into the "greatest light" from the Essene perspective. I believe that you and I are witness to that choice. The choice has been made.

The young child in the study did not know that he was supposed to succumb to a virus with a history of a one hundred percent mortality rate. In his innocence, he simply "was," in the purity and innocence of a child. Living his truest nature, he became that love and that purity. His body, his mirror of the quality of his thought, feeling and emotion, simply reflected his choice.

It only has to happen once for the possibility to become anchored among us.

It only has to happen once, and I suspect that it has happened many times. Perhaps it was this child, documented by the Los Angeles School of Medicine, that has become a living bridge. I suspect that it is happening many times each day, within us and among us; the choices have been made. Possibly, for the first time, we now have documentation for those who are more comfortable with proof. For others, there is simply a knowing.

Within a few years of the close of this 200,000 year cycle of experience, we are asked to move beyond the doing of our lives to become the inner technology of the second path. It is through the second path that we have the opportunity to move gracefully through the opportunities of the shift. Now, the language of our own science has shed new light on this ancient understanding. Our becoming is possible through our ability to attain specific qualities of thought, feeling and emotion leading to the balance of compassion. As a being of compassion, the maximum flow of information, our resonance, is allowed through the tuned circuit of the earth heart brain cell connection. The implications of this relationship between emotion, DNA and the relationships of our life are awesome and enormous. The questions seem endless.

Where does our earthly mother receive her signal from? What is our earth tuned to? Is it possible that the very nature of our feelings, the union of thought and emotion, are responsible for the quality of the sacred vibration that connects us to the earth...our creator...and beyond?

IF
we are resonantly linked to our home planet,
AND
our home is linked to another signal source, a greater "song,"
THEN
we are truly One with all that we know as our world,
and beyond!

Is this link the connection that we have intuitively suspected for so long? Is this vibration the song of the earth, the harmony of the spheres and the song of creation referenced in the ancient texts of the masters who have come before us? I believe that the answer to each of these questions is a resounding "yes!" Now, collectively, we have arrived at a point where we have defined a mechanism for the flow of energy information light that we know as the codes of life. We have defined through a language that is acceptable to us in the context of the world that we have created for ourselves. The circuit has existed all along. Its existence was held for us in the sacred songs, hymns, parables and prayers of those who have come before us, preserving such knowledge. It was always there. We are simply rediscovering it for ourselves. As we rediscover our truest nature, we redefine our wisdom through our own language, science and understanding. Life continues, moving forward, the timetable intact and on schedule.

Wisdom is defined as the living of knowledge acquired. As we live the knowledge of our sacred circuit, our vibratory connection to all life, what will we do with that knowledge? What will our collective wisdom look like? As initiates of the highest order, my prayer for us is that we allow ourselves to remember the gift of life within our own lives. Through re-defining what our life, and our relationship with all life, means to each of us, we become the living bridge to those that we hold most dear.

CHAPTER FIVE

JOURNEY OF INITIATION
THE SEVEN TEMPLES OF RELATIONSHIP

Plate VI: *Orchid*
Japanese symbol represents The Life of Man

"It is easy to love others..."

"The challenge is to love those who have seen our anger,

seen us in our rage,

and our nakedness;

our challenge is to love ourselves

as we love our families..."

THE ESSENE GOSPEL OF PEACE [1]

L aying in bed under the damp summer sheets a young boy hears the living room door slam shut. It is 10:30pm and his window is open, allowing the meager breeze to offer some relief from the stifling heat and humidity of a summer night in Missouri. The familiar sound of his mother's shoes against the concrete walk is broken only by her sobs. He hears her crying as she quickens her pace toward the parking lot behind their tiny "garden level" apartment. Still reeling from the experience his younger brother is laying in a bed, identical to his, just a few feet across the room. Crying into his pillow, his brother believes no one will hear him. The footsteps fade into silence. For what seems like minutes, there are no sounds. Has his mother left? Is she just standing there under the streetlight of their "secure" apartment parking area, perhaps waiting, thinking crying?

He has never really thought of their apartment as home. His home was the house where his mom, dad and brother had lived just a few months before. Home is where his dog Sparky had a doghouse in the backyard, where he and his brother would climb the hill in the evenings to empty and burn the trash after dinner, where mom did laundry in the basement. That was home. This place, this tiny apartment with funny linoleum floors and another family on the other side of the wall, just inches away from his bed, this was not his home. This was just a place to be, for now.

The young boy in this story is me. This particular incident occurred while I was eleven years old, shortly after my parents had separated for divorce. Mom and I had just had another painful fight, a barrage of poorly understood emotion, flying carelessly back and forth at one another. It had gone on for hours. Mom was the object of my anger, my rage, while she was in the house. Ever since we had moved there were fights, terrible fights, between mom, my brother and myself. I did not really know what the fights were about. They never made much sense to me. They were real enough though. Mom would say that we were "making her crazy," that she had to get away. Still, we continued arguing, bickering and screaming. Tonight, something was different. As our fight reached its usual peak of rage and chaos, mom had picked up her car keys, put on her shoes and left the house. She said that she "had to get out." Where was she going at 10:30pm on a school night? Maybe she has changed her mind and is coming back. Maybe we can hug and say our "sorrys" and everything will be all right before we go to sleep. Suddenly, I hear our family car, the unmistakable whine of our Plymouth Valiant station wagon as the engine revs and shifts into gear. The sound of the engine fades as the car disappears down the street.

She is gone!

She has left!

At an insane pace, the fears begin to race through my mind. Before I can rationalize an answer to one question, the next begins.

Where is she going?

Is she alone?

She was so angry at us that she was crying.

How can she drive while she is crying.

What if she is in an accident?

How will I know?

What if mom is so mad that she never comes back?

My mother's leaving had thrown me into a panic that quickly escalated into sheer terror. My question is "why?"

Why was it that I did not feel relief as I heard her leave? After all, I had "won" the fight, hadn't I? Why was I laying in bed, soaked with perspiration from the intensity of the exchange, terrified at the thought of never seeing my mother again, the very person that I had just directed every ounce of anger and rage within my being, toward?

Why?

In the Spring of 1990, I had left my corporate position with a large aerospace company in Denver, Colorado. Living temporarily in the San Francisco area, I was developing seminars and writing during the day. By night I would work with clients who had enlisted my help in understanding the role of emotion in their lives and relationships. One evening I had a scheduled session with a client who I had worked with many times before. Our session began as usual. As the young woman in her mid thirties relaxed in the wicker chair in front of me, I asked her to describe what had happened during the course of the week since we had last talked. She began telling me about her relationship with her husband of nearly eighteen years. For much of the marriage they had fought, sometimes violently. She had been on the receiving end of daily criticism and invalidation of everything from her immaculate appearance and dress, to her housekeeping and meal preparation. The belittling even extended to the rare instances of mutual passion and lovemaking.

During the week that had passed her situation had escalated to a point of physical abuse. Her husband had become angry when she confronted him with questions about his "overtime" and late nights at the office. She was miserable with the man that she had loved and trusted for so long. Now, the misery was compounded in the danger of physical harm and emotions that were out of control. In the heat of their most recent fight, after throwing her across the room, he had left to live with a friend. There was no phone number, no address, no indication of when or if they would see one another again. The man who was wreaking havoc in my client's life, after years of emotional abuse ending in outbursts of potentially life threatening beatings, was gone at last. As she described his leaving, I waited for some display of relief. In its place, something very astonishing began to happen. She wept uncontrollably in the realization that he was gone. She felt as though she was "crushed," "absolutely devastated." Now, in the opportunity to live free of abuse, free of the daily criticism, insults and invalidation, she was devastated.

My question is "why?"

I remember an incident that occurred in a Safeway grocery store while I was shopping with my wife one evening in 1989. As we wandered through the aisles, crossing off items on the skillfully prepared list that would feed us through the week, we were both searching for ways to expedite our shopping adventure and end our long day that had started nearly fifteen hours earlier. She had asked me to go off into another part of the store for canned items and meet her quickly at the checkout stand. As I arrived at the canned food section on my mission, I noticed that there was no one else in the aisle except a young mother with a small girl shopping in the same aisle. I began reading the labels of the canned ingredients near the soup section when our peace was broken by an ear-piercing scream that would have rivaled Ella Fitzgerald's "is it real or is it Memorex™" commercials in its intensity. Looking up from my label reading, I noticed that the mother had momentarily stepped away, leaving her daughter of possibly 2-3 years of age, alone with the shopping basket. The girl was terrified.

My question is "why?" Why would a young child, left alone in the world of shiny, colorful cans, pretty labels and no one to discourage the exploration, be terrified at the prospect? Why would she not say, "Look at these beautiful soup cans with red and white labels" and ravage the Campbell's soup display? Why would the opportunity of being alone, even for a moment, touch something so deep in her at that early age that her first instinct would be to scream in terror at the top of her lungs?

PATTERNS OF THE WHOLE

The answer to my "why" in each of these situations, as different as each appears, may have a common thread of explanation. Additionally, my fear of mother not returning, my client's devastation at the prospect of her husband leaving and the young girl's terror of being alone probably have very little to do with the people that have left each of us. My mother, my client's husband and the girl's mother each served as catalysts for a powerful, yet subtle, pattern that runs so deep within each of us that it is nearly unrecognizable and forgotten.

That pattern is fear.

Fear has many masks in our culture. Playing a dominant role in the way that we structure our relationships of business, career, romance and society, each of us are asked to address the disguises of fear on a daily basis! Frequently, fear will surface as a pattern in your life that you do not recognize. Commonly, the pattern is not even yours.

Through the opportunity to work with many people over the years, an interest-ing phenomenon has surfaced regarding the masks that we have created for fear in our culture. I will describe the phenomenon by detailing a process that I invite seminar attendees to experience for themselves. Following guidelines on a pre-printed series of charts, participants are asked to detail information about a specific time in their lives. In this example, I ask each participant to describe behavior patterns from their pri-mary childhood caretakers, as they remember them. The purpose of this exercise is to allow each participant to see themselves, and their caretakers, possibly in a way that they have never considered before.

If you are reading this book the chances are good that you have already explored the many relationships and subsequent emotions of your life to some degree, in an effort to know why you behave as you do. In fact, you probably know yourself so well at this point that, if asked direct questions regarding your past, you can provide just the "right" response appropriate to the given question. Inherent in the acceptable answers, there is a good chance that you will miss the single, deep and continuing pattern that has permeated your life from the moment that you were born. It is for this reason that I invite seminar participants to complete a preprinted form asking them to identify pat-terns of their primary childhood caretakers that they would consider to be negative.

Rarely have I seen someone stuck or impeded in positive patterns of joy in their lives. It does happen upon occasion, however, when one individual's idea of joy is very different from the range of experience accepted as joy in surrounding neighborhoods and societies. Nearly all of the patterns where people feel stuck are rooted in what they con-sider to be negative feelings. These feelings are their unique perceptions of past experi-ence. For this reason only, our focus is on the perceived negative characteristics. It is our perceptions of negativity that hold the greatest personal potential in their redefinition.

I begin by acknowledging the bias inherent in the terms of "positive" and "negative." These words are for purposes of clarity and identification only. Clearly, the characteristics identified through this exercise do not necessarily reflect events as they actually occurred in life. Often, multiple participants of a common experience will have very different views of the experience. The uniqueness of each description mirrors the way that the events were perceived and remembered by the individual at the time of the occurrence.

After completing this exercise, I ask the audience to randomly "shout out" char-acteristics that they have noted on their charts under the "negative" column for their primary Male and Female caretakers. Suddenly a room full of people from diverse geo-graphical, social and ethnic backgrounds lights up with comments. Ranging in age from twelve to eighty nine, most of the participants have not met previously. The com-ments are sincere and emotional. As accurately as I can, I quickly record the terms on a white board as they are shouted out to me.

angry	cold	unavailable	critical
judgmental	abusive	jealous	strict
controlling	invisible	fearful	dishonest

Immediately, we begin to see an interesting pattern develop. As one person shares a descriptive word describing their family memories, someone else is offering the same feeling, often the identical word, possibly from a very different age group, social, geographic and ethnic background. There is a levity, a discernible lightness that fills the room, as we journey together through memories of our young lives and see the similarity of our experience as the list before us. If we did not know better, based on the descriptive characteristics of the chart, we could have easily come from the same family!

Following a brief discussion clarifying what the terms and experiences meant to specific individuals, I display a slide that brings nods of approval and broad grins from the faces of those who recognize what is happening. The slide is from another seminar, composed of different people, from a different part of the country. The slide was made years earlier. The similarity is striking. In some cases the words of the group list match those of the slide precisely.

How can that be?

How can so many people, of such diverse backgrounds, have such similar experiences and common perceptions of their childhood caretakers? To answer this mystery is to remember a pervading pattern that runs deep into the fabric of our conscious makeup. That pattern may be described as our core, or *Universal Fears.*

DISCOVERING OUR UNIVERSAL FEARS

Examining our workshop exercise again, a second pattern unfolds. As diverse as the fears of each person may appear, there is a thread that gathers fear's many masks under a common umbrella of experience. I seldom say "never" and "always" in describing the workings of creation as they are shown to me in life. Having said that, I know that there are always exceptions of possibility. In my experience of working with several thousand people over the last eight years, each expression of fear that I have seen appears to stem from one, or some combination, of three underlying patterns of perception. From this perspective, each symptom, regardless of how extreme or unique, becomes the mask of a subtle yet powerful system of belief. These patterns are so pervasive through the social, political, economic, ethnic, cultural, romantic and business relationships of our world that I refer to them as the three "universal" or core fears.

The patterns of universal fear may be so subtle in our lives, yet so painful in their memory, that we masterfully create acceptable masks of their expression. Like a painful family memory that is seldom discussed, we have unconsciously agreed among ourselves to disguise our memory assuring that our past is never forgotten. The disguise has become our collective defense mechanism allowing us to experience the fears on subtle levels of acceptable hurt. By distancing the expression of the fears from the fears themselves, we have removed the experience of our lives from the very pattern that we have come to heal.

So successfully are these fears masked, for example, that for all intents and purposes the original patterns that propel life forward are forgotten. It is this distancing that allows life's hurts to appear as discrete, random and unrelated experiences. Frequently, these experiences have been interpreted as betrayal, violation and disappointment. It is the same distancing that masks life's healings as we express them through ecstasy, joy and laughter.

FIRST UNIVERSAL FEAR: ABANDONMENT AND SEPARATION

Almost universally there is a feeling that runs through each individual, of each family, in every culture and society that we are somehow "separated" from the creative intelligence that is responsible for our being here to begin with. We feel that somewhere in the forgotten mists of our most ancestral memory, we were brought here, then left or abandoned without explanation or reason.

Why would we expect to feel any differently? In the face of our engineering mastery that has placed us on the moon and allowed us to see the genetic codes of our creator, *we still are uncertain as to our origins and true history.* We sense our truest nature from within, while we look to our world of external technology to prove and validate our feelings. Reflected in our literature, cinema, music and culture we make the distinction between our experience of earth, and the distant memory of heaven as some place other than earth. We even consent to, and affirm our separation from our creator through our translation of an ancient prayer to our creator, our Lord's Prayer.

For example, the common Western translation begins with,

"Our Father who art in Heaven..."

acknowledging a separation between us and our creator. In this translation we are "here" and our Father is somewhere else. The original Aramaic texts, however, offer a very different view of our relationship with our Heavenly Father as

"Our Father who is everywhere..."

reinforcing the ancient concept that "Our Father" of heaven is not separate, distinct and distant from us here and now. Rather, the creative force that is our Father, whatever that means to you, is not only with us, *the force is us,* permeating all that we may know as this world. Our Father is the vibratory field of intelligence that oscillates as each sub-quantum field of our wave particle point grid matrix reality. Our Father is the stuff that lives in between the nothing.

Inherent in the experience of fear is the *charge* of what fear means to us now and has meant to us, as our lives. For the purposes of these discussions, charge may be defined as an emotional bias pertaining to the rightness, wrongness or appropriateness of the outcome for a given experience. Charge attracts the experience of bias, so that it may be healed and relieved of its charge. Your charge of universal fears, though often unconscious, are your promise that you will create patterns of relationships showing you your fears. Through these relationships you will come to recognize your charges and remember your core patterns. Do you have the wisdom and the courage to recognize what your relationships are showing you?

If you do not remember your feelings of separation and abandonment, or have chosen to defer their balance and healing, there is a good possibility that your fears will express themselves to you in ways that you would never expect, reminding you of your deferred commitment, through the relationships that you masterfully create in your life.

In your personal relationships, are you the "leaver" or the "leavee"? Are you the one who is always the last to know that your relationships are over? Do "perfectly good" marriages, careers and friendships crumble before your eyes, without warning for no apparent reason? Are you devastated as these relationships fail and break?

Perhaps you are on the other side of the relationship. Do you always leave the relationship when it is going great, before you get hurt? Do you say to yourself, "This is a perfect job, perfect marriage, perfect friendship. I had better leave now while things are good before something happens and I get left behind (hurt)."

If these or similar scenarios are, or have played out in your life, there is a good possibility that they are your socially acceptable, skillfully and masterfully created masks of your fear of abandonment and separation. Through living these patterns you reduce your level of pain to a manageable level. The tradeoff is that the pain of the relationship becomes the diversion, your way of looking away from the core fear that you were left behind, separated and abandoned from your Creator. Your healing will not be found in diversion.

SECOND UNIVERSAL FEAR: SELF WORTH

Almost universally there is a feeling that runs through each individual of each family, in every culture and society of this world that we are somehow "not good enough." Through logic and rationalization we create scenarios describing why we are not worthy of our greatest dreams, highest aspirations or deepest desires. Though we may wish, want and dream, there is a doubt from deep within that we will ever "have" because we collectively question our deservability.

Why would we expect to feel any differently? For at least the last two thousand years, we have been told by those that we trusted and respected, that we are somehow "lesser beings" than our angelic counterparts. We have convinced ourselves that by virtue of being birthed into this world, we have committed an act from which we will always be seeking redemption from a force that we are told is beyond our understanding.

Through the faint memory of Jesus of Nazareth, for example, we are compared to a distorted memory that we can never live up to. Though sometimes offered in a joking manner, words reminding us of our inadequacy are common, touching something deep within.

"Who do you think you are, Jesus Christ?"

"How will you get there, walk on water?"

How many times have you heard these or similar admonitions in your lifetime? How many times have you been told that you may try to live the best life possible and still you will never be good enough. Still you will never be viewed as an equal with Jesus of Nazareth or other ascended masters?

On some level you may believe these suggestions. On some level we all do. We have agreed to collective expressions of limits to our worth. In the acceptance of these illusionary limits, we question our gift of life and our qualifications to accept the eternal nature of our gift.

Again, inherent in the questioning of our worth is the charge of what our worth means to us. Our fear of inadequacy and worth promises that our relationships will mirror our fear. If you do not remember the value of your life as a part of this world there is a good possibility that your fears will express themselves to you in ways that you would not expect. For example do you settle for relationships that are not truly what you choose to have in your life, yet rationalize your situation by saying, "...this isn't the 'love of my life' but it is good enough for now?" Do you find yourself saying "I would love to have a partner in my life that I can share the joys of my life with, but ..." or "This is not the job where I really feel that I can express my gifts, but..." followed by all of the reasons that your desires can not be met at the present time?

If these or similar scenarios are, or have played out in your life, there is a good possibility that they are your socially acceptable and skillfully created masks of you questioning your self worth and deservability in this world. The relationships are your way of reminding yourself of your core patterns. Your life expression of each pattern will offer you the opportunity to live in the lack of "not good enough" settling into a pattern of complacent acceptance, or recognize what your relationships are showing you and choose a higher option.

THIRD UNIVERSAL FEAR: SURRENDER AND TRUST

Have you ever experienced a relationship of any kind, where the level of trust was so complete that you were able to surrender your "personal self" in exchange for the experience of knowing a greater self? I am not addressing the giving away of personal power in this experience. Quite the opposite, the experience that I am suggesting is regarding such a strong sense of personal power that you are able to let go of your constructs of self and what your relationship "should" look like in exchange for a higher, grander view into what the relationship may become. You are willing to live the possibility.

Almost universally there is a feeling that runs through each of us that, for some unknown reason lurking somewhere in our distant past, we believe that this world is not safe. Possibly through the perceptions of separation and abandonment or in the questioning of our worth we have grown to a place that demonstrates to us that to survive this experience, we have to live in suspicion of the processes of life.

Why would we expect to feel any differently? Trust is given such a narrow bandwidth of acceptance that any outcome beyond our expectation is perceived as betrayal and violation. Each day, your life asks you to demonstrate your level of trust in this world. Do you trust in the process of life, as it is shown to you? Do you trust in the divinity of life processes, regardless of their outcome? Do you trust in the intelligent force that expresses as each being sharing this life experience with you? If your answer is "no," then my question to you is "why?" Who or what experience taught you that it is not safe to trust? Why did you choose the belief of "no trust"?

Your charge upon "trust" is your promise that you will create patterns of relationships that prove to you your expectations. You may possibly find yourself in relationships that mirror your belief that to trust is not safe. Additionally, you may find yourself in relationships where others will question your worthiness of their trust. Close and intimate relationships will push the boundaries of the way you define trust, providing you the opportunity to prove to yourself that life is safe. Do you have the wisdom and the courage to recognize what your relationships are showing you? If you do not remember your feelings of "no trust" and "not safe" or have chosen to defer their balance and healing, there is a good possibility that the fears will express themselves to you through relationships in ways that you would not expect.

Each of the universal fears may express themselves through a variety of relationships and life opportunities. Each expression may have a name and mode of healing unto itself. Jealousy, anger, rage, alcoholic or codependent behavior, for example, are expressions of universal fear seeking resolution. Healing each of these symptoms one at a time can be a laborious path that may take years to complete. Choosing this path, healing one at a time is a choice to know yourself, and those with whom you have experienced, very well. I bless this path and all that have benefited from this path.

There is another path which begins where the laborious path will eventually lead, the path of healing the three universal fears. With few exceptions, our experiences of pain, suffering, illness, disease and emotional trauma of many descriptions have their roots in these core patterns of trust, separation and abandonment and self worth. You may ask,

"Is that all that I have to 'do,' balance three perceptions to heal my life?" Deceptively simple, from the perspective of Walking Between the Worlds, the answer is yes. Again, the healing is less about what you do and more about what you become.

You must become that which you choose to have in your life.

You must become trust to have trust in your life! You must become your worth and feel union to experience worth and heal separation in your life. Each relationship, every career, job, friendship or concept of yourself, is you reconciling for yourself your beliefs of separation and abandonment, trust and self worth. Your willingness to address your universal fears determines how much time your healing requires. You may choose to stage your healing, over many years, as old concepts melt away in the face of situations where they no longer work. You may embrace your healing in a single heartbeat if you are willing to allow for the possibility.

There is a good chance that some combination of these patterns has played a significant role in your life. Recognizing the role of these three patterns is a powerful step toward your highest levels of mastery. You, living your knowledge, becomes you as your wisdom. This is the part of life that cannot be taught. You are asked to become trust, worth and union. In your healing, each of the relationships that you have ever held in place by the charge of universal fear fall away. There is nothing remaining to hold them in place.

Our universal fears appear to be so well disguised and accepted, that it is often easy to overlook them or to rationalize them as something other than their true nature. Following is a chart identifying each of the three universal fears and the characteristic patterns of relationship rooted within each.

"Universal" Fear Expressed As:

Abandonment and Separation	• Relationships where you are devastated when they fail or break. • Always being the one who gets "left" in the relationship. • Being the first to leave a good relationship, so that you are not hurt.
Not Worthy	• Issues of low self esteem • Creating relationships of career, friendship and romance that match your expectations of not being "good enough."
Surrender and Trust	• Inability to surrender to our experience. • Relationships that mirror your expectations of this world being unsafe and unworthy of your trust.

Any fear perceived is only a fraction of yourself in wholeness. In your totality, you are of greater substance than any one fragment of fear standing alone.

TEMPLES OF RELATIONSHIP

Almost universally throughout ancient and indigenous cultures are memories preserved as locations of sacred experience. In modern times these sites are called *temples*. Perhaps more accurately, it is our modern interpretation of history that has established the role of the temple as a place of "worship" in the lives of those who have come before us.

The prevailing view of Egyptian history is an excellent example. Our modern interpretation of Egyptian history is largely the product of French archaeologists and their interpretations of excavations during the time of Napoleon. Though the stories of early archaeologists depicting gods and warriors are certainly interesting, in some cases at least they may be incomplete. In their inaccuracy, is it possible that we may be missing powerful clues to our past? The structures that we call temples may represent tangible links between thousands of years of experience and our lives today. Is it possible that the temples were actually powerful devices constructed to teach us something of ourselves, two thousand, thirty five hundred, even four thousand years ago?

Ancient texts, codices and calendars remind us that we are living the close of a grand cycle of experience. Our cycle they tell us, began before the beginning of our recorded history, over 200,000 years ago. At the same time, modern researchers show us that earth as well as our solar system, is in fact, moving through an experience of unprecedented change. A myriad of data, measurements, charts and graphs depict a change within the earth and every living system that is resonantly tuned to the earth. That change is characterized largely as powerful shifts of magnetics and frequency. Researchers have demonstrated that each cell of the human body is working diligently to match earth's new magnetics and frequency. In doing so, our bodies maintain a tuning to the reference signals of our home planet. Recent reports have demonstrated emotion's role as our "switch" to turn specific codes of DNA "OFF" and "ON." How we allow ourselves to feel our world determines, in large part, how we function in our world. This relationship between emotion, DNA and our ability to change our tuning now sheds new light on the relevance of ancient temples throughout the world.

The ancients demonstrated their knowledge of this time in history through the traditions of the mystery schools. They knew that individuals living in these days would experience tremendous change in their lives. We are reminded that we may expect those changes in sleep patterns, dream states and our sense of time. We are cautioned that our immune systems may be taxed and that we may see new disease and a new intensity of emotion in our relationships. Clearly, the ancients knew of our time in their future history. In their knowing, they planted the seeds of knowledge that have become our wisdom. In many instances it is their knowledge that has become our teaching, training and preparation for this quantum shift of human expression. Beyond speculation and theory, those that have come before us carried the knowledge one step further, insuring that you and I would remember the tools to carry us gracefully through our experience. The ancients built their massive structures of external technology to induce emotion and know themselves in that emotion. That was their path. That was their mastery. Imbued with the knowledge of shifting magnetics and frequency that was to come, they built their tuned chambers, simulating and modeling in their time the very parameters that we experience now.

There is an undercurrent of their memory within us today. Many people feel as though they must go to these temples for their healing, to have the experiences that will prompt the change within their bodies. While the temples have certainly been valid, and have obviously worked for others in the past, I believe that we have outgrown the exterior temples. They have served us well, bringing us to the point where we are now, the place where we let go of the outer temples and remember that this is the time of inner technology. This is the time of the temple within.

The initiates of our past would immerse themselves into their chambers of altered perceptions and record what the conditions meant to their feelings, emotions and physical body. They recorded their experiences for us, in the only language that they knew. They passed their records to us today, so that we would have them as a map to prepare ourselves, as we move collectively into the shift.

From their perspective, the history of Egypt is not a story of powerful gods and goddesses represented by stone statues in earthly structures. Rather, each Egyptian temple was dedicated to the mastery of human emotion, the inner technology of the second path. Within each temple the initiate had the opportunity to isolate some combination of human emotion to be known, experienced and mastered. The vibratory technology of the temple allowed the initiate to remember his/her inner technology. Their remembering meant mastering the codes of emotion within a safe and healing environment. Over unspecified periods of time each initiate would have the opportunity, the luxury, to immerse themselves into the fields created by the passive dynamics of the chambers themselves. These conditions simulated for the people of their time the same parameters that you and I are living now. The difference between the initiate of 3,500 years ago and you today is that it is no longer necessary to enter into a specialized chamber to have the experiences. We live the conditions today that were modeled for us 3,500 years ago!

Do we have the wisdom to recognize their words?

Do you have the courage to honor your feelings?

It is no longer necessary to step into a chamber of altered experience to know what low magnetics and/or high frequency feels like to your body. You are living those conditions in your homes, schools, malls and offices. You know the conditions and have mastered them well. Today you no longer have the luxury of isolating a single emotion within an artificial temple and spending months, or perhaps years there, knowing yourself in that emotion. You no longer have the luxury of entering into the temple of trust, for example, and completing the mastery of trust before moving into the temple of love, fidelity or darkness to know yourself in those ways.

Today, your relationships have become your temples. You have outgrown the outer temples of stone and masonry. You and your personal interactions with others have replaced the ancient structures of simulated experience. Today you may enter into the temple of *love* for example, in the relationship that we call marriage. Within this temple of love, in all probability you will have the opportunity to see yourself in additional temples. The temple of *trust* for example, or the temples of *anger* and *fidelity*. Quite possibly, you enter each temple without conscious knowledge that the temples are preparing you for something much greater than the relationship itself.

It is through your relationships that you masterfully create for yourself. In relationships you have the opportunity to experience just the right kind of emotion and feeling, just the right "switches," allowing your body to respond to shifts from within the earth. Your feelings about the loss of relationships, finances, health and friendships for example, provide the opportunity for change within your body. Through knowing yourself in these ways, or supporting others as they know themselves, you become the change.

Do you remember that you are not your experience? Do you remember that you are not your AIDS, you are not your cancer, you are not your successful marriage or your failed marriage? Your success, failure, abundance, lack, health or disease are your indicators, powerfully mirroring your qualities of thought, feeling and emotion.

Relationships are your opportunity to see yourself in all ways. Each relationship mirrors a reflection of your beliefs, judgments, bias or lack thereof, as you interact with others. Even if you live upon a mountain top having no human interaction you still must interact with yourself. Within yourself you will see the reflection of your beliefs. Do you have relationships with different people that seem to follow common and recurring patterns? What switches are you reminding yourself of? It is through the temples of our relationships that we remember our truest nature. In that memory, once again we return to a sacred place of wholeness. We know that place as *union*. In union, we become compassion.

The previous example of attracting adult relationships that exhibit the very characteristics that hurt you as a child is one expression of the complex and subtle dynamics that play a key role in each of our lives. This system guarantees that we will continue to remind one another of who we are through demonstration, in addition to words. This system is called *mirroring*. Mirrors of your beliefs, that which you expect to be true and that which you hold a charge upon, surround you daily in the relationships of your life. They will begin as extremely subtle patterns, tremendous gifts to you, if you have the wisdom to recognize them. In the non-recognition, mirrors will become less and less subtle until the mirror manifests in your life in a way that you can no longer ignore.

Ancient traditions indicate a series of mirrors that each man and woman will encounter on the path to know themselves. Through their many translations and interpretations over time, to some degree those paths have become distorted, sometimes to the point of non recognition. Rediscovered in 1947, the Essene texts of both the *Dead Sea Scrolls* and possibly lesser known *Nag Hammadi library* have had only forty nine years of interpretation and translation to become distorted. Consequently, I believe that these pre-Christian texts provide a powerful perspective from which to view the later traditions and teachings, developed over the last 2,500 years.

THE SEVEN ESSENE MIRRORS OF RELATIONSHIP

The "Mystery of the Seven Mirrors of Relationship" will be presented to each person regardless of age, sex or culture, through the relationships of their lifetime. In all probability, you are living these mirrors. Interestingly, there is a sequence to the way that you will recognize the mirrors. Subtle mirrors will be recognized and resolved before the powerful mirrors of even greater subtlety are acknowledged. From the perspective of the ancient initiate, emotions that lead to compassion are mastered, in sequence, through consciously acknowledging and mastering the seven mirrors of human relationship. How would it be possible for the initiate of 2,500 years ago to become trust, for example, if the fears that prevent trust had not been mastered? How is it possible today?

How can you change the cycles of fear and hate without mastering the patterns that allow fear and hate to exist?

It is through your relationships that you will be shown the greatest examples of your core beliefs, regardless of what you "think" those beliefs are.

You are living the same patterns, the same temples as the ancients, unfolding to you in the same sequence as it has to each initiate who has ever embarked upon the path of mastery. Recognizing *what* the sequence is saying to you, and *why* you repeat similar patterns with different people, may be your most powerful steps toward your highest levels of mastery.

For this reason, I offer these mirrors to you in order, from the least to greatest degree of subtlety. Multiple expressions of these mirrors may cross your path in the same day, in the same moment, and remain unrecognized until the sequence is complete. The resolution of each mirror, in sequence, is the coded equation that allows biochemical change within your body. These changes are you, holding your tuning to the earth. The science of emotion and relationship is your "vibratory technology" of life and compassion.

A word of caution is appropriate here. Once the mirrors are identified, you will begin to see them everywhere. It is like searching for a particular vehicle to test drive before you purchase one. Once I test drove a Jeep Cherokee, I suddenly began to see them everywhere. Miraculously they appeared in grocery store parking lots, on freeways and inside of parking garages. I could look at them and tell you whether or not each was a middle or top of the line and what equipment came standard, all because I had noticed them. Of course they had always been there. Until I considered purchasing one, I had no reason to recognize the pattern as significant.

Your mirrors are for you only. Without intimate knowledge of another individual's history, life path, choices or intent it may be inaccurate to identify a life mirror for that person. Your mirrors work for you. They have always been there, patiently awaiting the time when you would notice them. You noticing is you waking up to the subtle patterns in your life. From my perspective, this is the most sacred aspect of the science of sacred geometry. Your projected patterns of joy, lust, rage, and compassion form as energetic imprints of charge. Each imprint forms as one, or some combination of the five sacred forms known as the platonic solids. *(Appendix II)*

I have chosen the traditions of the ancient Essenes to portray the mirrors as they were left for you. Illustrated as real and intimate examples, taken directly from the life of myself and others, you may see for yourself the mirrors existing and developing in your life at present, as well as what each is saying to you.

THE MYSTERY OF THE FIRST MIRROR:
REFLECTIONS OF THE MOMENT

"You read the face of the sky and of the earth,
but you have not recognized how to read this moment."
THE NAG HAMMADI LIBRARY[2]

My first experience with cats began in the winter of 1980. I was working as a computer geologist, living in a small apartment in Denver, Colorado. As a member of the Technical Services Department, I spent most of my days, evenings and weekends learning new technologies and applying them to the traditional concepts of geology. I had not considered owning a pet, as I was never home to honor the commitment of stewardship.

One weekend, a friend brought me a "gift," a beautiful orange and blonde kitten approximately five weeks old. His name was Tigger, after a cat in a children's television program, and though I was not allowed pets in this particular apartment I was immediately drawn to him. Even if an exception to the "no pet" rule was made, I would not be home to give Tigger the attention that I felt he deserved. It did not take long for me to discover that the kitten probably needed me around much less than I had imagined. It was still winter in Colorado, and Tigger quickly became an expert at burrowing under the comforter, quilts and sheets of our bed creating a warm spot where he would spend much of his day. Often I would come home from work and he would not move from under the warm sheets and pillows, even to see who had just come into the house.

After a couple of weeks I became very attached to Tigger and chose to bend the rules of the apartments, temporarily, and keep him. The manager of the apartments had explained that the incentive for their pet rules was based on past experience. Cats had been hard on his apartments, especially so on carpets, drapes and vertical blinds. Immediately, I trained Tigger to honor specific places in our home. He was taught to stay off the couches, counter tops and refrigerator and out of the window sills. Each day, I would come home and he would be sleeping on a designated approved zone. I was keeping my pet with no problem.

My position with the oil and gas company was relatively new, with an equally new and ambiguous job description that left many tasks open to interpretation. As I explored this new position and the resulting levels of responsibility, I noticed that I was encountering greater and greater amounts of friction with those whom I had been asked to supervise. Technicians and aids who were assigned to support me on our projects became arrogant, angry and hard to work with. Some proceeded directly against the instructions that I had given them, in blatant defiance of my guidelines.

One day, I left work and arrived home earlier than usual. As I opened the door to my apartment, Mr. Tigger was awakened from a deep cat sleep, on the kitchen counter next to the sink. This was not an approved zone for him and he was as surprised to see me come through the door as I was to see him there on the counter! Immediately, he jumped down and retreated to his place on our bed and waited, watching to see if I would reprimand him. Now I was curious. Was this a one time incident representing an error in judgment, or did he explore any region of the house that he desired including the off limits places, when I was gone? Could he "know" my patterns and timing so well that he would be certain to move to a approved zone just before I arrived home each evening?

Normally, when I would leave the house I was in a hurry, off to somewhere with no looking back. That day I tried an experiment. As I walked out onto my balcony overlooking a beautiful green belt below, I slipped back the drapes and waited. Within minutes, Tigger left the bed and went directly back into the kitchen and his perch high upon the kitchen counter, next to the toaster and juice machine. He believed that I was gone. Closing his eyes, he began to nod a couple of times and soon was asleep next to the kitchen sink, a place that he would never go if I were present. After weeks of similar experiments and training techniques, I became very frustrated with his lack of respect for our house. It was not until I spoke with friends who owned cats that I learned something that probably every other cat owner has already discovered.

You do not train a cat.

Cats do what cats do. Cats will generally gravitate to high places such as countertops, refrigerators, window sills. They may honor your requests while they are in your presence. When alone, they own their world.

The reason that I share this story is because of what my friend Tigger "did" to me. In his being who he was, I became frustrated, almost to the point of anger. He would look me directly in the eyes and I knew that he "knew" where his boundaries were. Still, he acted directly against my will and did what he chose, wherever he chose. At the same time the relationships at the office were becoming even more tense. There were additional instances among my aids of disrespect for my direction and instructions for our projects.

After a particularly rough afternoon, one employee came to me asking why I did not "let her do her job?" I had given her an assignment, and was "micro managing" her expression of that assignment each step of the way. That afternoon, as I walked into the apartment, Tigger, once again, was in a forbidden zone of the kitchen counter. I became furious.

As I sat down on the couch to think about what was happening I noticed the parallel between Tigger's disrespect for my requests and the disrespect of those with whom I was working.

In frustrated desperation, I threw my hands up into the air and said to Tigger, *The house is yours, do what you do!*

Changing clothes to go for my evening run, I came to a similar conclusion regarding my coworkers. In my mind, I said the same thing to each of them, *I will stop "helping" you to do your job!*

The run felt good and I did not think of Tigger or my job for the rest of the evening. In my office the following morning, I called a meeting and expressed to the project employees my feelings. Immediately there was a feeling of lightness in the room and a few audible sighs of relief. Someone said to me, *At last, you're going to let us do our job.*

Through two simultaneous, though seemingly unrelated experiences, both Tigger and my coworkers had shown me something very significant about myself. Each had mirrored a pattern so subtle that I had not recognized it until that very moment. That pattern was to become the first in a series that I would have to recognize within myself before healing powerful, yet even more subtle aspects of relationships.

During the 1960's many self help professionals said that if you do not like what someone is showing you, look to yourself. There is a good chance that others may be reflecting back to you the very patterns that you have become within yourself. These are the patterns that you identify with so strongly that you often do not see them.

When this scenario applies, it will often be expressed as others mirroring you back to yourself, in the moment.

With regard to Tigger and my co-workers this is precisely what was happening. Without consciously realizing the dynamics of our relationship, each was showing to me a mirror of myself, as I presented myself, through our interaction in that moment. At the time, these particular moments mirrored for me my *control*.

This is not to say that control is good or bad. In and of itself control is benign. It is simply a pattern of energy applied toward a desired outcome. How the control is expressed is the issue that is demonstrated in the mirroring. Each time that my world reflected to me my patterns of control it was simply an opportunity for me to see the immediate consequences of those patterns. The mirrors occurred in the moment, rather than hours or days later, so that the correlation between the pattern and the outcome could be recognized.

The value of this immediate feedback may be seen through an example of anthropological studies of hidden tribes found in Asia. Upon discovering one of these "lost" tribes, researchers were surprised to find that the members of the tribe made no correlation between the act of sexual intercourse and the advent of pregnancy and birth. The lag time of nine months between the act of sex and the birth of the child was so great, that the connection between the two events was not obvious. Herein lay the value of our mirrors of the moment.

If we are seeing our mirrors, then they are current patterns, happening *now*. The mirror becomes our moment of opportunity. Once recognized, the pattern may be healed in a heartbeat. It can happen that quickly. To recognize the pattern is the clue as to the underlying source of the mirror. More often than not that source is some combination of the three universal fears.

In our example, my patterns of control were saying to me that I perceived the need to control external factors in my life to feel safe in my world. My corporate actions mirrored my belief that I must control each step of our project to assure the success of its outcome. Why? What was it within myself that did not believe that my coworkers were capable of, or had the initiative to, perform as well as I would on our project? Ultimately, my issues were mirroring to me something much deeper, my universal fear of trust. My control said that I did not trust in the process of life as it was shown to me, in the processes of others, or my safety within those processes.

Tigger's refusal to obey my requests in our house angered me, only because I had a charge on being in control of my house. To others who would visit me, or who shared their lives with cats, the very same behavior from their pets did not bother them. They took the action of their cats as a sign of "independence." They had come to terms with what it meant to invite a cat into their world. The owners realized that the invitation included all of the characteristics and all of the traits that have followed cats through thousands of years of evolution. These traits included climbing to high places to monitor their world, regardless of whether that place is forbidden to them or not! For these owners, a cat on the refrigerator was no more of a problem that the same cat laying beside the fireplace on the living room floor.

"What is the problem?" they would ask. "Cats do what cats do."

Cats are great mirrors for triggering the subtle patterns of emotion that we call "issues." The way that we feel regarding the outcome of an event, circumstance or relationship is one of those subtle patterns. A strong feeling as to the rightness, wrongness or appropriateness of an outcome has been previously defined as our charge on that experience. Mastery describes how and to what degree we hold charge in our body. Do we trust in life as life is shown to us? Having accomplished all that we can possibly accomplish in a given situation, are we able to let go of the outcome and trust in whatever follows?

In the example of my coworkers, my emotion was one of fear. I was afraid that "they" would not perform correctly. My fear was that in their imperfection, I would be judged. As my thoughts were directed "to the negative," I mirrored those thoughts with words such as

"Don't be late with this project,"

and

"If you don't do a good job, we are all in trouble."

Each statement was intended as an incentive for the employees to perform well on this assignment. In both cases, by offering the incentive in the negative, I created the charge.

It certainly was not intentional. At the time, it was my way of being certain that all went well on a project under my direction. Using different thoughts and words, I could have conveyed the same idea without the negative connotation in the sample above. For example, by saying

"Please, don't be late with this project,"

what I have accomplished is to give power to the "lateness" of the project. Energy follows attention. Through my statement, I have directed a focus to "not being late." My focus has created the charge. A higher option of stating the identical incentive may have been to offer the idea in the positive,

"Please be on time with this project,"

or

"Thank you in advance for your timely completion of this project."

The same idea is conveyed, with a very different sense. In this example the focus of attention now is "on time" and that is what creation promises we will have the opportunity to experience.

When you find yourself reacting with a charge to the words, actions or life expression of someone else, human or otherwise, there is a good possibility that you are experiencing a powerful opportunity to know yourself on a deep yet subtle level. If you find that your response is a particularly strong reaction, I invite you to bless that moment. You may be experiencing the first step in a powerful series of initiations that will lead you to the greatest levels of personal mastery, the Essene Mystery of the First Mirror: the Mirror of the Moment.

THE MYSTERY OF THE SECOND MIRROR:
REFLECTIONS OF JUDGMENT

"Recognize what is in your sight,
and that which is hidden from you,
will become plain to you."
THE NAG HAMMADI LIBRARY[3]

A heavy mist surrounded the valley, hanging close to the base of the mountain as I walked in the morning sun. I began to recall teachers from my past, masters from my years of training in the martial arts of Karate, Aikido and Judo. It is interesting how clearly the memories return and how clear the message appears, when it is time. I saw my Karate instructor, Charles, in his midwestern dojo instilling within me the virtues of concentration and focus. One evening, in demonstration of the power of focus, Charles had called our class to attention and asked that we give him three minutes of "meditation time" before we approached him. After the three minutes, by any means necessary, as a class we were to move his outstretched arms or dislodge him from his cross legged position on the mat in the center of the room. We agreed believing that even this powerful man, the object of honor and respect from each young man and woman in the room, would be no match for a class of fifteen or so working in unison to budge him from his position.

Closing his eyes, we watched Charles begin to shift his breathing. Within a few seconds he had gone from deep rhythmic breaths that caused his stomach to fill and flatten, into a breath that was so subtle it appeared as if he was not breathing at all. At the mark of three minutes we began. Two of us at first approached the man sitting there on the mat, deep in meditation. We reasoned that with two of us, we would "give him a chance." Together, we pulled, pushed, heaved and tugged. Absolutely nothing happened. We could not even budge our instructor's rigid arms as they extended from his shoulders like a human letter "T." Two more students from the edge of the mat joined in, then two more. Soon, everyone was grabbing and holding Charles, pulling, twisting and grunting in an effort to move something, *anything!* We could not even flex our instructor's fingers, let alone move him to another location on the floor. For all intents and purposes, in that moment, our Charles was a part of the floor of his dojo, organically anchored through some mysterious force that was invoked through his concentration and focus.

We later learned that, during his meditation, Charles had visualized a chain between each of his arms and a distant and imaginary mountain. As long as the chain was present, nothing could move him or his arms, *until he willed it.*

As I walked down the road I thought to myself,

If such feats could be demonstrated, purely through focus, what if that focus were applied to a situation, belief or concept that was demonstrated in my life? Immediately, my Judo instructor, John, came to mind. John's message to me had been simple." Never take life, or yourself, too seriously," he would say. Entering into his dojo each evening three times a week, John would greet us by asking if we wished to "play" judo. It was to be fun as well as instructional. In the fun, I recalled a discourse that he provided to me following an especially discouraging sparring demonstration one evening. Though I had been "defeated" in a sparring match with another student, I was still presented a belt award signifying my mastery of specific hand and foot techniques. As I questioned my worthiness of receiving the award that evening, John shared with me his reasoning.

"Each person in competition is a mirror to you," he began. "As your personal mirror, they will always show you who you are in that moment. By observing how your opponent approaches you, you are seeing your opponent's reaction to what he or she perceives you are offering."

I had chosen the correct techniques in response to my opponent's offering. For that correctness, I was awarded. It was in the demonstration of my techniques that I had been defeated. I remember John's words and think of them often. Later in life, I had broadened the context of that one way discussion, to include each personality that came into my life. Applying that wisdom to the situation that had become the focus of this particular walk, it made no sense at all.

In the fall of 1992, three people came into my life within a short period of time. Through these people I would experience three of the most powerful, as well as painful relationships, that I have known as an adult. Though I did not recognize them at the time, each of the three in their own right was to become a master for me in a way that I had never imagined. Together the single lesson that they offered me, though subtle in its nature, became a compelling catalyst that assured my life would never be the same again.

Though each relationship served as a mirror for me at precisely the right time, I did not immediately recognize the timing of each teaching. The first relationship was a romantic relationship. A woman had come into my life who I believed demonstrated such similar goals and interests to mine that we chose to live and work together. The second relationship was a new business partnership that was to provide much needed support for the setting up of seminars and workshops in cities throughout the country. I perceived this as a welcome relief for many of the administrative routines that were so vital to a successful seminar. The third relationship was a combination of a new friendship and business arrangement. This agreement revolved around a gentleman living on my property while I traveled in exchange for overseeing the property, as well as additional carpentry that would support the renovations that I was undertaking at the time.

It was not long before each of the three relationships began to exhibit characteristics that provided me the opportunity to demonstrate patience, assertiveness and resolve. These relationships were absolutely "driving me up the wall." With each there were arguments, disagreements and a general tension between us. Because I was traveling extensively at the time, offering seminars and workshops, I had a tendency to neglect the timely resolution of these relationship hotspots. I would rationalize the arguments as stress related and assume responsibility for the tensions, taking a "wait and see" attitude until I returned from my next trip. Upon returning I would find things just as they had been before I left, with tension and disagreements occurring almost daily.

At the time there was a routine that I would follow upon arriving at the airport after each seminar. I would collect my gear from the baggage area, withdraw enough money from the automated teller machine (ATM) to pay for parking, pick up my cat from the vet and buy food on the way home. On this particular trip home, however, my routine would change. After collecting my bags and seminar materials, I went to the ATM to withdraw my travel money. To my horror, the machine politely printed a slip informing me that my account did not even contain enough money to give me a twenty dollar bill for gas and the three and one half hour drive home.

Spring in Northern New Mexico is a short season lasting possibly two to three months. During this particular Spring in 1993, I had scheduled contractors to begin renovation of the buildings on my property. Checks had been written against funds deposited, for a variety of reasons ranging from family members, mortgage on my property, monthly bills, to renovations on the property. To my amazement and disbelief everything was gone. The ATM was telling me that there was nothing, absolutely nothing. I knew that this had to be a mistake. I also knew that it was an error that would not be remedied at 5:30pm on a Sunday afternoon in Albuquerque, New Mexico. After convincing the airport parking attendant that I would repay the long-term parking bill that had accumulated during my trip, I began my three and one half hour drive north and thought about what had happened.

Calling my bank the next morning to rectify the "mistake," proved to be even more of a surprise. To my disbelief, I discovered that an unauthorized withdrawal had been made from my account. The account now was empty with an additional negative balance incurred by overdraft charges and the associated penalties for seventy one checks. I felt shock and disbelief. Within minutes my emotions moved quickly to anger and the anger turned to rage. I thought that I had known rage before in my life. Now I knew that it had only been anger. My mind raced with thoughts of the consequences, bounced checks, the dishonoring of all that I had written the checks to. The violation of trust and complete disregard for me, as well as those to whom the checks had been committed, was more than I had expected.

Later that day, the business relationship reached a boiling point as I opened my mail and examined a hand written ledger sheet of expenses that were deducted from a series of seminars that I had completed in good faith. Pouring over the tabulation of charges against the proceeds for the events, I began to see items that I felt were not justified as being taken from the workshops. I found myself on the phone with those who I had believed were representing my best interests, fighting for my share, line item by line item. Clearly, these people and I were not working from the same perspective toward the same goals.

During the same week, I discovered that the gentleman living on my property was pursuing a series of interests that were not only in direct opposition to the agreements that we had made, they were frowned upon by the state of New Mexico as well. I could no longer ignore what was happening in these relationships.

The next morning I walked down the dirt and gravel road leading away from my property to the large mountain that loomed over the valley behind my home. Ute Peak, at 10,039 feet above sea level, had always been a source of clarity and mystery to me. That day I walked toward Ute Peak in an effort to understand the lesson that my life was showing me, the lesson that I could no longer ignore. I stepped in silent prayer over the ruts and broken gravel, asking for the wisdom to recognize a pattern so blatant that I could not see it. What was the common thread between these three different, yet related, relationships? I called to myself the memories of those who had demonstrated their wisdom in my life.

"Each person," John had said, "is a mirror to you, showing you who you are in that moment. By careful observation, you see your opponent's reaction to what you are offering."

I looked at the three individuals, my relationship with them and I asked myself, *What characteristics have each of these people shown to me in their actions?*

I made mental notes of each as the traits emphasized in the relationships fluidly raced through my mind. Some passed so quickly that I never thought of them again. Others returned, again and again, until there were four that stood silently above the others.

Honesty, integrity, truthfulness and trust were etched clearly on the white board of my mind. I asked myself the next question,

If each person in this situation has mirrored to me that which I am in the moment, am I being shown that I lack honesty?

Have I somehow violated integrity, trust and truth in the course of my work or somewhere in my life?

As I asked the question in my mind, a feeling welled up from somewhere deep inside of my body. Inside of me a voice screamed. It was my voice, saying

No, of course I am honest.

Of course I have integrity.

Of course I am truthful and trustworthy.

These attributes form the very basis of the work that I offer to others!

At the same instant a realization came over me, fleeting at first, then clearer and stronger until it was there, crystallized for me to see and know. In that moment the mirror suddenly became clear. Those three people that I had so skillfully drawn into my life, each a masterful teacher in his or her own right, had not mirrored to me that which I was in the moment. Rather, each one had shown to me a very different reflection, a subtle mirror that no one had warned me of.

In their uniqueness each of the three had shown me quite clearly, not what I was, rather that which I judged.

They had demonstrated to me those qualities that I had a charge upon in the moment. The qualities were those of trust, integrity, honesty and truth. Suddenly I realized that I had a tremendous charge upon all of these characteristics. In all probability, the charge that had been building since my childhood. Immediately I began to recall all of the times that one, or some combination, of trust, integrity, honesty and truthfulness had been violated in my life. Past romances that were not truthful about others in their lives. Adult promises that were made and never honored. Well intentioned friends and corporate mentors who had made promises that they could not keep. My list went on and on. My charge, my judgments, regarding these issues had been building for years on such a subtle level that I had not recognized them. Now something had occurred in my life that I could not ignore. The repercussions were deep and vast. The blatant nature of this experience was my assurance that I would move beyond merely looking at my pattern. This time I would have to see my pattern.

This was the day that I learned the subtle, yet profound Mystery of the Second Mirror of Relationship, the Mirror of that which is Judged.

The following day I visited a friend who lives and works on a nearby pueblo. One of the oldest indigenous dwelling sites in North America, this particular community has been continuously occupied for at least 1,500 years. Robert (not his real name) had a shop within the pueblo itself and was a tremendously skilled artist and craftsman, as demonstrated by the dream catchers, sculptures, music and jewelry on display inside. As I walked in he was working on a large sculpture, nearly seven feet tall, standing in the aisle behind him. After saying our "hellos," I asked about his family, business and catch up talk. He asked me what was happening in my life and, after hearing the story of the three people and the missing money, he told me a story.

"My great grandfather," he began,

"hunted buffalo on the plains of Northern New Mexico."

I knew that he must have been talking about a long time ago, as no buffalo had openly roamed this part of the state for years.

"Before his death, he gave to me his most valued possession, the head of the first buffalo that he had ever taken as a young boy."

Robert went on to tell me how this buffalo head had been a valued possession of his as well, one of the few tangible relics connecting him with his great grandfather and their common heritage. One day a gallery owner had come to visit Robert from the nearby artist community of Taos. She asked him if she could use the buffalo head for a display in her jewelry gallery and he agreed. After a few weeks had passed, Robert had not heard from his friend and went into town to see how she was doing. To his surprise, when he arrived at the gallery, there was nothing there. The doors were locked, the windows covered and the shop was out of business. She was gone. Robert looked up from his work into my eyes and I could see that he had been hurt in the experience.

What did you do?,

I asked, expecting to hear how he had tracked down the gallery owner and retrieved his prized possession. As his eyes met mine, the wisdom of his answer was not lost in its simplicity.

"I did nothing," he said.

"She lives with what she has done."

I left the Taos pueblo that day, thinking about the story and its relevance in my life. As I explored my legal options for recovering at least some of the money that had disappeared from my account, I learned quickly that regardless of the course of action, it would be a lengthy process. Attorney after attorney advised me that there was certainly a case, and a good one at that. Due to the nature of the complaint, theft from a federal banking institution, I would be required to turn it over to the authorities as a criminal rather than a civil suit. From that point on, the fate of the person charged would be out of the hands of myself and my attorney. If convicted, there was a good chance of incarceration. Before that, however, there would be preliminaries. These pretrial particulars included hearings and trials at the convenience of the court, regardless of either of our schedules. There would be fees for the attorneys, fees for court costs, fees for attorney's aids and an investigation. All of this added up to a prolonged relationship with someone who I no longer felt any connection with, leading to the possibility of probation or imprisonment in the event of a guilty verdict, and a lot of money.

I did not feel good about the options. As enraged as I had been, I did not feel that imprisonment was warranted, nor the emotional expense of a pretrial investigation. As I pondered the options and opportunities as they had been presented, I reached a conclusion that immediately felt "right." I reflected once again on the conversation with my friend at the Taos Pueblo, as well as the lessons that the incidents that the previous days had afforded me.

There was a common thread that bound the meeting of each of the three individuals together. Upon first meeting each one, I had experienced a feeling that something in the relationship was not right, something was amiss. There was no logical reason to feel any suspicion. I did not even know the people. Still, there were the feelings, feelings that I ignored. There were even blatantly obvious clues. I ignored them as well, rationalizing them as insignificant or my suspicious judgments. For example, upon first meeting the man with whom I would enter into an intimate business partnership, I had asked a question that I seldom ask of anyone. Within minutes of our meeting I abruptly shifted the course of our conversation with a question.

When were you born?

I asked the question from a place within me that did not even think about this exchange.

"June 28, 1954," had been the reply.

To my amazement, June 28th, 1954 was the exact day, month and year of my birth as well. The man with whom I was about to trust with sensitive details of business and scheduling, my business, was born on the exact day, month and year that I was only five hours earlier. I thought that two people with such close dates of birth, both water signs of feeling, could not go wrong in a partnership.

At that moment, something happened that I remember well to this day, though I discounted it at the time. My business "partner to be" looked me directly in the eyes, probably without even realizing the clarity of his message, laughed and said to me

"I am your evil twin."

His very words could have been a clue for me, if I had heard what he was saying rather than listening to what I chose to hear. Before the echo of his words had faded from the room, I discounted them, rationalizing them away as joking with me, though I admittedly found little humor in that conversation. Within a few short months I would remember those words, and it would be too late.

Taking into consideration all that had occurred, and the context of each of the events, I reached a conclusion with regard to the money. In the present situation, I would do nothing. In doing nothing, I would allow the momentum of the chain of events to cease, the pattern would be changed and it would be done.

Just one week earlier I had spoken to a group in California stating my sense that 1993 was a year of "Truth." As a year of truth, anything lacking the integrity of its own truth would collapse under its own weight. I recognized the opportunity for me to demonstrate this principle to myself by allowing each of the parties, as well as myself, to forever live with the consequences of all that had unfolded. It was complete. Reaching that decision with my body as well as my logic was the work. Having made the decision I did nothing, and felt good about it.

Almost immediately, something interesting began to happen. Following the conscious choice to "do nothing," each of the three people mirroring my judgments began to fall away from my life. There was no intentional effort on my part to drive them away. Each simply began to fade from my day-to-day activities. Suddenly there were fewer telephone calls from them, fewer letters from them and fewer thoughts about them throughout the course of my day. I was not angry with them. I did not resent them. I began to sense a very odd feeling of "nothingness" with regard to each of these people. Having reconciled the events that had transpired between us for what they were and not what my judgments would like for them to be, there was simply no charge to hold the relationships in place.

Within a few days, something perhaps even more interesting began to occur. I realized that there were people who had been in my life for a long time, that also began to fade away. Again, there was no conscious effort on my part to end relationships or drive these people from my life. Communication between us became almost nonexistent. What conversation did exist required an effort and seemed artificial and pointless on my part. Where there had been common ground previously, there was an emptiness that was uneasy for them, as well as myself. Almost as soon as I noticed the shift in relationships I became aware of, what for me, was a new phenomenon.

Each of the relationships that were now falling from my life, as diverse as they appeared, had their roots in the same pattern that each of the three present relationships had shown to me. That pattern was judgment.

The charge of my judgment regarding trust, violation and discernment was the glue that had held all of these relationships together. Having recognized the path of compassionately allowing each individual to demonstrate their mirror of me, rather than resisting through actions of retribution, and "getting even," the attraction began to fade. In the absence of my charge of judgment, the glue dissolved. I noticed what appeared to be a cascading effect. Once the pattern of judgment was addressed at one place on one level, in one relationship, its echo faded on many other levels. What a beautiful validation of the Mystery of the Second Mirror; the Mirror of Judgment.

I invite you to examine your relationship with the people that you hold most dear in your life. Acknowledge the characteristics and traits that you are most drawn to in these individuals. Additionally, recognize the patterns and characteristics they exhibit that absolutely irritate you to no end. Having identified the patterns that they show you through their actions, ask yourself the question:

"Are these people showing me myself in this moment?"

If you can honestly and truthfully say "No," then there is a very good possibility that, laying at the core of your irritation, you will find a clue regarding yourself. The source of your irritation with their actions may be the mirror of those qualities of character that you judge in life.

The challenge in relating this story has been to convey the patterns of charge as opposed to the emotion of "whom did what to whom." People have said to me, after hearing this story,

"They took your money."

"They violated your trust."

"They left you with nothing."

"They did it to you."

On one level, these observations may be accurate, as the experience is relative. Viewing and responding to life from this level, however, promises that we will remain locked into the patterns of thinking that perpetuate this kind of experience. On another level, each of the three individuals, simply in being who they are, taught me one of the most potent and empowering lessons of my life. Each, in his or her own way, was a great teacher for me. I choose to take the experience of our lives to the next level.

The mirrors of judgment are subtle, elusive and will possibly not make sense to all who become aware of them. The recognition of judgment as a reflected action is not an insignificant achievement. For the lessons I give thanks. To the individuals who have shown me my humanness, my deepest respect and gratitude for impeccably holding the mirror.

THE MYSTERY OF THE THIRD MIRROR:
REFLECTIONS OF LOSS

"The Kingdom of my Father
is like a certain woman who was carrying
a jar full of meal.

While she was walking on a road,
still some distance from home,
the handle of the jar broke
and the meal emptied out behind her
on the road.

She did not realize it;
she had noticed no accident.
When she reached her house,
she set the jar down and found it empty."

ESSENE PARABLE FROM THE NAG HAMMADI LIBRARY[*]

Your love and compassion are like the meal in the jar of the preceding Essene parable. As you journey through the waking dream of life, pieces of your life may be lost, innocently given away or taken away by those who have had power over you. These portions of you are your compromises, exchanged for surviving your experience of life. When you reach a time in your life where you truly choose to love, share and give of yourself, you may find that nothing is left. You discover that you have lost yourself, little by little to the very experience that invites you to share. Recognizing the patterns and masks of survival as they play out through your relationships is an accelerated path of choice. Calling back those pieces of you that hold dear may be your highest expression of personal mastery.

It was a warm night in July, even for northern California. In the small town of McCloud, about nine miles from the city of Mt. Shasta, I had rented a combination retreat center, bed and breakfast for the purpose of offering a new workshop. Based on my experiences from Egypt's Mt. Sinai two years earlier, this intensive was to focus upon the sacred aspect of sacred geometry and the role of relationships as reflections of ourselves. My group filled the bed and breakfast to capacity, allowing us unrestricted and private access to the entire facility including the reception and greeting areas with comfortable couches, assorted chairs, and a large screen television. It was on this television that I was previewing new video documentation of the significance of sacred geometry in ancient and sacred sites, terrestrial and otherwise.

Sometime during the video, the screen door to the lobby opened and two young women walked in, having just completed a long day of travel. They were acquaintances of a third woman who was working at the B&B in what was called "selfless service." Selfless service is performed by individuals through their work supporting the retreat center in exchange for meals and lodging. Noticing the room full of people engrossed in the video, one of the women asked me if she could stay and watch, what by then, was some of the most compelling information in the video. I agreed and she found a seat on the floor, quickly melding into the group with questions and discussion until the program was complete.

As the lights came on following the video, for the first time I could see the young woman who had just shared the better portion of two hours with a group of strangers. There was something familiar about her, a strange familiarity that immediately put me at ease while being drawn to her at the same time. Apparently she felt the same, and after saying our good nights to the others in the lobby we agreed to go for a late night walk through the streets of McCloud. If you have ever been to McCloud, you know that the walk did not take long. To our surprise we were back at the inn within minutes, neither of us feeling like ending the evening. She made arrangements to stay with her friend that night and we walked the "McCloud circuit" many more times, familiarizing ourselves with the city's landmarks, the railroad and mining museum, ice cream shop and lumber mill, while we shared travel stories, names and family histories. Her name was "Chris" (not her real name) and she mentioned that after getting her old Volvo station wagon fixed, she would be driving alone, back to the East coast. We said good night and I believed that I would probably never see this woman again.

The following morning, I drove up and down the side streets of Mt. Shasta look-ing for a pet store. As I had decided to take Merlin, the young kitten gifted to me by the inn, I knew that there would be certain supplies that would make our travel time to New Mexico much easier. I was on a mission to locate a kitty food and water bowl, a leash for road stops and disposable kitty litter pans. Coming to a stop at one of the few lights in town, I glanced at the pedestrians in the walk and saw Chris standing there waiting to cross. She saw me at the same time and ran over to my open window to say hello just as the light changed. Behind us, drivers vented their impatience. Amid the blasting horns and shouts from inside the cars, I asked Chris if she had lunch yet, she said "no," I asked if she would like to, she said "yes" and in a heartbeat she was in the car and we were off. It had happened in just a few brief seconds. Finding a pet store close by, we found Merlin's accessories and were off to lunch, both a little surprised at the spontaneity and synchronicity of finding ourselves together again.

Stopping at a small cafe on the south end of town, we were seated quickly, apparently the first to be interested in lunch. We began to talk. As our conversations wove around our life experience of marriages, divorces, travel to foreign countries and the pursuit of God, I watched the cafe fill for the lunch rush. Soon the crowd thinned and we were the only two in the restaurant, thoroughly enjoying our time together. I glanced at a clock on the wall as we finished our meal. Nearly three hours had passed since we had been seated for an early lunch. Her car was parked close by and we walked to the now repaired Volvo, still talking. With a hug and a kiss on the cheek, we said our good byes and she drove away. Once again I suspected that I would never see her again. As I watched her car disappear down the road, something began to happen inside of me, something quite unexpected.

A tremendous emptiness began to well up inside of my chest and stomach. Sud-denly, waves of emotion flooded my body. My eyes began to tear and I realized that something unbelievable was happening. I was missing this woman! If I had not known better, I would have believed that I was in love. I knew that love, in the romantic sense of the word was probably not likely. We had known one another for a total of maybe five hours. Regardless of what it was, or what I was choosing to call it, something very real was happening to me. There was no denying that.

As I reached my car I sat there in the early afternoon sunlight, staring down the road to where her car had vanished just moments earlier. Was she feeling the same thing that I was feeling? Would she turn her car around and drive back, or was the entire event happening within me only, within my mind? A barrage of thoughts and emotion ran wildly through my mind as I sat and waited. After a few minutes, I started the car and drove back to the inn to pick up my new friend Merlin and begin the drive to New Mexico. I never saw Chris again. What had just happened to me?

During the early part of my career in the aerospace industry, I worked as part of a team of software engineers. We shared a relatively small work space in typical Steele-case™ Air Force regulation desks, chairs and cubicles. Spending long hours together in close proximity, we quickly became very familiar with one another and our personal, private and family lives. Several times per week we would go for lunch together, sometimes cashing paychecks or doing quick lunch time errands.

One of the engineers who worked with me experienced a frequent phenomenon that wreaked havoc throughout his life. Almost on a daily basis he would "fall in love" with someone that he had met during lunch. It might be the waitress that had taken our order or the bank teller that had just cashed our checks. It may be the saleswoman in a department store or the clerk at the grocery checkout line. He would fall in love multiple times per day. The reason that this became a problem was that he was happily married to a lovely wife with a beautiful child. The feelings of love for these other people would become so strong following the encounter, however, that he would not be able to focus on his work. He would think about these people for the rest of the afternoon, sometimes pursuing them with telephone calls and invitations to coffee. If they agreed, he would meet them after work to talk. Then he would fall in love with the waitress who was waiting on them. He was compelled to initiate contact with these people, to explore what he believed his feelings of love were telling him. What was happening to this man?

Have you ever had similar experiences, perhaps to a lesser degree? Have you ever been in a perfectly happy, committed relationship or perhaps no relationship at all and not looking for one, walking down the street of a busy city, in an airport, shopping mall or grocery store and suddenly "it" happens? Someone, possibly a complete stranger, walks past you. In the passing your eyes meet and, click, there is a feeling. Perhaps it is simply a feeling of familiarity. It may be an almost overwhelming impulse to know this person, to initiate conversation or possibly just stand close. As people feel comfortable sharing intimate portions of their lives in workshop situations, I have discovered that this is not an uncommon occurrence.

What commonly follows is this: even though their eyes have met and they have felt the "feeling," one of the parties will discount the event. For a few brief fractions of a second, however, there is an altered state, perhaps a sense of unrealness. For just a moment beyond a casual glance, their eyes will communicate. Each being will say something to the other in that moment, probably without even knowing it. Then, almost as if on cue, their rational minds will create a distraction, anything to break the contact. It may be the sound of a car passing or possibly gum on the street. It may be a toss of their hair or a sneeze. The other person will shift his/her attention and the moment will be gone, just like that.

If you have had this experience, what has just happened to you? An awareness of life patterns will demonstrate that you probably have this experience commonly, possibly on a daily basis. Hopefully, your feelings will not be as intense as my engineer friend. Each of these examples, Chris in Mt. Shasta, my friend the engineer and you walking down the street have a common thread. Each is illustrating a powerful opportunity to know yourself, if you have the wisdom to recognize the opportunity. The secret to this opportunity lies hidden in the Mystery of the Third Mirror.

For you to survive in your life, until this very moment, you may have compromised huge portions of yourself in exchange for the continuation of your experience. Those portions were innocently given away, lost or taken away as you learned to cope with the challenges of life. You learned that it was easier to "give in" or to change instead of navigating your life into the face of opposition. The compromises have been masked as socially accepted courses of action that, while not always approved of, have been allowed or overlooked in our society. The forcing of children to perform in adult roles of business or family, the loss of racial history as cultures are forced together, the survival of childhood and adolescent trauma through numbed emotions are examples of giving away portions of yourself.

Why would you do such a thing? Why would you compromise huge portions of your uniqueness, knowing that you would need to retrieve them at some later time in your life? The answer is simple. Survival.

As a child, you may have discovered that it was much easier for you to remain silent, rather than voicing an opinion at the risk of being invalidated by parents or peers. As the object of abuse and trauma in the family, it is much safer to give in and forget, than to resist those who have power over you. As a society we accept the killing of others in special circumstances, through conditioning. We have been conditioned to give our power away and feel helpless in the face of conflict, illness, disease and overwhelming emotion.

In each of these examples, I am describing a pattern of behavior rather than illustrating a wrong, right, or the appropriateness of a feeling. Specifically, that pattern is the losing, giving away or having a part of you taken away to survive life.

That pattern is also a path. With any path there are consequences. To the degree that you have compromised pieces of yourself to get where you are today, for each piece lost there remains an emptiness waiting to be filled. That void may be thought of as an empty charge. The key to understanding what happened in each of the above examples is this:

As you encounter someone with a charge complimenting parts of you that have been lost, taken away or given away, their charge may feel very good to you.

We are continually searching for that feeling, either consciously or subconsciously. The complimentary charges held by others is what makes us feel "whole" again, until we remember the portions of ourselves that lay dormant within ourselves. As you feel in another the patterns that you have forgotten within yourself, you may believe that you feel love for that person. With them, you find the awakening of your dormant virtues, qualities and characteristics. The same feeling of love that you experience may not be true for the person standing next to you in the grocery checkout line, a friend or some other member of your family. The chances are that other people have not given themselves away in quite the same way that you have.

The key to your mastery is to recognize the feeling for what it is, and not what your conditioning will make the feeling out to be. If you do not know better, you may believe that you are in love, and you may very well be. What is the unexplainable magnetic attraction, the fire that we seek with others allowing us to feel alive and complete? *That fire is the charge of our compliment.* That feeling is what it feels like when we find someone with the complementary pieces that match our voids. Romantic love is the name that we give to the feeling of finding our missing pieces. Sometimes we call those pieces "our other half." With that in mind, lets go back to our examples and answer the questions of "What has happened?" and "What is happening?"

Without consciously knowing it, there is a good possibility that my friend the engineer was seeking within others the very pieces of himself that he had lost, had taken away or had given away throughout his life. In addition to the portions of himself that he retained, the qualities that allowed him to be the engineer father husband and friend that he was in that moment, the pieces lost were so prevalent that he found at least one in nearly every person that he encountered.

Not understanding what his feelings were saying to him, he was compelled to act upon his feelings in the only way that he knew how. He honestly believed that each encounter was an opportunity for happiness because he felt so good while he was with these people. He still loved his wife and his son very much. When I asked him if he honestly wanted to leave them, he looked shocked. He had no desire to end his marriage and yet, the force of his feelings led him into compromising situations until the loss of his marriage became a very real danger.

When Chris drove away from me in Mt. Shasta, I had a very deep emotional and physiological reaction. I actually felt a part of myself "ripped" away as her tail lights disappeared over the horizon. As I asked within myself for the wisdom to understand what was happening to me, I realized that in Chris I had seen a part of myself that I had given away years earlier. In that particular moment, Chris was mirroring to me my lost innocence and spontaneity.

I knew that this was true as I had just been thinking about that very topic during the drive into Mt. Shasta. I loved her innocence and the wonder with which she viewed her life, as well as the lives of those around her. Through years of academia, two corporate careers and the rigors of a "broken" marriage, I certainly had lost a portion of my spontaneity and innocence. It may happen commonly to each of us, perhaps on a daily basis.

For example, years ago before becoming a geologist, I used to drive West on Interstate 70 from Denver in complete awe of the beauty in the road cuts through the mountains. I had never known that rocks could have such vivid colors; bright reds, shimmering pinks and deep greens fading into blues and grays. The banded sections of rock stood almost perpendicular to the ground. After receiving my degree I still drove Interstate 70 West through the road cuts. Now, however, those road cuts did not look the same. They had not changed. Each band of color was still there as brilliant as ever. I had changed, however, something within me. Now I saw geologic examples of dip angles, beautiful Cretaceous strata and metamorphic processes in place of the bright colors and beautiful stripes. I had compromised a degree of my innocence in exchange for the wisdom of my knowing.

Each of us has skillfully given away the portions of ourselves that we determined in the moment, were necessary for our survival or mastery of that moment. In doing so, we may have become trapped within the limited expression of what remains. For some the trap is greater than for others.

One afternoon, while working in the aerospace industry, I received a very unexpected invitation on my desk to an informal presentation by high ranking military and corporate officials. They were to tour a portion of our research and development facilities related to a weapons program that was being tested at the time. During a conversation following the presentation, one of the C.E.O's, in unusual candor, answered a question that someone asked regarding what it took to rise through the military ranks, through the civilian ranks, through the Pentagon bureaucracy into a tremendous position of power and authority afforded as Chief Officer of a large multi-national corporation. I listened intently as this man, honestly and consciously, began his answer.

"To get to where I am today," he began,

"I had to give myself away to the journey. Each time I advanced in rank, I lost another piece of myself in life, time after time. One day I realized that I was on top and looked back at my life. What I discovered was that I had given away so much of myself to the journey that there was nothing left. The corporation and the military own me. I have given away the things that I love the most, my wife, my children, my friends and my health. I traded those things for power, wealth and control."

I was amazed at his honesty. Though this man had lost himself in the process, he had done it consciously. To him it was a price worth paying for his position of power. Though probably not for the same reasons, we each may do something very similar over the course of our lives. For many people, however, the goal is less about power and more about their very survival.

When you do encounter someone on the streets, in the stores or in the office and begin to feel that feeling of familiarity, I invite you to immerse yourself in the moment. Something powerful is happening for both of you. You have just encountered someone who exhibits a portion or portion(s) of you, that you are searching for. Will you recognize it the moment? If you feel that it is appropriate, initiate conversation. Begin talking about anything, anything at all, to maintain eye contact. While you are speaking, in your mind ask yourself this question:

What do I see in this person that I have lost, given away, had taken away or forgotten within myself?

Almost immediately, in your mind, the response will come to you. It may be as simple as a feeling of realization or as clear as a familiar voice that has spoken within you since childhood. Answers are often single words or short phrases. Your body knows what is meaningful to you. Perhaps you simply recognize the beauty within this person, a beauty that you feel is absent within you in that moment. Possibly it will be their innocence, the grace with which they move down the grocery aisle, their confidence and organization in performing the task at hand, or simply the radiance that surrounds a person of vitality. Through eye contact, feel the "feeling" and recognize what is happening. In all probability, as you have these experiences, you have just found someone who has the potential to show you portions of yourself that you have lost or forgotten. In the recognition lives your mastery.

For some individuals, having these feelings of attraction without understanding the mirror may seem awkward or inappropriate. You may even believe that you are in love and feel all of the guilt of the inappropriateness of the encounter. Knowing what your feelings are saying to you will allow you to act consciously, rather than following some mysterious and compelling force that you cannot explain.

When you encounter someone through eye contact, feel the feeling and recognize what is happening. There is a good possibility that you have just found someone who has the potential to show you something of yourself that you have sought for years or possibly lifetimes. If the situation involves someone that you see regularly, such as a coworker or office mate, feelings of attraction may become a problem. You may find yourself in situations that compromise your career, family or personal integrity.

If this experience happens frequently to you, I invite you to try something. This simple exercise may prove to be very empowering for you, as well as the other person involved, should you choose to share your process with them. If you sense that the other individual is open to discussing the obvious feelings, you may approach the subject in the following manner. Express your feelings to them by simply stating the truth:

I find myself drawn to you. Then continue with an explanation.

In asking myself why, I have discovered that in you, I see something of myself that I lost a long time ago. It is that part of you that I am attracted to.

Having offered this to employees and practiced it myself, I can say from experience that something magical happens in simply and honestly saying the words. The powerful charge surrounding the attraction dissipates, opening the opportunity for a new and different kind of charge, something greater than was present before. In the acknowledgment of the feelings, together you may determine the appropriateness of how the feelings are resolved. More often than not, in sharing the three sentences offered above, or their equivalent in your own words, an even greater friendship born of deep respect and understanding may emerge. If this occurs in an office environment, the chances are that the two of you may be working together for a long time. What a powerful alternative to the resolution of the feelings, rather than acting on what is perceived as love only to find disappointment in the relationship and tension in the office or classroom.

Through the seminars, people have asked me about these mirrors relative to female and male attraction. Herein lies possibly one of the best kept secrets of the Third Mirror. Within your being, as a soul essence you are neither male nor female alone and both combined. Without a body you are essentially genderless. Now, consider the magnitude of your expression through a body in the earth experience. To descend into the earth plane of polarity, you must choose between one or the other of two polarities. You must choose to express as either male or female, compromising the other in order to even begin this life! Before you emerge from the womb, you have given away fifty percent of your identity, placing it on a back burner, unable to fully express that portion of your life.

This being the case, you will generally seek the compliment to that which you have given away, your other half. You now begin to see why sometimes you are unexplainably attracted to someone of the opposite sex, for no apparent reason that you can identify. While you may rationalize the attraction as the beauty or sexual chemistry, in all probability you are feeling what it feels like to be whole again as you hold and touch your compliment.

Ideally, the relationship will awaken that portion within you that lies dormant, and for you the charge will be balanced. From that moment on, you must make a powerful choice as to whether or not you choose to continue the relationship. I say that this is a powerful choice because only when the charge is gone, are you able to make the choice without the magnetic force compelling you to remain in the relationship.

What about "same sex" relationships? You now have the information that may provide an answer to this question for yourself. We generally seek the complement of that which is lost, taken away or given away within ourselves. Prior to birth fifty percent of our identity is given away to begin our earthly experience.

For example, consider a soul that chooses to experience earth as a male body. The feminine aspect of that soul is de-emphasized for the sake of the experience, a choice that is made before birth. As the soul is polarized into a male expression, "male" may be all it knows to begin with.

Now, the question: What happens, if through the experiences of life, that soul's maleness is lost, taken away or given away? What is left? The feminine was compromised before birth and the masculine is compromised after birth. The polarized soul will be drawn to reinforce the polarity that it was born with to reclaim at least fifty percent of its identity. The male will seek the companionship of other males, mirroring its loss, as it strives toward wholeness. The mirroring of this possibility may last for days, years or for a lifetime.

The key here is that in the past our society has emphasized the compartmentalization and labels of relationships. Inherent in the labels is the judgment, separation from families and guilt over a very natural process of seeking the compliment to that which has been lost. We discover completeness within ourselves as others mirror to us our nature. Collectively we seek wholeness. Individually, we create varied and unique paths to attain our wholeness.

For those who dare to allow themselves feeling, the Third Mirror, the mirror of loss, probably faces them nearly every day of life. Clergymen, teachers, elderly people watching young people, parents watching their children, all are catalysts of feeling.

It is natural.

It is human.

Understanding what your feelings about others are saying to may become your most powerful tool toward a high level of personal mastery.

THE MYSTERY OF THE FOURTH MIRROR: REFLECTIONS OF YOUR MOST FORGOTTEN LOVE

"That which you have will save you,
if you bring it forth from yourselves."
THE DEAD SEA SCRIPTURES[5]

In 1992 a man called me one evening and asked if I would be willing to help him through what he perceived as the greatest challenge of his adult life. He had just been diagnosed with an "aggressive" cancer and it was the opinion of the medical professionals that he had a very slim chance of long term survival. I returned the call to "Charles" (not his real name) and explained that I had no medical credentials and could do little more than offer insights into possible patterns of emotion underlying his condition. He agreed, made an appointment, and we met two nights later.

As Charles walked into my office that evening, a flood of emotion filled my body. Though he did not "feel" well to me, at the same time he did not feel like someone who had given up on life. My sense may best be described as a dichotomy surrounding his life, his condition and the relationship between the two. Following a warm embrace and our greetings, I asked Charles to tell me about himself and his life. Immediately, he launched into a description of his "disease" and what doctors had told him. A flurry of diagnostic terms tumbled from his mouth as he detailed diagnosis, prognosis and survival statistics regarding his condition. His voice cracked and his hands trembled as he described to me what "they" had said to him. Sensing his need to say these things, I listened for a few moments. Finding a courteous breakpoint in his conversation, I interrupted.

What you have offered is a description of the way that others have seen you, from their perspective, I began.

Please Charles, tell me about your life.

Who are you?

What do you Feel?

Charles stopped. He stopped crying. He stopped speaking. He simply stared at me. "What do you mean?" he asked.

"How do you think I feel?"

That is a fair question, I replied. *I have chosen to understand you. To do so I must hear from you how you perceive yourself.* Nodding his head, Charles began by describing the pain in his chest and lower abdomen, his fevers, the stiffness of his muscles.

Now, I said, *you are describing body sensations. To the best of your ability, describe to me your emotions. Please let me see your eyes.*

He turned and offered his eyes to mine in what I sensed was an act of compromised desperation. There was a noticeable shift in the energy of the room as Charles sat back in his large wicker chair and began to fumble with the seam of the Afghan cushion beneath him.

"I feel scared," he said.

"I feel lost and alone. My family does not know how to be with me. They don't know what to say. My boss has asked me to take a leave of absence so that I don't disturb other employees. My friends are scared and have quit calling. I am alone. I have no one."

Good, I said, *you're doing good. Now, tell me about your life.*

Not surprisingly, Charles chose to begin with his early childhood at the age of six. Listening to his story, I began to hear of a man who had been in pain most of his life. It was an all too familiar story of abandonment in childhood. At the age of six, Charles' birth father had left the family quite suddenly. One day, after weeks of terrible fights with his wife, Charles' father just left. He went to work one day and never returned. At six years of age, without the benefit of understanding the adult dynamics of marital relationships, Charles felt that he was somehow responsible for his father's disappearance. He never knew quite how, he just knew that he had driven his father from the house.

For years as a young boy, each time that he saw his mother cry in the loss of her husband, Charles felt guilt for her pain, as well as his own. He and his mother grew distant as he developed friendships with other boys in his neighborhood with similar backgrounds. Together, he and his friends discovered cigarettes, alcohol, sex and how to survive a tough childhood.

It was not long before he began to numb his pain with whatever was available. Whatever emotional anesthetic his friends had, Charles used to help him stop feeling. Throughout junior high and high school he experimented with a variety of chemicals, and alcohol. He categorized each for me in detail, by their desirable and undesirable properties including side effects. By the time he was in the military, Charles had forgotten the reason why he drank each day. His drinking had become a habit, a very powerful force in his life without reason. Though he "dried out" briefly while he was in the service, it was not difficult to locate whatever he needed to get him through his day, regardless of what city he was stationed in.

Throughout this time Charles went through a number of romantic relationships. More often than not, the women would leave him, just the way his father had left his mother. Suddenly, for no reason, they would stop returning his phone calls, letters and correspondence. I asked Charles how he took the breakups. Each time, he said, "I was devastated in the break ups. I felt as if someone had taken something from my gut."

Now, in his early fifties, the doctors attributed the cancerous condition that was claiming Charles' life little by little, to a combination of factors largely related to years of alcohol, chemicals and nicotine and their effect upon his respiratory and immune system. Having read a few self help books as a last resort, Charles now was asking "Why?"

"What was happening to him?"

"What had he expressed in his life choices and why was his life being 'taken' from him?"

I offer Charles' story because it illustrates so beautifully a path, for some an unconscious path, that many have chosen at this time. The ancient calendars and mystic texts tell us that this lifetime is a time of cyclic completion. The close of this grand cycle of experience and the condition of Charles' body are not separate. To complete this cycle of experience Charles' life is asking him to come to terms with, what for him, represents his greatest fear of this lifetime. In coming to terms with himself emotionally, Charles will create the "program" that will allow his physical body to heal and survive. If we are to believe the ancient texts, there is a good possibility that the quality of Charles' emotion was determining the quality of his physical expression of life.

For many people, as with Charles, their greatest fear is so painful that they have skillfully masked their fear in a very clever way. Each fear is disguised as a socially acceptable pattern of behavior. In its disguise, the pattern may be acted out publicly, because its masked expression is accepted. If the mask of your greatest fear is acceptable in the eyes of your community, family and society, then it becomes safe to deny, numb and anesthetize your fear with others who have similar fears. To clarify this concept, lets examine Charles' patterns, step by step, to develop a sense for what his life was saying to him.

Charles began his life summary by describing how he was devastated in his father's leaving the family. His exact words were,

"My father left me. He left me alone."

Why was Charles so devastated at his father's leaving? The family relationship had been one of tension and anger. Why wasn't Charles relieved at his father's leaving? Without knowing what he had done, Charles had just described to me what was quite possibly his greatest fear in life. He even described it to me in the language of the first of the three universal fears, the fear of *Abandonment*. The pain that Charles felt when his father left him probably had very little to do with his earth father walking out on he and his mother. That incident was the catalyst that pushed the "buttons" of abandonment that Charles had come into this world with, the charge of separation. Each time someone left him in his subsequent relationships, romantic or otherwise, they were reminding Charles of his original feelings of separation. The ending of the romantic relationships felt more devastating because he had allowed a greater degree of intimacy and trust. Is it any wonder that it hurt so much when his father left? Look at the words that he chose to describe his experience. What was he really saying to me when he said,

"My father left me. He left me alone."

As we continued, Charles admitted to me that this single sentence described the feelings he had regarding his father in heaven, in addition to his earthly father. "How could a creator that loves me allow so much pain in my life?"

"How could a creator that has not forgotten me, allow this cancer in my body that is taking me, little by little?" he asked.

Perfect, I said.

Perfect response.

Perfect language.

I could not have stated the condition better myself. You have created for yourself the opportunity to discover, in this moment, what very probably is the part of yourself that you have least remembered, that part of yourself that you hold most dear. This is the part of yourself that, for you alone, will represent Your Most Forgotten Love.

Charles had done his work. He had taken a chance with me, someone that he had just met thirty minutes earlier, and allowed himself to trust me. In that trust, he also allowed me to feel his fears. In his innocence as he shared with me his most forgotten love, he discovered for himself the Mystery of the Fourth Essene Mirror of Relationship. Now I invited him to sit back, listen and consider the possibilities.

ADDICTION'S "GIFT"

Within each of us lives the hidden seed of our truth. Locked inside of each seed lives the memory of who we are, our relationship with the forces of creation, and our role in this world. Also, within each of our lives, lives the perception of what that seed means to us. The difference between the truth of the original seed, and the perception of our current reality is the distortion. The equation may be thought of as follows:

$$(Original\ Seed) - (Present\ Perception) = Distortion.$$

For some individuals, the present perception has become so painful that the distortion is unbearable. Skillfully, these powerful individuals create patterns of behavior that allow them to survive the distortion. These masterful diversions allow them to get through life with minimal pain. The reality is that the behavior pattern that "gets them through" actually numbs their pain, again and again. Today we call these repetitive patterns of behavior **addictions.**

Definition: For the purposes of our discussions, *addiction* may be defined as a repetitive pattern of behavior, that you rearrange the rest of your life to accommodate.

Upon hearing the term addiction in the workshops, immediately many people think of drug, chemical and alcohol. While these are certainly common expressions of behavior patterns that individuals rearrange the rest of their lives to accommodate, there are others that may not be so obvious. These subtle patterns may be masked as socially acceptable choices of lifestyle and behavior. Following is a partial list of addictions from a recent seminar.

Relationships	Nicotine	Making Money
Power	Control	Sex
Spending Money	Living in Lack	Illness

Each of these terms describes a pattern, without judgment of good or bad, that the individual shifted the priorities of their lives to make room for. The expression of the addiction itself is probably of less importance than the thought behind the addiction. For example in the addiction of "making money," is the money being made at the expense of loosing a family and loved ones? Is the money being made for the "joy" of making money or the "fear" of not having money? Clearly, we have just touched the tip of the iceberg when patterns of this nature are identified.

What does addiction have to do with the Essene Temples of relationship and the example of Charles? Herein lay the beauty of the gift of addiction. *Addictive and Compulsive Patterns of behavior, in their extreme, provide the opportunity to experience exactly the opposite of that which you most desire in life.* Your Addiction is your way of providing yourself the opportunity to experience your greatest fears, little by little, as you drive from your life the very things that you hold most dear. Once begun, an addictive and/or compulsive pattern will continue in your life until one of two possibilities occur.

- You recognize the pattern as the things that you hold most dear slip away, resolve the underlying fear, and release the charge holding the pattern in your life.

or

- You allow the pattern to continue for so long, that your greatest fear manifests in your life, over time, by degrees.

I invite you to consider what I have just offered to you. This is a perspective only. In discussing perspectives, there are seldom *always* and *nevers* with patterns of behavior. There are generalities. In the reflected reality of addiction, generally the very things that you hold most dear slip away from you little by little. There is a good possibility that the things that you value most in life are the very things that your "addiction" takes from you a little at a time. Recognizing your addictions will identify your greatest fears. It is the charge placed on the "not losing" of jobs, family, relationships, health and loved ones that promises the charge will be experienced.

The key here is to appreciate the gifts and qualities that life has offered, without the fear of losing those things. We never really *have* anything. We simply share time, experiences, lives and emotions. Inherent within each moment of your life is a choice. Inherent within each choice you affirm life or deny life within your being. What do you choose?

What life affirming words do you choose as you address others? What life affirming words do you allow others to use as they address you? What do you take into your body as life affirming nourishment? What do you feed those that you love to nourish them? These are examples of the choices that you and I make each moment of each day. I invite you to choose life, and live your choice, whatever that means to you!

In the instance of Charles, his greatest fear (most forgotten love) was a common fear of being separate and abandoned from his Father in heaven. The charge on his most forgotten love became so great that his father's leaving at age six was devastatingly painful. Each time someone would leave him in a relationship, he felt his original pain all over again, magnified by the complex distortions of whatever that particular relationship had meant to him. In his attempt to anesthetize his pain he numbed his emotions through the habitual use of chemicals, alcohol and nicotine. Each time that Charles chose to indulge these behavior patterns, consciously or otherwise, he chose to deny life in his body.

By the time I met Charles, his addiction was taking from him, little by little, the one thing that he held most dear in his life. For Charles it was life itself. Expressed as a cancerous condition, his body was reflecting back to him the quality of his thoughts, feelings and emotions about his own life. There was little that I could offer to him, beyond the opportunity to become aware of his choices and the power of his choices.

From that moment forward, Charles had heard the words. He could no longer say that he "did not know" of the relationship between his choices of lifestyle and their mirror within his body. From that moment forward Charles would have to choose each time his habits beckoned to him. In his choices would be the real workshop; the workshop of his life. Though various forms of therapy could certainly prove useful in delaying and pushing his body's expression of denying life into remission, clearly his highest option was to change the code driving the cancer. There is a good chance that the choices Charles had made in his life had brought him to this very point, the opportunity to choose again. He did. This time he chose life.

MYSTERY OF THE FIFTH MIRROR:
REFLECTIONS OF FATHER/MOTHER/CREATOR

"Whoever does not hate his father and mother as I do
cannot become a disciple to Me.
And whoever does not love his father and his mother as I do
cannot become a disciple to me.
For my mother gave me falsehood, but my true mother gave me life."
ADAPTED FROM THE NAG HAMMADI LIBRARY[6]

In early 1990 I was living in the San Francisco area, doing private counseling while researching *Awakening to Zero Point*. A woman that I had seen for several months regarding relationship issues had made an appointment with me one particular evening. Throughout the months that I had known her, she had been working through her feelings regarding a man that she had been involved with for many years. While she and her significant other had chosen not to marry, they could not seem to find completion for what she called the never ending date.

That evening as she sat across from me I asked her how she was and what had happened in her life since our last meeting.

"My life is terrible," she began.

"So many weird things have happened. We were sitting in the living room watching television and suddenly heard a loud crash in the bathroom. We ran in to find the door of the under sink vanity blown off its hinges, laying on the bathroom floor with water shooting out from the pipes under the sink. The next morning, we heard a loud noise in the garage. When we opened the door, the garage was covered with steaming water. The hot water heater had blown up. As we got into the car to shop for a new water heater, the radiator hose broke, spilling coolant all over the driveway."

I listened intently to what she was describing. When she had finished, I asked her the questions.

What is happening in your life right now?

How is your relationship with your never ending date?

Without stopping to think about an answer, the words fell out of her mouth, spilling over the last syllable of my question.

"The tension is almost unbearable," she said.

"Our lives are like a pressure cooker."

Her eyes met mine with a simultaneous look of acknowledgment and disbelief. "You don't think that my relationship had anything to do with my bathroom sink, hot water heater and radiator hose, do you?"

In my mind, there was no question.

The mirrors of life run much deeper than human relationships. We live in a world of resonance. Our lives mirror tuned patterns of energy tuned to other patterns of energy. We are tuned to our homes, our automobiles, appliances, office equipment, pets and weather patterns. Even the functioning of our world, the smoothness or lack thereof, of our electrical, mechanical and hydraulic realities reflect patterns of energy mirroring our expression of life. When one of these realities "fails," it may be asking us to look at the function of the failed component for insight into a belief system in our life. When the brakes go out on our car for example, what reality do we perceive as "out of control" or "can not be stopped" in our life? In this reality, friendships, jobs, animals and relationships are constant indicators, describing the quality of our thinking, feeling and emotional world.

Through the Essene traditions, we are shown that the mirrors of our relationships are in constant communication with our awareness. Our relationships serve as direct windows into the thinking, feeling and emotional postures that we assume in our world. As we have the wisdom to recognize the language, we may look to our world "out there" for precise, and sometimes graceful reminders of our beliefs. In light of this reflected reality, possibly the single most powerful mirror for me is so subtle, that I lived nearly forty years without seeing it.

In working one on one with clients, and more recently with many people in a workshop setting, I invite participants to complete a series of forms describing their primary childhood caretakers. Using single words or short phrases they list the positive and negative qualities of these people as they remember them. This is the work portion of the work shop. Similar to forms completed earlier in the program, this form emphasizes the participants perspective regarding health and disposition of their caretakers from an adult viewpoint. Ample time is offered to complete this exercise as the words that are chosen will become precise indicators to each participant of a subtle, yet powerful pattern, and the role it plays in their lives.

As they complete their forms I ask the group, in no particular order, to share a few words from their charts. The result is a list describing their primary childhood caretakers, similar to the following example:

POSITIVE	NEGATIVE
loving	angry
nurturing	controlling
understanding	sick - cancer
	- heart condition
	- diabetes
available	judgmental
compassionate	abusive

Following this list, and any discussion that arises surrounding each descriptor, I invite participants to listen carefully to what I am about to offer them. There are no absolutes, no always and nevers in the world of relationships. There can not be. Each person is unique in their viewpoint, interpretation and expression of life. Through these exercises we look for generalizations and patterns. If they apply, the recognition of these patterns as they play out in your life provide rapid insights and serve as powerful catalysts toward high levels of personal mastery. Having said this I offer the following.

There is a good chance that the way you see your mother and father have very little to do with the person that you call "dad" or "mom" in this world. All of the love, joy, nurturing and compassion that your parents have shown to you, as well as anger, judgment, distance and fear are only possible as they mirror to you, your expectations of your relationship with your heavenly "Mother/Father" creator.

The first time that I say the words there is little reaction to the mouthful that I have just offered. As I repeat the words the second time, the possibility begins to sink in. I will hear an "ah ha" or "wow" from somewhere in the audience, and still most are still reeling from the possibility of what I have said. Through similar words, I will offer this concept once more.

There is a good chance that the way you have perceived your mother and father in your life has mirrored to you, your belief of how you feel your creator views you.

I invite you to read and then re-read the previous sentence, slowly and carefully until you have allowed the intent underlying the words to be known within you. This single concept may provide you more insight into why you have lived the kind of life that you have, than any other reason based in rationalization or logic. Consider the implications.

There is a strong possibility that the way you see your earth father/mother mirrors your expectations and beliefs of your relationship with your heavenly Father/Mother, positive as well as negative. How you regard your parent's love, nurturing, being there for you and understanding as well as their anger, not being there, judgment and criticism may be providing you with key insights regarding your relationship with your creator. If applicable in your relationships it works as follows.

Through their lives, your father and mother have loved you so much, that they have lived precise indicators of those things you believe to be true within yourself. Because they are your parents, holding your mirrors, another person may not see your parents in the same light. They can not because your parents do not mirror the depth of the patterns to anyone other than you.

For example, the abandonment that you perceive in your father who is never home or there for you, may be viewed by your father's peer as dedication to a corporation and career. Neither is right or wrong. The abandonment is your issue, triggered by your father's actions.

Inherent in the responsibility of becoming a parent lay an unspoken agreement. Each parent acts as a surrogate of the male or female aspect of our Mother/Father creator. Our earthly parents hold these mirrors of our most sacred relationships until the time that we are able to recognize the mirrors on our own. The moment of recognition signals the completion of that level of commitment from our mother and father. As we remember the message coded as our relationships, we have served one another well in life. We may recognize our mirrors early in life, or not until after the passing of our parent(s), and still we have fulfilled our commitment to one another. Our earth mother and father allow their lives to be this service, because on levels that they may not even acknowledge they love us that much!

Your parents may have taken extreme measures to mirror to you how you believe your creator sees you. My experience with clients and friends suggests that the nature of the demonstration is in direct correlation with the strength of the individual remembering their power. In the anger, judgment and wrongs that your parents may show to you in this world, you are prompted to come to terms with the anger, judgment, separation and trust issues between you and the force responsible for your being here. You will only see in others that which the filters of your belief allows you to see. What you see as your parent's judgment of you may very well be them mirroring to you, your belief of your creator's judgment of you. If you have forgotten the nature of their commitment to show you your beliefs, you may blame them for being judgmental. As you come to terms with how you believe your creator sees your actions, the judgment of your earthly parents will diminish. Similarly, you can only see the joy, compassion and love shown to you by your mom and dad through eyes that allow for the possibility of these qualities, the same qualities offered by the creative force of your origin.

The perspective offered here does not condone or support violence and abuse in the family unit. I offer this perspective as just that, a viewpoint intended to shed understanding on the nature of our relationships. The actions of your parents, by their very nature, beckon to you for a healing of the feelings that they invoke; feelings of separation, trust and self worth.

The mirror works for all expressions of life, positive and negative alike. You are in resonance with your world. The degree of your resonance may be seen as your patterns of behavior mirroring the validity of your words, actions and intent. What mirrors have your parents held in place for you, possibly for your entire lifetime? How have they been there for you, constantly reminding you of the single most significant relationship that you will ever experience? In healing tangible issues with your earth parents you heal the sometimes nebulous relationship between you and your heavenly parents.

Lets look at a case history as an example to see how this subtle mirror may work in real life. A client, "John" (not his real name), is single and in his mid forties. He has no career or career aspirations at the present time. John works occasional jobs such as landscaping, painting, light construction and maintenance. Though he has had steady and long term relationships with women in the past, the idea of "marriage" is frightening to him because of what past examples of marriage have shown him. At this point in John's life, the focus of his attention revolves around the controlled substances that he uses daily, placing him into an altered state of numbness. Denying any problem with his "pastime," John proves to himself that he is all right by waiting until mid-afternoon to administer the anesthetic of alcohol. In his comfortable zone of alcohol induced familiarity, John does not have to prove himself or his worth to anyone. He also does not have to feel.

John's relationship with his parents, particularly his father, may best be described as adversarial. For as long as he can remember, his father has reminded John of how worthless he is in this world. His father has told him, time after time, that if he were to leave this world today, "no one would notice," "no one would care," "no one would miss him." John readily describes his father as sick, cruel, unavailable and unloving. Still, they stay in touch. John frequently spends time with his parents, has meals with them and shares sports such as tennis, golf and fishing. Underlying each encounter are his issues of esteem. Sometimes they are spoken, sometimes they are not.

With respect to the Fifth Mirror of Relationship, what dynamic is playing out in this relationship? If the Fifth Mirror holds true, then there is a strong possibility that John's view of his earthly father mirrors to him, and him only, his ideas of his relationship with his Father creator. This particular mirror does not suggest the reality of the relationship. Rather it reflects John's perception of the relationship.

Note how interesting this example is. John's father loves him so much, on levels that he may not even be conscious of, that his thought and action toward John constantly push buttons of universal fears so that John may remember and heal them. In these examples, the buttons are primarily those of self worth. By virtue of fathering him in this lifetime, John's father has agreed to and accepted his role on earth as surrogate to John's Father in heaven. John came into this life with a charge on the universal fear of self worth. His sense of being worthless in the eyes of his creator, of having failed somehow at something that he has forgotten, is mirrored by his father's actions.

John's descriptions of his dad accurately reflect his view of his relationship between he and his heavenly Father. He feels that the relationship is "sick" and needs healing. He feels that his Father in heaven is "disappointed" and "unavailable." Because of the disappointment he feels that he is not loved. To numb his pain of perceived failure John administers to his body, on a daily basis, the anesthetic of chemical or alcohol products. In his earth father's eyes, this only serves to validate his suspicions of John's lack of worth. The is the cycle that was playing out when I met John as a client.

The opportunity in this case may come from John's choice to recognize and remember the gift of life and discover his worth, independent of his father's perceptions. The relationship between he and his father may become so strained, that John reaches a point where he says,

"Wait just one minute. I am valuable. I am a life of worth, no matter what my father says about me."

The day that this happens, John's father has accomplished his task. He has pushed John to a place in his being where John is able to overcome the mirror of his father's expectations and reclaim himself.

The opportunity also exists for John's father to come to a place of peace in his life by accepting John for whoever John chooses to become in this life. In loving acceptance, he holds John in wholeness, completeness and success, regardless of how John chooses to express his life.

Key in either opportunity is the willingness of each to change the pattern that has held them in the gridlock of expectation and allow one another to simply "be." As John is able to forgive his earth father, holding him in the light of perfection, he has healed his relationship with his heavenly Father who never let him down in the first place. It is John's perception that is healed. The reality of his wholeness has always existed. Both are opportunities. Each is a choice. In either instance, John and his father are playing out for one another the Mystery of the Fifth Mirror of Relationship.

Lets examine the chart from our workshop closely. Look at the words that were used to describe our parents. Words such as loving, angry, nurturing, controlling, understanding, available, judgmental, compassionate, abusive are commonplace. They are very similar to words used for the same chart in response to the same question from other cities throughout our country! Is there a common denominator of an underlying pattern? If our parents mirror for us our unique perceptions of how we view our creator relationship, then what is the pattern saying?

Do you now, or have you in the past, seen your creator as angry, controlling, judgmental, compassionate, loving or "not there"? Look at the illness as we have described them in our parents. Do they love us so much, possibly on an unconscious level, that they are they holding a mirror of our own perceived "sickness" in our relationship with our creator? Are they showing us our "blindness," our "deafness," our "cancerous feelings" and contracting, life defeating patterns of emphysema, arthritis and "loss of memory" so that we will "remember" our relationship with our creator?

Clearly, I am not suggesting that these patterns of disease mirror your true relationship with your creator. Rather, I am asking you to consider the possibility that they may mirror your perceptions and beliefs of that relationship.

Perhaps the Fifth Mirror of Relationship is the key to the mysterious quote at the beginning of this section. The subject of controversy since its re-discovery, this quote has been questioned, referenced, discounted, scorned and praised, by scholars as well as churches. As recorded in the Nag Hammadi texts, Jesus of Nazareth is quoted as suggesting that we must hate as well as love to know ourselves. In hating as well as loving our earth father and mother, we have the opportunity to recognize the single most powerful and precious relationship that we can know in this world. That relationship exists between you, myself and our Mother/Father creator. When we feel anger at our earth parents for their actions, we are knowing ourselves in our perceived anger with our creator. In their accessibility our earth parents bear the brunt of unseen and sometimes forgotten feelings for a source that may be perceived as intangible. When we love our earth parents, we are knowing ourselves as the vast love that we feel for our creator.

How, then, do you apply this mirror in your life? If it is true that your mother and father of this world have held to you a mirror of your beliefs regarding your relationship with your heavenly Mother/Father, what happens if you choose to see the mirror differently? What happens if you hold your "ill" and "diseased" parents in the vision of perfection, without judgment of the physical illusion that they project? Acknowledging their choice of life expression, what happens if you choose to see through the illusion?

Herein lay the beauty of the hologram and the surrogate expressions.

By virtue of healing your illusions and relationships with your earthly mother and father, you have healed your perception of your relationship with their heavenly counterparts. Your earthly surrogates of mother and father allow you to work through the greatest relationship that this life will ever offer, taking as long as it takes within the span of their lifetime. When their lives are complete, you will continue on your own until the relationship is clear and it makes sense to you.

This is your opportunity. I invite you to examine the way that you feel about the mirrors of your parents. What universal fear(s) are they showing you? You allowing for the vision of wholeness in your mother and father, allows them to release the charge that they have had on the vision, possibly to the point of miraculous recoveries of disease associated with "old age." See your relationship with your creator as healed by seeing your earthly parents whole and complete!

In truth, there is no illness, sickness and disease in our world. There are powerful illusions of illness, sickness and disease in our world because we collectively consent to them.

Do you believe in this possibility? Can you find a place within you that allows for the possibility that each soul is whole, intact, new and shiny and that anything other than that newness is a powerful projection of illusion, group and collective, that we have consented to. You and I consent to the illusion of cancers in our bodies, each time we say to ourselves or one another,

"So and so has cancer and will live for three months."

"How," you may say, "do I contribute to the illness of my loved ones by simply acknowledging that they have cancer, for example?" The answer is simple and at the same time beautiful in it's elegance.

Consciousness, and our verbal mirrors of consciousness, are taken as literal commands by our bodies.

In the statement, "So and so has cancer," we have just decreed a command to creation. We have consented to it being so. In the consenting, we actually contribute to the illusion of illness in those that we hold most dear. Any time you "see" another individual as anything other than the perfection of themselves, you "consent" to their expression of their belief regarding themselves.

For example, if the mirrors work in this way, then my mother and father have never been sick. Each has however, projected powerful illusions of disease, possibly without knowing that they have a choice. Their essence is not sick, ill or diseased. It is the projection of their beliefs that their body holds as the mirror. As I "agree" to their illusion of illness, it is only possible to the degree that I choose to see anything other than perfection in their lives. How can I see a "diseased body" for my father, for example, if I am seeing him through eyes that allow for perfection in his life expression? If I see him as "ill," what have I compared him to in judging his "imperfection"? As I see my father's wholeness, while allowing for perfection in whatever he shows me as his life, I heal the illusion of separateness between the Father aspect of my creator and myself. You are asked to see beyond the projections of your loved ones, into the essence of those that you hold most dear. This mirror paves the way for the last mirrors of relationship, in which you are asked to see perfection in the perceived imperfections of life.

For many individuals, the loss of their parents lights up for them their greatest fear of abandonment. This fear is echoed in their descriptions of their loved one's passing. "My mother or father has left me." "I am alone in this world." There is a powerful process that I offer in our workshops wherein I ask the following question.

What is the one thing that you would most choose to hear from your parents before their passing? If you had thirty seconds left with your mother or your father, and all of the reasons for all of the actions that "need explanation" were complete, what is the one thing that would allow you completion and freedom to move forward in this world, alone?

Though the answers that come to me are unique in their wording, there is an underlying pattern common to each. Almost universally, "we" say that we would choose to hear from our parents something similar to the following:

"I love you my daughter (son)."

"I am proud of you."

"You have done well."

We spend much of our lives seeking the approval from our mother and father of this world. The reality may be that they are the closest thing that we know to our Mother/Father creator! It is the love and approval of your creator that you truly seek, and have sought through the mists of our forgotten history. Today, through the Mystery of the Fifth Essene Mirror of Relationship, you have awakened your memory. Perhaps of even greater significance, you have a choice.

MYSTERY OF THE SIXTH MIRROR:
REFLECTIONS OF YOUR QUEST INTO DARKNESS

*"All are born and must walk in the two spirits
that the 'One' has created in man, the spirit of
light and the spirit of darkness."*
ADAPTED FROM DEAD SEA DOCUMENTS[7]

There was a gentleman who came to see me during an open night of client meetings one night in 1991. I was developing techniques of managing emotion based upon principles of sacred geometric patterns and their relationship to the meridians of the human body. An open night was the opportunity for individuals to show up without appointments for a brief consultation and possible follow-up scheduling, if desired. This particular man seemed extremely agitated, describing an urgency for direction as some unknown course of action in his life. Even before he was seated in his chair, he was relating sequences of experiences in short bursts that made little sense to me. I invited him to take a deep breath, slow down and as concisely as possible describe to me the events that had transpired in his life. He began.

I saw the man, just inches away from me, constructing his thoughts. Meticulously he pieced together the events that had unfolded over the last three months of his life. He was in his middle forties and appeared fit, with the exception of a general anxiousness. As he began his story I listened intently to the words that he chose and the inflections in his voice. I watched the postures of his body shift, almost with each new thought. I knew that whatever I would hear, for this man in this moment something very big was unfolding in his life.

"Gerald" (not his real name) was an engineer for one of the big computer companies in Silicon Valley. He had two beautiful young daughters and was married to an equally beautiful wife. They had been together for nearly fifteen years. The company had just given him an award for his fifth year with them, having worked his way through the ranks to a high level "troubleshooter" for a unique kind of software. His position made him a valuable asset to the company and his expertise was required during much more of the day than the 8:30am to 5:30pm that he had agreed to when he accepted the position. To meet the demand for his skills, Gerald began to work late evenings, weekends and travel out of town to trade shows and expositions. It did not take long before he found himself spending more time with his coworkers than he did with his family.

I could see the hurt in his eyes as he described to me how he and his family had grown apart. When he arrived home at night, his wife and children were sleeping. He was at his office in the morning before they had begun their day. Soon, he knew more about the lives of those in his office and their families than he did his own. He felt like a stranger in his own home. When he did take an occasional day or weekend off, he discovered that conversation was difficult. He had little in common with his daughters or his wife. Unaware of his children's activities and accomplishments in school, he felt that he could no longer discuss the challenges of his work with his family, nor theirs with him. He no longer knew who his family was.

Among the engineers in his office was a brilliant young programmer about his age. This programmer was a woman. Gerald found himself teamed up with this woman for assignments that lasted for days at a time in cities across the country. Before long, he felt that he knew this woman better than he knew his own wife.

At this point, I suspected that I knew where the story was headed. What I did not know was why Gerald was so upset and why he had come to me.

Soon, he believed that he was in love with this woman and made a choice to leave his wife and daughters to begin a new relationship with her. To Gerald, it made sense at the time as they had so much in common. Within weeks, he had moved out of his home and into her apartment. Though the separation was painful for him and his family, all appeared to be going well. He saw his daughters when he could and his wife agreed to a divorce with "no contest."

Shortly after his move, his new significant other was transferred to Los Angeles on a project that was scheduled to last three years. He applied for, and was granted, a transfer to the same facility and moved to Los Angeles to set up housekeeping. In his divorce, Gerald had lost more than he had bargained for. Friends that he and his wife had know for years suddenly become distant and unavailable. His coworkers thought he was "off the wall" for leaving the position and projects that he had worked so hard to attain. Even his parents were angry that he had broken up such a beautiful family. Though he was hurt, Gerald rationalized. He was off to a new position, with a new woman in their new home. What more could he ask for?

I could tell we were getting to a crucial point in the story as Gerald's voice began to waver. Within weeks of his transfer, his new love announced that their arrangement was not what she had expected. She ended the relationship and asked him to move out, just like that! Gerald was crushed. After all that he had done "for her," how could she do such a thing to him? After all, he had left his wife, his home, his children, his job, his friends. In short, he had left everything that he held familiar and close. How could she do this?

He began to perform poorly at his new office. Following warnings and a poor performance review, the department laid him off until further notice. At the same time, he discovered that other companies with similar jobs would not consider hiring him for "personal reasons." He later suspected that he had been excluded from those positions by those that knew of his situation.

As the story unfolded, I began to see what had happened to Gerald. His life had gone from the highest of highs, with all of the prospects of new relationship, new job, greater income and a new home to the lowest of lows, as all of those dreams disappeared. Gerald had given away all of the things that he loved, not because he was willing to let them go. Rather, he gave them away believing that he had discovered something better to take their place. Should you ever find yourself in a similar position, here is the powerful key to this story.

Energetically, there is a tremendous difference between leaving that which you hold dear because you feel complete with it and leaving that which you hold most dear for something you believe is better.

In his innocence, Gerald gave away the friendships, security, trust, love and respect of those that he held most dear in exchange for something that he believed was better. He was not complete with the relationships with his wife and daughters. When his new love, home and job did not work out, and prospects for another job, fixing his new relationship or securing a solid source of income all had fallen through, Gerald began a painful, yet powerful path. He had given away everything that he had held dear. Now, with absolutely nothing left except himself, huge tears rolled down his cheeks as he focused on "what to do."

"How can I get back my family and my job?"

"Please tell me, what is it that I have to do?"

Handing him the box of tissues from the nearby table, I said something that caught Gerald completely off guard.

Congratulations, I said in all sincerity.

This is a time of tremendous opportunity in the course of your life. You have just begun the time that the ancients called your Dark Night of the Soul.

He wiped his eyes and said,

"What do you mean, the Dark Night of the Soul?"

"How come I've never heard of it?"

I offered a perspective that he seemed surprised to hear.

This time in your life is not about recovering your lost family, security, or friendships, I began, although each of those things may happen. What you have skillfully created for yourself goes much deeper than your job or your family. You have awakened within yourself a dormant force that may become your most powerful ally, a gift toward the highest levels of mastery for you in this lifetime.

Gerald sat back in his chair and listened intently. I invite you to consider the possibilities of what follows, as I offered them to Gerald. With few exceptions, nearly everyone will experience a Dark Night of the Soul at some point in the course of their lives. The experience does not have to be painful, as the ominous sound of its namesake suggests. The pain, if any, comes from the innocence and possible resistance, of what the experience is and the possibilities that it offers.

Definition: Your "Dark Night of the Soul" is a time, as well as an experience in life, wherein you may be drawn into a situation or circumstance representing, what appears for you, to be your worst fear. To experience the Dark Night of the Soul is to live the Mystery of the Fifth Essene Mirror of Relationship: Your Quest into Darkness.

Corollary: You are capable of entering a "Dark Night of the Soul" only when you have amassed all of the emotional tools necessary to see you through your experience, intact and with grace.

Your personal mastery of life is the trigger, signaling to creation when you are ready to demonstrate your mastery of what life has offered to you. You can not fill a cup full with water from the faucet until you turn the faucet "On." The filling of your emotional tool box is the faucet that signals the water of experience to issue forth. Until you turn the switch, it will not happen. Conversely, when it does happen, you may rest assured that you have turned the switch. Your mother knew this. She shared her memory of this ancient Essene wisdom with you each time she reminded you

"God will never put more on your plate than you can bear."

FROM THE ADVICE OF MOTHERS EVERYWHERE.

From this perspective, as I see individuals and sometimes groups of individuals, experiencing what for them appears to be the most undesirable situations of feeling and emotion that they could ever imagine, I know that without exception, that each is a wonderfully masterful being. I also know that each is remembering their power, living an opportunity rather than a test, in which they will be asked to draw upon their power to demonstrate to themselves their mastery of themselves in this world.

I believe this and have found it to be true in the lives of those around me as well as my own life. If this perspective is meaningful to you at all, then you must reconsider any judgment that you have ever harbored, regarding any condition of life that any human has ever experienced. Is it possible that the "dreaded conditions" that plague us as individuals, as well as a society are opportunities to demonstrate mastery? This is where context is so important. Without context, AIDS, Cancers, Hantavirus, emphysema and every health crises experienced, appears as just that, a random set of circumstances in the lives of unfortunate individuals. I believe that we are much more than that. How could beings of such power and magnificence experience random and unfortunate circumstances in their lives?

The Context: We are living the completion of a Great Cycle of Experience that began nearly 200,000 years ago. Each individual, without exception, must come to terms with what life, the gift of their life and the experience of their life has meant to them. You must come to terms with your life and what the gift of your life means to you!

Is it possible that as powerful individuals, becoming powerful masses of individuals, that we have consented to extreme catalysts of experience, pushing us rapidly into a place in our lives where we are forced to embrace life, or lose life? Is it possible that we have consented to "Group Dark Nights of the Soul," such as AIDS, Cancers, epidemics and starvation to remind us that in each moment of life we affirm or deny life within our bodies?

Clearly, I am not condoning social, political or economic actions resulting in the enhancement or encouragement of these conditions. Underlying all of the expressions of life, beyond the obvious, is it possible that we have consented to the conditions of life, however those conditions are expressed, to know ourselves and reclaim our power in those conditions.

As I faced Gerald, he asked,

"Are you saying to me that I have lost my wife, children, new relationship and career, all that I have ever loved, because I didn't want to lose them?"

Searching within myself for the right words to mirror clarity, I began.

What I am saying to you, Gerald, is that to lose the things that you have held most dear, you had to have held a charge on not loosing them. Rather than living each day in the appreciation and expansive expressions of what life has offered to you, you were living the contraction of a fear, either consciously or unconsciously. Your fear was that of not having those people and experiences in your life. More generally, you have lived a fear of being alone and separate.

I continued.

This is very different from allowing yourself to share time in this world with those that you love. You never 'had' anything. You simply shared time and experience with your loved ones. At the point in time that you created the space for a new love to come into your life, you set the trigger for a new chain of events. In trust, you allowed your new love to carry you to the very edge of who you believe you are. In your instance your new love not only took you to the edge, she pushed you a little harder right over the edge, leaving you alone to find your way out. On a level that is probably not conscious to her, she did that because she loves you that much. The new woman in your life loves you so deeply that she agreed to work with you in your recovery of your power.

This experience is your opportunity to demonstrate your mastery of who you have become. It is not about the woman who left you, the companies that refuse to hire you or getting back your wife, friends and family. This is about you, Gerald. This is your way of redefining your universal fear of abandonment. It could not have happened unless, through the course of your life, you had accumulated all of the tools required to find your way out. Your loss says to me that you are a being of tremendous power seeking to demonstrate your power to yourself.

I believe that you and I work this way. I believe that we love ourselves and one another so much, that we consent to the extreme expressions of life, even to the loss of life, to remind ourselves of the sweetness of life.

Interestingly, each of us has a different worst fear. For some, the worst imaginable fear in life may appear as an insignificant concern to someone sitting next to them. For example, Gerald admitted that his worst fear was that of being alone in this world. I had just spoken with a woman earlier in the evening that stated "being alone" was her greatest joy. Someone such as Gerald, who fears being alone is a master at creating relationships that could never work in a million years. In a breakup, he may perceive the relationship as having failed. The reality is that the relationship has successfully allowed him to see himself in his worst fear.

Through your Dark Night of the Soul you will be asked to draw upon every particle of wisdom available to you, from the depths of your innermost experience, to negate the power that you have given to the fear. The Dark Night of the Soul comes about at times in our lives when we least expect it, usually without warning. With few exceptions, nearly everyone will have an opportunity to experience what for them is the loss of that which they have a charge on not losing. Whether it is a relationship, health, financial security or some combination of "things," the charge assures that you will have an opportunity to know yourself in the absence of those things so that you may balance that charge. Therein lay the power of the Dark Night of the Soul. If we knew it was coming, we would turn away. Who would not? Who, in their right mind, would ever get up in the morning have a cup of coffee, feed the dog, send the family off on their day and say to themselves,

"I am ready now for my Dark Night of the Soul?

To know ourselves in our greatest darkness is our opportunity to heal that part of ourselves that we least choose to experience. To find our balance we must know our extremes. Perhaps more accurately, we must know ourselves as we respond to our extremes. We must know how we respond in the darkest of the dark as well as the lightest of the light, and embrace both, to heal the judgment of our experience and find the power of our truest nature. Our Dark Night of the Soul is an example of our quest to know ourselves in all ways, our quest into darkness as well as our quest into light.

You are asked to come to terms with all experience and each expression of your life. To give the gift of yourself, in wholeness and completeness, you must know yourself within the context of all possibilities, all the extremes. All of your joy, all of your pain, all of your anger, rage, jealousy, and judgment. Each of these precious feelings are your gifts of darkness and light to help you to know yourself. Kahlil Gibran states so eloquently in his book, The Prophet,

"No man can reveal to you aught but that which already lies half asleep in the dawning of your knowledge. And even as each one of you stands alone in God's knowledge, so must each one of you be alone in his knowledge of God and in his understanding of the earth."[8]

Your unique experience allows you to push the boundaries of who you believe you are, as you approach the reality of what you are truly made of. In that knowing, you have the opportunity to see yourself in situations that you may never experience again. These are the extremes that will help you to know and redefine your point of balance. Your endpoints are constantly shifting.

Please consider the following hypothetical example. At the age of fourteen, perhaps the most ecstatic experience that you may be aware of is that of being asked to a very important school dance. Having been asked, you have been accepted and validated by another, and it feels good. At the same time in your life, the worst pain that you may have felt up until that time in life is the death of your family pet, a friend that has been with you throughout your childhood. At that point in life, the extremes may look like this:

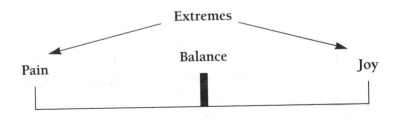

The boundaries of how you see yourself, within the context of joy and pain, are defined by the extremes of those experiences that you have known in your life. It is pointless for someone else to impose the boundaries of their experience upon you. Your extremes must be experienced to be known. Let us carry our example one step further. Perhaps later that same year, you lose your entire family in an accident. The pain of the loss from your family pet pales by comparison.

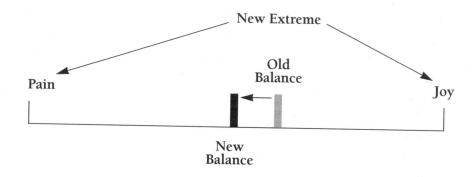

Within the context of the new loss, you are forced to redefine pain, moving your personal knowledge of pain to a new extreme. The loss of your family has had a far greater impact than the significant, though less painful, loss of your family pet. With the new extreme shifting your perception of pain, your point of balance has shifted accordingly. No one could have conveyed the feeling of that sense of loss to you. It had to be experienced.

Though this is an extreme example, you begin to see how each experience has allowed you to see yourself from a slightly different viewpoint of joy and pain, light and dark. That difference allows you to redefine your definition and limits of experience. As difficult as it may have seemed in the past you always have the ability to see beyond the pain, into what the pain is saying to you. Your life is a gift through which you may come to see yourself from many viewpoints, and know yourself as all possibilities.

Whatever you have allowed to express in your life, without exception, I believe we work this way. The Sixth Essene Mystery of Relationship: Our Quest Into Darkness, does not have to hurt. The pain, if any, is our mirror of the degree of charge that we have placed on "not losing" the very things that we hold most dear in life.

I bless each of us in whatever path we choose to remember who we are and our relationship to the One. If I have described you in these scenarios, then I bless you and your knowing yourself. I honor your gift of the Dark Night of the Soul.

MYSTERY OF THE SEVENTH MIRROR: YOUR GREATEST ACT OF COMPASSION

*"Show to me the stone which the builders have rejected.
That one is the cornerstone."*
ADAPTED FROM THE NAG HAMMADI LIBRARY[9]

In the late 1980's my office was in a huge, multistory building on the outskirts of Denver, Colorado. Though the building was enormous, cutbacks in government spending had required that my company "down size" and consolidate. As other divisions moved to our facility, office space was at a premium. I shared my office with another employee, a woman performing a function very different from mine within our department. There was no competition or shared responsibilities and we quickly became good friends, sharing stories of our family weekends, friends, joys and sorrows of life outside of the company.

On this particular day, we had just returned from lunch when she retrieved the messages that had arrived on her voice mail while we were gone. From my peripheral vision I saw her become very still, then sit down abruptly with a glazed look in her eyes. Her face had turned pasty white, except for the makeup on her lips and cheeks. As she hung up the telephone, I gave her a minute to compose herself, then asked *What has happened?* She looked at me and began a story that I found sad, and at the same time powerful.

A good friend of hers had a young daughter with a much envied combination of beauty, athletic ability, material skills and artistic talents, each of which she had cultivated and excelled at since early childhood. Searching for a way to use all of her gifts in a single career, this young woman had chosen a modeling career following graduation from high school. Her family supported her choice, helping in whatever way they could to promote the fulfillment of her dream. As she "shopped" her portfolio to the ad and modeling agencies, many responded immediately, with enthusiasm. She had offers of travel, education, finishing classes and more optimism and support than she had dreamed of. In appearances, life could not look better.

After traveling to New York to accept a position with one of the agencies, she completed a series of modeling assignments. She was assured that this was the beginning of a promising career in fashion. On a subtle, almost imperceptible level however, those that knew her began to see a change. Her enthusiasm was showing signs of concern. The agencies that she was working with were searching for a certain "look" in the women that they would promote. While this young model certainly had a unique beauty, it was not quite what the agencies were looking for. Haunted by the requirements of that special look, my office mate's young friend enlisted the support of her family and began a series of medical procedures that she felt would allow her body to fit the requirements of the agencies and her career.

She began with the most obvious procedures, having her breasts enlarged and lifted, with some minor "tucks" and "nips" around the thighs and stomach. While these procedures brought her closer to her goal, she still did not fit the bill and continued with more extreme procedures. Since birth she had always had a slight overbite, with her chin and jaw recessed slightly. She agreed to a re-structuring that involved a breaking and re-setting of her jaw, to create a greater symmetry. Her mouth was wired shut for six weeks while the bones healed. She could eat only liquids through a straw and subsequently lost weight during that time. When the wires were removed and the bruises had subsided, she did indeed have a beautifully symmetrical face, with accentuated cheek bones and the overbite eliminated. Looking at a photograph that my office mate had of her friend's daughter, I personally could see little difference between the before surgery and after surgery pictures. I reasoned to myself,

If that is what it takes for this woman to come to terms with herself, then I support her in her choices.

Having lost the weight from weeks on a liquid diet, this beautiful young woman began to notice that her lower abdomen did not have the same shape, the "V" as before the surgery. The *reality* was that in the weight loss, her upper body had lost mass and muscle tone, making it appear to be of similar proportion with the lower body. Her *perception*, however, was that there was a problem that could be surgically remedied and she underwent a special procedure to have her lower "floating" ribs, removed to give her greater definition in her hip, waist and bust proportions. At the same time, noticing that her recent loss of weight had brought approval from her peers, she embarked on a program to enhance the effects of weight loss.

If you have ever experimented with weight loss, you may have noticed a peculiar phenomenon regarding the way the body discourages or enhances your process. In my Junior High years, I had briefly participated on the wrestling team. To qualify for specific events within specific weight classes, I had to weigh in prior the match. I noticed early on that when my body would get into a "gain weight" mode, I would rapidly add pounds, and in a "lose weight" mode, I really lost weight. It would begin slowly at first, gaining momentum as the days passed, until suddenly my body was losing or gaining pounds, seemingly of its own accord. On weigh in day, if I were losing weight, I would come in well under the target, not just slip under by a thread.

The young model had a similar experience. She had reset her jaws, changed her hair, enlarged her breasts, lost weight and even had her lower ribs removed and still she was unhappy with her appearance. She began a program of weight loss that never turned back. In her lose weight mode she discovered quickly that something had changed within her body. She could no longer control the addition or loss of pounds. She was losing weight on a daily basis. By the time her parents recognized what was happening and hospitalized her, it was too late. Attributed to a series of complications rather than a single event, my office mate's young model friend had passed away that morning. That was the telephone call that she had received after our lunch.

You may know of people who are on a similar path, though hopefully less extreme. I use this example to emphasize a point. The young woman in this story had an image of perfection in her mind's eye. This image became her reference point of comparison. She constantly held herself in the shadow of that reference point, using her mental image as the yardstick by which to gauge her physical appearance. Her belief system said to her that somehow she was imperfect the way that she was. Her imperfections could be fixed, however, through the gift of modern medical technology designed to remedy such conditions.

What was happening with this young woman runs much deeper than the procedures used to fix her perceived flaws. This story is not offered in judgment of the technology available to change physical appearance. The procedures themselves are benign. The wisdom of the procedures must come in their application. This example demonstrates a distortion of the intended use of these powerful tools.

The question is why? Why did the young model feel that these extremes were necessary for her success? Why was she supported by family and friends in her choices? Why did this beautiful young woman feel compelled to become something other than who she was at birth? What fear was so dominant in her life that she sought to change her outward appearance to meet the expectations of others? More importantly her expectations of herself? Perhaps an even greater question follows.

What do you use as your yardstick of comparison?

What is the point of reference that you hold yourself accountable to, as you gauge your 'successes' and 'failures' in life?

Though this example is an extreme, to a lesser degree the same thing happened frequently. An unrealistic ideal becomes the model or the yardstick by which our lives, accomplishments, physical expression and earthly capabilities are gauged.

Following this story in the workshop, I often ask participants to complete a simple chart before we continue our discussion. On the chart I ask them to rate themselves in a number of areas including education, physical fitness, romance, corporate and athletic accomplishments. The rating system is composed of four possible categories ranging from Highly Successful, to Moderately Successful, Average, and Failure. Typically, I give very little time to complete this sheet. I do so for a reason. The actual responses on the chart are of less significance that the thought behind the response. The reality is that whatever their response, any response indicating anything other than perfection, is the participant in judgment of him or herself. The only way that you can possibly rate yourself as success or failure is through comparison to something external to your experience.

Often, our toughest judge of ourselves, is ourselves. For this reason, the Seventh Mirror is known as our Greatest Act of Compassion. It is through the mirror of ourselves, that we are asked to compassionately allow perfection in each expression of life, regardless of how the experience is viewed by others. Why is it that so many find it easier to demonstrate compassion for others that it is to have compassion for themselves?

Our definition of compassion from Chapter III reminds us that compassion is the result of specific qualities of thought, emotion and feeling. Thought without attachment to the outcome is perhaps our greatest challenge in a world viewed as cause and effect.

Without attachment to an outcome, each experience becomes an opportunity to express, and nothing more. How would your life be different if you allowed each expression of your life to be perfect in its outcome, regardless of the outcome? If we have expressed life to the best of our ability within a given situation in a given moment, then without comparing to another expression, how can we have failed or had success? It is our thought about ourselves, our performance, our appearance, our achievements that determines the direction of our emotional energy. The greatest act of compassion that you may ever be asked to demonstrate may well be compassion for yourself, in your choice of life conduct and life expression.

- Your view of yourself in anything other than perfection will reveal your greatest doubt (universal fear of least trust) in the perfection of your experience.
- Your actions to change yourself born of anything other than the love and respect for the gift of life through your body will reveal your greatest question of esteem (universal fear of self worth) in the perfection of who you have come to be.

Applying the codes of compassion to your sense of self, you must ask yourself the questions:

If You:

1 **Acknowledge** that there is a single source of all that is or may ever be; that every life event, without exception, is part of the One.
2 **Trust** in the process of life as it is shown to you; divine timing with no accidents.
3 **Believe** that each and every experience drawn to you, without exception, is your opportunity to demonstrate your mastery of life.
4 **Believe** that your life mirrors your quest to know yourself in all ways, knowing your extremes to find your balance.
5 **Truly believe** that your life essence is eternal and that your body may experience eternally as well.

Then:

How can you, at the same time, judge your choices as right, wrong, good, bad or of anything other than an expression of the One? How can the body that you were gifted be anything other than Perfection?

IF
you believe that have come to this world
to know yourself in all ways
AND
if your experience of extremes allows you to know your balance
AND
if you choose each commitment of life carefully, with intent and fully
present doing the best that you are capable of in the moment
THEN
how can you be anything less than perfect in any category?

You are not your experience. You are the energetic result of that which your experience has shown to you. You determine how your experience is interpreted. Your choices in life simply offer to you the opportunity of experience. Experience has no success, failure, good or bad until you compare your accomplishment to someone or something else. With respect to your uniqueness, who could possibly qualify as your yardstick?

How many times have you been in a public place, perhaps a restaurant or shopping mall, and heard the comments of those around you toward individuals passing in the room? Perhaps the comments echoed expressions such as the following.

"Look at that, he should be ashamed of himself."

"Why doesn't she 'do' something with herself?"

I remember an instance in the Dallas/Fort Worth airport while waiting for a TRAAM car to carry a group of people from one portion of this huge "city within a city" to another. Standing in line, I noticed an elderly couple next to me. The man obviously did not hear well. As the train approached and we prepared to enter, an extremely large woman came down the escalator toward the train. The elderly man next to me looked at her and commented to his wife regarding the woman's size.

"Isn't that terrible," he said.

"Why doesn't she do something about her size?"

Possibly because he was hard of hearing, possibly because of the acoustics in the room, possibly because there are no accidents in this world, his comments were louder than he had intended and everyone heard, including the woman who had to weigh close to four hundred pounds. I know that she heard him. I know because she never said a word.

As the words left his mouth, she turned to face him and in doing so gave me the opportunity to see her also. As she looked our way, I accepted the invitation to look into her eyes. I could tell that she did not travel much. Her luggage was outdated, the old vinyl linoleum type with hard sides and brass fittings on the corners. I sensed her travel to be a difficult combination of uncertain connections, special accommodations due to her size, dining and rest room requirements, all complicated by one hundred plus degree temperatures in Dallas during August. I thought to myself,

She must have a really good reason to travel today.

Her eyes were reddened and welling up with tears form the hurt of the comments that she had just been the object of. She was not angry, or even surprised. I'm certain that she had heard similar comments before. Her eyes definitely betrayed the pain that had just been touched within her body. As I looked into her eyes, I sensed the perfection of her soul in the illusion of a large body. How brave for a woman of that size to place herself in the position of public scrutiny. What memory was her body protecting her from? What had happened in her life that said to her body,

"I now require layers and pounds of 'protection' to make this world safe?" Possibly, just the kind of comment that the gentleman next to me had offered. As we walked into the train, I looked at the man and his wife and smiled a "hello." I felt no malicious intent as he continued speaking to his wife. This appeared to be something that they did all the time, discussing with one another the differences between themselves, their expectations of life and the reality of what life showed to them. From this elderly gentleman I sensed an unconscious innocence. He certainly had not intended to hurt this woman. He was not even aware that his words had carried beyond the privacy of he and his wife. I thought to myself,

What a powerful experience the four of us have just had.

Each in our own way had just been given the opportunity to ask ourselves the identical question. "Do we love enough to allow for the possibility of perfection in the 'imperfections' of life?" The man and his wife in consideration of the large woman. The large woman in consideration of the man and his wife. Myself in consideration of each of the three. From very different perspectives, each of us had just experienced for ourselves the Seventh and most subtle, yet profound mystery of relationship. The Seventh Essene Mystery :Your Greatest Act of Compassion.

I invite you to ask yourself the same question. Do you love enough to allow for the possibility of perfection in whatever life shows to you? Can you allow for perfection in the asymmetry of life?

Now I invite you to consent to it being so.

BEYOND THE TEMPLES

While there may certainly be additional, even subtler mirrors that are shown to us through our relationships, to the best of my knowledge at this time, these are the primary keys. Each may be considered as a stepping stone toward a high level of conscious, personal mastery. Once you know of the possibilities, those possibilities become a part of you. Once you have seen them, you can not un-see them. Now you will be asked to live the meaning of the words.

Each time you recognize a mirror of relationship, an energetic opportunity of opening is created. The opening is available merely from your allowing of the possibility. With that opening comes an additional opportunity for you to demonstrate, to yourself only, the meaning of each particular mirror as it is presented in your life. Having read the descriptions, case histories and true stories, you have been able to see how the energetic patterns are presented to you through relationships.

Not long ago I met a friend who had just left a career, family, friends and a relationship in another state to move to the wilderness of the Rocky Mountains. I asked him why he had left so much behind to come to the desolation of the high desert. He began by telling me that he had come to the mountains to find his "spiritual path." In the same breath, he shared with me that he had not been able to begin his path because nothing was going right. He was having problems with family, business plans and contractors in the renovations of his property. His frustration was obvious. Listening to his story, I turned and offered an insight.

Maybe this is your spiritual path, I offered.

Maybe the way that you resolve each of your challenges is the path that you have come here to know.

Glancing back to me with a surprised look on his face, he echoed,

"Maybe it is."

From my perspective, we are capable of only spiritual activity. Life is a spiritual endeavor. As varied and diverse as each path may seem, I believe with the power of my entire being, that each path is leading to the same place. Without exception, I believe that each life, every death, all of the hurt, all of the joy and each experience in-between, brings us closer to the same whole, to the same One. Our relationships are not separate from our spiritual evolution. Our relationships are our spiritual evolution.

There is a good possibility that once a pattern is recognized anywhere in your life, in any relationship, the same pattern will be seen in varying degrees through other relationships. The control issues that are the object of tremendous emotion in the home, may be seen, with very little emotion in dealing for a new car, for example. Nonetheless, the pattern is there. You and the car dealer do not know one another as deeply, you do not share the same level of intimacy, as you do with your children, for example. Still the pattern remains.

Interestingly, in finding resolution to your dealings with the car dealer, you very probably have found resolution to your expressions of control in your home. This is the beauty of the hologram of emotion and consciousness. Once a pattern changes in one relationship, all other relationships that are based in the same pattern benefit from the original change.

Your relationships have become your temples! You no longer require isolation in artificial structures to isolate and master specific patterns of emotion. You have out-grown those structures! Today, within a few years before the close of this great cycle of human emotion, you have moved beyond the outer temples. Today, you enter into the temple of love in a relationship where you believe that you are in love. Then, having entered the temple you will discover additional temples, possibly some that you never even knew existed.

There is a possibility that no one has reminded you that these temples are your stepping stones to the highest possible levels of human mastery. You have simply felt, thought, had emotion and moved forward in life based on those thoughts, feelings and emotions. This is precisely the point. Perhaps no one has reminded you that you are an initiate of the highest order, immersed in a world of logic and emotion to know your-self in all ways. Still, perhaps without knowing "why" you have moved forward, mastering your life in the process.

That is how powerful you are.

You master overlapping and intermingled emotions, survive the highest of the highs as well as the lowest of the lows, without ever knowing precisely why. You have outgrown the external temples. In many ways, you have outgrown the lessons of the outer masters. Their lessons prepared you and trained you for precisely this time in our history. You are moving into a time when there are no reference points to compare to, no previous experience to determine appropriate response. You are moving into a time when all that you have is yourself.

"You" is all that you will ever need.

Your temples of relationship are preparing you for precisely that experience, precisely that moment. Each of the Seven Essene Mysteries of Relationship is sequential, building upon the realization of the one previous to it, until, through each of the seven mysteries you have healed your universal fears. In doing so, you have prepared for yourself the path that allows compassion to be a Force in your life. In the story of his search for truth in his life, Gurdjieff came to a point in a remote and hidden monastery in an unnamed country where he was offered the following words.

"You have now found the conditions in which the desire of your heart can become the reality of your being. Stay here until you acquire a force in you that nothing can destroy."[10]

I believe that force to be compassion. As our relationships demonstrate to us our true nature, the fallacy of darkness, fear, and hate are exposed. Once healed all that is left is compassion.

CHAPTER SIX

ALL OF OUR ANCESTORS
EMOTION, COMPASSION AND CRITICAL MASS

Plate VII: *Chrysanthemum*
Japanese symbol represents Soul of Man

"May I become an inexhaustible treasure
for those who are poor and destitute;
May I turn into all things they could need
And may these
be placed close beside them."

SHANTIDEVA,
A GUIDE TO THE BODHISATTVA'S WAY OF LIFE[1]

I t was nearly 9:30pm as we turned from the washboard dirt and gravel road onto the county highway. Instantly, the car became quieter as the tires rolled onto the smooth asphalt two lane. It was a Sunday evening in October of 1987. My wife and I had just spent the weekend with meditators and researchers living in Northern New Mexico, discussing the nature of life-force, the human soul and the Shift of the Ages. Returning to my corporate world of software engineering, I was scheduled for a 7:30am staff meeting in my office the next morning. My wife had an early morning in her office as well. At best, the five hour drive would place us in our South Denver home by 2:30 the following morning. Accelerating onto the highway, I pushed in my favorite "U-2" cassette and my wife curled up for a long drive. Neither of us would sleep much that night.

We had crossed the Colorado state line and were on the mountain road leading into the small town of Walsenberg. It was here that we would find Interstate 25 and a legal speed limit of 55mph most of the way home. As we rounded a mountain switch-back, I could see the tail lights of another car in front of us pulled off on the side of the road. I began to slow and pulled to the shoulder to see if anyone needed help. As our car rolled to a stop, I could see two people huddled in front of the headlights, staring down onto the road. I quickly ran to their car, and found two women standing in the lights staring at a young deer that they had struck moments before. The deer had apparently stopped on the highway, frightened by their lights. Though the women had tried to stop, it was too late.

The fawn was still breathing. She was laying there in the right lane of the highway, silent and motionless except for an occasional breath. She appeared to be in shock. I looked with my flashlight and could see no obvious injury. Why didn't she jump up and run away? Asking the two women to help me, we gently rolled the deer to one side to check for damage. As we turned her body into the light of the high beams, suddenly I could see why this beautiful young animal was laying motionless in the road. The impact of the collision had compressed many of her internal organs, forcing them through a large opening in her abdomen. I knew that she would not live long. We pulled her off to the shoulder of the road, and then further until she was propped up against a cattle fence. Elevating her neck slightly seemed to help her breathe. As I looked up, I could see the silhouettes of the two women standing over me in the headlights. Each of us, including the deer, created a small cloud from our breath in the cold mountain air. The women were nurses at a large hospital in Denver. Trained in saving lives and limiting suffering, they felt helpless in the presence of this gentle young animal dying in front of them.

As I looked back down at the deer, she remained motionless. There was a peace that had come over her as her eyes followed me. I sensed that she somehow "knew" we were trying to help. She did not appear to be afraid. Now I was the one who felt helpless. Here on this deserted mountain road were two registered nurses, my wife a certified massage therapist and myself, a degreed engineer. Each of us was a master in our respective fields. Each felt powerless to do anything in the moment. I knelt down, cradling the deer's head in my lap and offered a silent prayer.

I ask that this animal be blessed with a graceful passing. Please allow her to begin her new journey of exploration without suffering.

Suddenly, something began to happen. It was happening to me. I felt a familiar sensation, the feeling that I had felt before in my near death experiences. Now I was having the feeling here on this cold October evening, in the presence of the passing of a life. In that feeling, I knew that we were not alone on that roadside and that everything was right. As I placed my hand on the deer's forehead over her eyes, her breathing became shallow. With one last sigh she stopped. Lowering my hand her eyes were still wide open, I knew that she was in transition.

At once, I realized that I had never been present at the actual moment of the passing of a life. I had certainly paid my respects during memorial services of friends and at funerals for loved ones. I had attended to friends until mere moments of the time that they died. On each occasion something had happened. There was a distraction or diversion and I had left their presence at the moment of passing. Perhaps their choice to be alone at the time of death. Perhaps it was my choice not to witness. Never had I been present at the actual moment of transition, until now.

As I held her in my arms, warm waves of emotion surged through my body. They were like undulating pulses of heat radiating from my chest out to my extremities. With a gentle burst of warmth, the undulations stopped. I knew that she was gone. In her passing, this young deer had given me the gift of experiencing her passing. I had felt the essence of her life as it left her body and briefly, shared mine. Though I have always *known* of our connectedness with one another, in that moment I had moved beyond knowing. In the moment of transition with this beautiful animal resting in my lap I had *felt* her passing. For a matter of seconds as she stopped breathing, she had somehow been a part of me. Her passing had an effect upon me. She never made a sound and still, she had affected me deeply.

During that moment, it would have been a challenge for me to describe where the life force of the deer stopped and where I began. During those brief seconds, she and I were the same being. Without knowing why, I cried. Tears rolled down my cheeks and onto the still, warm face of this animal that I had never known. I remember thinking to myself, *How could the life of this single animal, unknown to me previously, here at seven thousand feet in the mountains of Southern Colorado, be making a difference in my life?* Asking myself these questions, I felt an emptiness. Knowing that she along with many others of her kind, are "out there," I missed her. I missed her presence in my world. With her passing something now seemed different in my life.

I have always known that we are a part of all life, connected through the threads of a force that binds all in its creation. Though I have always known, it took the passing of this particular life for me to feel the difference. That difference is the reason that I share this experience.

BECOMING: OUR TECHNOLOGY OF THE SECOND PATH

We have chosen. As a collective memory of all that has ever been, and all that is yet to be, we have made our choices. We have spoken to one another and said,

"No more hunger, no more pain."

Still, many of our kind wait for the hunger and the pain to "go away." We have looked into one another's eyes and echoed,

"No more sickness and disease."

Still, many of us watch as new diseases, immune to modern technology, remind us of our past vulnerability. We have shaken hands with one another in agreement to

"No more killing."

Horrified and feeling helpless, we have witnessed unprecedented acts of violence and atrocity to peoples of all faiths, cultures, ethnic, age and social backgrounds. We have chosen. Our choice is a first and necessary step toward creating that which we desire for our world and ourselves. To believe that the choice alone makes the difference, however, may not be enough. Making the choice is the signal to creation that an opening has occurred. Your choices have created energetic openings of potential, spaces of possibility, in your experience of creation. The question now becomes

"What will you place into the openings that you have created?"

Having made the choices that create the void of possibility in the fabric of human consciousness, how will you fill that void? Having chosen to change is fifty percent of the process. In choosing, you have exercised one half of the great gift offered to you as your lifetime. Now in this time that the Mayans called "no time," the days of life in between the close of one great cycle and the opening of another, you are asked to move beyond choosing.

Today, within a few short years of the time that the ancients called the Shift of the Ages, you are asked to *become.* You becoming your choices is you exercising the second half of your gift. It is your free will that allows you to bring your choices to fruition. Exercising your free will, you are asked to become the very conditions that you so desire for your children and loved ones. You are asked to become that which you most desire in your life. Your becoming is the secret to fulfilling your promise of this lifetime to yourself.

Our cultural predisposition to *doing* is an artifact of our past, the remnant of a paradigm that has served us well. Acknowledging our gift of a technology based in doing, it is possible that the very path that has served us so well in the past, may no longer be serving us in this moment. The ideas, beliefs and thoughts that allowed us to kill one another to prevent being killed, to conquer and own one another to prevent being conquered and owned, and to judge the things that are not understood have served us well. Each idea, belief and thought has paved the way to this very moment. Now, I ask you to consider the possibility that we have outgrown the path of killing, conquering, owning and judging. We began *Walking Between the Worlds* with a discussion of internal and external technologies providing an outline, a road map of where we were about to go. Now, having offered the bulk of this text, that discussion warrants revisiting.

Beyond the doing of our past, now we are asked to become our choices. Our becoming is the technology of the second path. Ancient tools were left to you, for this time in history. Those ancient yet sophisticated technologies were for the very purpose of mastering your life at this time, in these days. Alive within you, encoded within you, those tools are available now in this moment. Having heard the words of this text I invite you to ask yourself this question. *You may know of these tools as logical and emotional codes in your mind, do you remember them in your body?*

Possibly dormant, certainly living within you, is the capability to shift life within your body, as well as the manner in which you see that life. That change may occur as quickly as the space of a heartbeat as you remember to allow it. Shifting life patterns from within your body by shifting your viewpoint is, perhaps, the single most powerful tool that you have available to you for the remainder of this lifetime.

The second path of internal technology is a path that is remembered rather than engineered. The second path is your truest nature. You learned to build mirrors of yourself outside of your body, only when the memory of your truest nature began to fade. That is how strong you are, how strong your will is to know remember and live.

Our inner technology remembers our body as the sacred union between the atomic expression of mother earth and the electrical and magnetic expression of father heaven. We are reminded of this through the original texts of the Dead Sea Scrolls and the Books of the Essenes.

> *"...for as the Heavenly Father hath given thee His holy spirit, thy Earthly Mother hath given thee Her holy body..."*
>
> ADAPTED FROM THE ESSENE GOSPEL OF PEACE[2]

Your enormous force of potential is activated and regulated by you through the manner in which you choose to conduct your life. If you and I are truly who and what we say we are, powerful and masterful beings of wisdom and compassion, living just a few short years from The Shift of the Ages, why not become healing technology? Rather than engineer the technology "out there" to address the consequences of our past condition, why not become the technology? Why not feel the feelings, emote the emotions and think the thoughts that allow our shifting to a state of being where bacteria, virus, change and even death are of little consequence? Why not become the cures from within?

From this perspective viruses, bacteria, immune breakdowns, social and political upheaval and other conditions previously viewed as horrors may actually serve as powerful agents of change. Each may be viewed as a catalyst that you and I have consented to in an effort to propel us collectively into a higher choice of being. We consent by encouraging and allowing the technology, and the thought behind the technology, to be present for the creation of these conditions.

The ancients remind us that compassion is not something that we do or accomplish. Rather, compassion is that which we allow ourselves to become. The message of hope is not foreign, coming to us from an external source of experience. It is our own ancient/future message coming back to "we" who have created it. It is coming from within us, responding to the signal that we programmed for ourselves long ago. "When we reach a particular level of technological sophistication, we are ready for the next step." When we:

- reach the day that allows us to peer into the very essence of our creator's genetic code at the moment of conception.
- reach the time that we are able to project extensions of our senses into the cosmos around us, as well as the atoms that are us, to tell us what is "out there," then we are ready for the next level.

Now we are ready to become the very technology that we have created to remember ourselves. Within this moment of history lives the opportunity to remember ourselves as our truest nature. The machines, tools and gadgets are a collection of artifacts representing us mirrored outside of ourselves as a record of our collective past. Today you have the opportunity to bless the technology of the first path for all that it has offered, for the time it has afforded, the ease of life it has offered and all that it has meant to you. Bless the technology and move forward in the second path.

Far more sophisticated than any machines ever built by the most brilliant of our kind, the second path represents a tremendous upgrade of conduct and our very standard of living. We now have the opportunity to become the healing of the medicines, to become permanent and eternal health, to become the peace of the peacemakers, to become the compassion of the religions and vibrant companions of life, and to do so gracefully. I invite you to reconsider the teachings that speak of a potent force of life that courses *through* your body. Therein lives the separation.

That potent force is your body.

There is no separation between you and that force. Beyond flowing through your body, that force is your body. It is you who determines your response to the bacteria, viruses, ultraviolet rays from a depleting ozone, even the flu "bug" that circulates through the office. It is you that determines your threshold of anger, hate and rage at events that you have created in your life. It is you who is determining our outcome at this high time in history, by determining our response to this time in history. You, in your totality, have something far greater to offer to yourself, those that you hold most dear and to this world, than you will ever find in a machine mirroring a fragment of you "out there."

OUR TIME OF MASTERY

The time of our outer temples, outer networks, outer grids and external guidance is nearing completion. For many, what has come as an inner knowing, was stated clearly through the language of our time two thousand years ago, and even before. Our knowing reminds us that you and I live as an expression of a highly sophisticated union, a sacred marriage, between the elements of this earth and a directive non physical force. We call that force Spirit.

Defined as a quality of thought, feeling and emotion, compassion is the peace that we seek in our bodies to align those elements with our spirit. Peace through compassion is the technology to hold the alignment in place, the same peace offered in the Essene references to thought, feeling and body. The vitality of your body, the quality of your blood and breath, your choice of relationships and emotion, even your ability to reproduce appears to be directly linked to your ability to embrace the force of compassion in your life.

To the degree that you embrace compassion in your life, change passes gracefully, with ease. For those who require proof, that proof is now available. For others, simply knowing that there is a direct relationship between emotion and DNA comes as welcome validation for an inner knowing that has driven the course of their lives for years. Becoming is the ancient key that was left to us so long ago, in the hope that by the time we reached this point in our history and evolution, we would remember our truest nature of compassion.

The intent and purpose of each saint and reference being along our journey has led us to this point, encouraging us to move beyond the teaching of the outer master. Their path has prepared us for our time of becoming the master. Allen Cohen in his powerful work entitled, *The Peace That You Seek* suggests to us that "The time has passed for you to seek the Master. Now it is for you to be the Master...Be the Master now."[3]

We are further asked to consider the significance of this time in our history. In an additional excerpt from *The Peace That You Seek,* Cohen reminds us that

"All of the work, done by all of the saints has been directed to this moment to you."[4]

"Their" work was to prepare us for this time in our individual, as well as collective history. If we are truly who and what we say that we have become, this time in history is our opportunity to demonstrate our becoming. Someone must do it first. Someone must interrupt the cycles of thought and belief that have allowed the disease, hunger and killing in the first place. These patterns are a part of us. They originated within us, from among us, and that is precisely where the change must occur.

Someone must choose to rise above the very parameters that have led us to the edge of who we believe that we are. Someone must choose a view of what life has offered from a vantage point beyond right, wrong and "someone has to pay" to something more, something greater. Someone must live the truth of a higher response to life's offering, regardless of the offering. That someone is you.

Who else?

Who else could the someone possibly be? The examples have been lived. The choices have been made. The stage is set. Now, I invite you to become more than the circumstances that this world has offered to you as your life. I invite you to become more than the hurt that others have offered you as they violated your trust, your innocence, their promises. I invite you to become more than the disease, illness, and killing that we have inflicted upon one another. This is your path. You will find your strength in viewing the events of this world from a perspective that enables you to choose a response of something greater than your emotions have dictated in the past. Now, I invite you to remember the technology that allows the seed of your choice to blossom.

As our greater option of compassion, we have the opportunity to redefine our past response to life's offering. From our new perspective, we have the opportunity to choose again.

CONVERGENCE: HISTORY POINTS TO NOW

The ancients had a name for the people who would live in these days, in this time. The ancients had a name for you. They wrote texts, created systems of time keeping, passed down stories and offered suggestions, dedicating entire volumes to you. The texts describe a point of convergence of cycles within cycles, cycles of time, experience, technology and understanding. This convergence point in history is described as a shifting of time, as well as thought within that time.

Changes within the physical world are described to mark this point in history, signals to you, so that you may know that now is the time. Through their prophecy and foresight, you are told that you may expect shifts to occur in global patterns of weather, planetary sciences, geography and social structures. You are cautioned that your life may not function as it has prior to this time. You are reminded that shifts from within your own body, chemical shifts expressed as feeling and emotion, will be the key to experience tremendous change within your world, gracefully. The question has always been whether or not, by this time in history, you would gain the wisdom to allow the process to unfold. Signaling a turning point in human experience, the changes were prophesied, predicted, feared and welcomed.

Measurements of time, some dating to 18,000 years ago, end in these years, in these days. The makers of the calendars foresaw the birth of a powerful generation, masterful beings that would bridge the time of the ancient calendars with a new time. There is no name and there are no calendars as yet for this new time. Between the old time and new time, there would be a transition period, a zone of experience that was named "no time." The prophecies tell of a single generation with an inner power greater than their own knowing. The source of their power is that of a living force lying dormant within each being. It is this generation that will survive no time by bridging the way that things have always been with that which was yet to be. To gracefully move through the days of transition, a period that the Hopi call "the days of purification," this last generation will have to once again awaken the forgotten power inherent in their creation. Sleeping within them has always been the ability to live without illness, to age without deterioration, to transform the body into higher forms of energy rather than dying. The power will not be externally engineered as devices, inventions and "things" that are done. Rather, the power will be demonstrated as an inner wisdom, an inner technology, expressed as that which the beings have become.

Unless you were very lucky as a child, probably no one ever told you that "you are an initiate of the highest order." Unless you were one of the very fortunate, born unto parents so awakened that, they themselves recognized life as an opportunity to demonstrate who and what we believe we are - unless this was the case then probably no one has ever offered you a context from which to make sense of the extremes of your life. Possibly no one has explained why you can have heights of joy and ecstasy followed by the depths of fear, sometimes all in the same day.

I have met people who were, in fact, born with this awareness, though not necessarily the product of family wisdom. They have always known that they were different from those around them, preparing for something, training for some nebulous event that would occur within their lifetime. What would that event be? Their lives never seem to fit into the mold that their families, friends, educators and employers had prepared for them. Somehow, they always felt out of place, as if each day they were simply going through the motions. Perhaps you are among those people. Unless you were very lucky as a child, probably no one ever told you that you are an initiate of the highest order.

If you were, however, fortunate enough to understand your initiation then possibly, you began to see your life as an opportunity of demonstration. From the moment that you projected yourself into the growing cells of a fetus in your mother's womb, you have masterfully compromised pieces of your identity, as those portions were innocently lost, taken away or given away to survive the experience. Skilled in the art of survival, you may have stored these pieces along the road of your life for the time when you knew that it would be safe to retrieve them once again. These portions of you may be as subtle as "giving in" to the opinion and desires of others for the sake of peace in the family, to something as blatant as the emotional numbness that results from years of abuse and invalidation. Though the memory is often clouded, relationships with others and the resulting emotion, play a key role in helping you and those that you love claim yourselves in the power of wholeness. Quite possibly it is your hidden desire for completeness that drives you forward each day of your life, pressing on toward some felt, yet sometimes invisible goal.

The time of this transition is now, these days. The beings prophesied in the ancient texts are you. You are living the time of no time, an interface between worlds. You experience time without living exclusively in the world of time. You experience space, matter and non-matter without living within either of these worlds exclusively. It takes a being of extraordinary power to hold a focus between these worlds, without becoming lost in the experience. You are that being!

Just as an electron has the opportunity to shift to a higher shell of energy under certain conditions, your body and your world have already begun a process that will allow a shift to a greater expression of life. During the transition, there is a period of time when the worlds coexist with one another, a time of dimensional overlap. The ancients had a name for you who would live in these times, during these days. They left messages of hope and encouragement to you. They wrote texts, dedicating entire volumes to you,

"You who walk between the worlds."

By this time in history, the close of a 200,000 year great cycle of experience, you have had the opportunity to see the highest expressions of yourself. You know how to become the peace that you desire in your life. You know of the prosperity of friendship and loved ones in your life. You know that it takes a certain quality of thought, feeling and emotion to live disease free and vitally in your life. The peace, prosperity and vitality that you have experienced in your life is mirrored as your world. You "knowing" is your first step toward becoming a higher quality of belief system. This is you consenting to your expression of compassion.

OUR POWER OF CONSENT

We live in a world of *collective consent*. Sometimes consciously, sometimes not, we collectively agree to expressions of resonant patterns in our world. For example, the creation of a non earth resonant material such as plastic can only happen if we allow for its possibility. On a level that may even be unconscious, we must agree to the possibility of all of the chemical and molecular patterns that make plastic, before there can be a plastic. If, in one moment, every person in this world agreed that plastic would no longer be, then the patterns of energy that allow for the polymers and molecules of plastic would no longer exist. They could not. If, however, even one person held out and chose to allow plastic in this world, the memory would be planted and the possibility would be anchored.

It is our consent that will bring to our earth the quality of life experience that we most desire. To create something new in our world, someone must anchor the new something as a seed of possibility. For that seed to continue, there must be a consent, a vibratory license that the new will be so. The healing of our world, more specifically the quality of thought, feeling and emotion underlying our global healing, works in the same fashion.

Through an ancient Essene science, keys were left to you. Your life is the living bridge between times. In these days, the "switch" that will forever change the way in which you perceive yourself, and the world around you, is no longer demonstrated as what you create outside of yourself. Now, your mastery of life is demonstrated as what you become. The science of compassion is expressed as a molecular shift within your body, an intentional shift achieved through a sequence of emotional and logical codes.

OUR LIFETIME OF BODHISATTVA

In the ancient texts of the East, we are told of men and women who have come to this world for the sole purpose of living the lifetime of compassion, anchoring the possibility into the consciousness of person that will ever follow. These beings are conscious of their path. They have chosen their path of continuing and returning lifetimes, among the children of our creator, rather than continuing upon their own journey into higher realms of creation. The name given collectively to these benevolent beings of compassion is "Bodhisattva."

Of the many understandings and expressions regarding the lifetime(s) of Bodhisattva, a definition may be stated as the following:

"One, who foregoes the ecstasy of heaven for the enlightenment of others." The lifetime of the Bodhisattva is solely for the purpose of allowing others the gift of their own growth and enlightenment. In doing so, the Bodhisattva, him/her self, becomes enlightened to an even greater degree. To give you some idea of how complete the life of service of the Bodhisattva is, I will share with you the words to the Prayer of the Bodhisattva, as they were offered to me during a Sacred Journey to Egypt in 1987.

Prayer of the Bodhisattva

Alone, in the presence of others, I walk through the
    waking dream of Life.
Others see me. At the first sight of recognition, they turn away;
    for they have forgotten.
Together, through the waking dream of Life, we journey.
May the clarity of my vision guide your life in grace,
    for I am a part of you.
May my action remind you of your God within,
    my action is your action.
May my breath become the breath that fills your body with life.
May my soul become the food with which to nourish and
    quicken you.
May the words from my mouth find a place
    of truth within your heart.
Let my tears become water to your lips.
Allow my love to heal your body of the pain of life.
In your most healed state, may you remember your
    most precious gift; your divine nature.
Through our time together, may you know yourself.
In that knowing, may you find your true home,
    your God within.

For all intents and purposes, you are living the lifetime of "Bodhisattva." Each moment of your life is in service to those around you. Through simply being who and what you have grown to be, the gift of each relationship that you encounter, is the mechanism that allows you to see something of yourself. To see something of yourself in others requires your willingness to allow for the possibility.

As the magnitude of the opportunity has become clearer to you, you probably have seen how your lifetime has been a life of service. You live each precious moment of your life in service to others. By virtue of that service, you serve yourself and ultimately, your creator. Through life you demonstrate your mastery, your opportunity to become the living bridge of higher options of response to the offerings of life, regardless of how the offerings appear. The demonstration reflects your opportunity to become the greatest gift that you may offer to those that you hold most dear in this lifetime. Your greatest gift is you in wholeness.

Researchers now have demonstrated to the Western world that human emotion determines the actual patterning of DNA within our bodies. Furthermore, the demonstrations have shown that DNA determines how patterns of light (matter) surround our bodies. Stated another way, researchers have discovered that the arrangement of matter (atoms, bacteria, viruses, climate, even other people) surrounding your body, is directly linked to the feeling and emotion from within your body.

Now, I invite you to Imagine the implications!

Allowing yourself to "remember," signals the highest levels of personal mastery. Do you know how powerful your technology is? Beyond microcircuit technology, beyond genetic splicing and drug induced engineering, without exception this relationship between your physical body (DNA) and emotion represents the single most sophisticated technology to ever grace this world through the expression of our bodies. Our own science now has demonstrated that your DNA, is directly tied to your ability to forgive, allow and love through the expression of your life.

The science of compassion, loving, forgiving and allowing is nothing new. It is an ancient as well as universal science. Your ability to express forgiveness, allowing others the outcome of their own experience, without changing the nature of who you are, is a hallmark of the highest levels of life mastery. The quality of your life is directly tied, with the personal mastery of what your life means to you. All that has ever stood between you and your true power are your emotions and your feelings, interpreted through the filters of what your life has told you that they mean.

Within the life giving fields of compassion, debilitating disease is not possible, immune compromising viruses are not possible, your body turning upon itself is not possible. Through mastery, illness is redefined. Through your mastery expressed as forgiveness and compassion, disease and even death become choices rather than chances.

I have been asked the question:

"What if, after all of this work, the Shift of the Ages never happens?"

I will answer that question now just as I have when asked in the past. Those who spend their lives waiting and preparing for the Shift, miss the very life that they have come to experience. Because their focus and life energy is directed toward a single event, they will think, act and feel differently than they would in the absence of the focus. That difference is the living that is missed. The chance of the Shift of the Ages not happening appears to be small, as the shift has already begun. The magnetics, frequencies and their associated phenomenon are occurring at rates unprecedented in recorded human, as well as geologic, history.

From my perspective, whether the Shift occurs or not is irrelevant. The opportunity to seed the wisdom of compassion, and the possibility of nurturing that compassion into an state of consciousness, far outweighs any other "what if."

I believe that we are the generation spoken of in the ancient texts. Very possibly, we are the last generation to mature before the close of this cycle. We are also the first to "wake up" on the other side of the conscious membrane that defines the two cycles. What we have become by the close of this cycle, determines what is carried to the next. As the seeds of compassion awaken to a critical mass (the threshold of opportunity where a key number of individuals have become their greatest potential), the whole will benefit. The opportunity to become a world where love, wisdom and compassion have replaced hate, ignorance and judgment is us walking between the worlds.

CHAPTER SEVEN

REMEMBER
THE PROMISE OF ETERNAL LIFE

Plate VIII: *Lotus*
Hebrew script represents Good and Evil in Balance

Within the hearts of the children of forever lives the
seed that each planted for themselves long ago.
Their seed is a gift of truth,
sleeping...

Awakened, that seed rekindles the ancient promise
of those who have come before us:
the promise that each soul survives the "darkest"
moments of life
to return home once again, intact and with grace.

That Promise is the seed of truth that we,
today, have named
Compassion."

THE AUTHOR

What is the very last thing that you do at night before drifting into sleep after the lights are off, the sheets are arranged and you have found just the right position to cradle your body for several hours of rest? Very possibly your last act of each day involves taking at least one full deep breath. Coded within that one breath is a signal to your body allowing yourself to slip into an altered state of awareness that we call "sleep." Without sleeping I'll ask you to do the same now. With your eyes wide open, I'll ask you to shift your body's awareness with breath. One deep breath.

Quite often in the workshops there is a tendency for participants to close their eyes as they begin a meditative process. Closing your eyes is a natural tendency because that is when you feel closest to the familiar, closest to home. This chapter is both an experiment in the written word, as well as an opportunity to allow the concepts of the previous chapters to settle in. I invite you to leave your eyes open, wide open. This open eyed world of our reality is actually the altered state! From the perspective of the ancients, this is the dream. This dream is the world that you and I have chosen to master.

I'll begin our process by asking you to give yourself permission to *feel*. Say to yourself several times, out loud if possible,

I allow myself to feel.

I give myself permission to feel.

Stating this command out loud sets up a vibratory pattern of consent. You are giving your program of emotion permission to feel. Now say it to yourself one more time, quietly within your mind. Allow the command to rest silently within you, holding the sacredness of your allowing.

Now I'll ask you to give yourself permission again, this time consenting to *remember.* Say to yourself several times, out loud if possible,

I allow myself to remember.
I give myself permission to remember.

Stating this command out loud sets up a second vibratory pattern of consent. In doing so you give your program of consciousness permission to remember. Now say it to yourself, quietly within your mind. Again, allow the command to rest silently within you, holding the sacredness of your allowing.

Within you there lives a place, one special place, that you and only you know very well. This is a very sacred place that has remained untouched by any person or earthly experience. Throughout the course of your life this is the one place that has been spared from attack or judgment. This is the part of you that remembers trust and truth; the place within you where you have come before to validate yourself.

The memory of this place may be more you than any another memory of yourself. Less of a physical location in space and time, this place is more of a feeling in the absence of time. By simply having the feeling, you move your awareness to this familiar memory. Remember the feeling. Your body knows this place very well, it has been with you always, even before your beginning. You may consider this place as a seed, planted deep within the core of your being, as you were conceived as a thought in the mind of creation. It is this feeling that became the nucleus of your soul's essence upon entering this world of place, distance, and time. Free of any conditions of your earthly experience, your seed is as new as the moment that you burst forth from the heart of your creator, innocent and willing to experience what few have experienced before. In the reading of these words lay the vibratory access to your seed. This is the portion of you that remembers the ancient promise of eternal life made to you long ago...

Remember a time before the promise, when there was no separation between you and I. There was no here and there or today and tomorrow. In this world of all there simply "was," and you were. In this place of thought and no time, you were a part of all that you knew. You and your creative source were one in the same. You existed in this world of one for some period of time, perhaps millennia or perhaps a heartbeat. It did not matter.

Remember the feeling that you felt, as one day you heard the new song reverberate throughout creation. The song was a call, an invitation to all who loved so much that they would journey to an unknown world of all possibilities. In this world of potential, all would have the opportunity to know themselves through the eyes of experiences that were only possible in this world. This world would be an opportunity to find within you a power born of compassion, acceptance, forgiveness and blessing. Only in a world of all possibility could rising above your experience without judgment have meaning.

Knowing yourself in new ways, you would at last, know the full extent of the power inherent within your being and your capacity to love and forgive. Remember yourself, for if you are reading these words, there is a good possibility that you were one who heard the call and had the courage to follow the song of a powerful ray into an experience where none had followed before.

Remember the anticipation, the excitement and the sense of honoring yourself through an act of life that had never been offered before. When you look into the eyes of a young child and sense the joy within them in the morning, just because they woke up. When you see the innocence in the eyes of that child, trusting and allowing. That joy and innocence may feel familiar to you. That familiarity is your joy and your innocence, reflecting that portion of yourself that you have given away to the survival of life. It is with this joy and innocence that you began your journey into this world. No one had ever done what you were about to do and still you came...

You knew that at some point there was a possibility that you would feel a distance between you and the creative force that spawned your very life essence. Always remaining one in mind, you knew that you may begin to feel separate from those who had traveled with you, who had also heard the call to this new world of time and feeling. You knew of the possibility that you may even begin to feel separate from others, yourself and the world around you. You knew of the possibility though you never knew how separate. You could not because no one had ever done what you were about to do and still you came...

You knew that at some point there was a possibility that you would question your worthiness to have the experience, the opportunity to achieve the power of the very force that spawned your life essence. You knew that you may begin to feel inadequate in the presence of those powerful beings who had traveled with you, who had also heard the call, journeying to this new world of time and distance. You knew that you may even begin to doubt your own worth and value within the world to which you had traveled. You knew of the possibility though you never knew how great the doubt. You could not because no one had ever done what you were about to do and still you came...

You knew that at some point there was a possibility that you would mistrust, questioning the very processes of your life, as well as life itself. Growing suspicious of the nature and timing of life as it was shown to you, possibly you would question the existence of the creative force that spawned your life essence. You knew of the possibility, though you never knew how great the mistrust. You could not because no one had ever done what you were about to do and still you came...

Together, you navigated the undulating waves of motion, following the new song to this portal of experience that we call earth. A strange sensation flooded your awareness as you saw your memory began to separate in body while remaining one in mind. What an odd experience of distinctiveness and unity all at once! Looking at your memory you began to see "you" emerge as others, becoming individualized clusters of your oneness. As these fragments of you disappeared into the mists of this world, do you remember saying to one another,

> *This is an illusion!*
> *This is the dream!*

As you begin your new experience, a portion of you whispers to yourself,

> *Please, feel my presence.*
> *Remember my essence.*
> *Please, remember me.*

You watched in silence as that portion of you faded from feeling. Then another. Then another. Until you were alone. In that moment, how did you feel? When do you have that feeling now? There is a good possibility that your feeling of unity in the presence of another that you love is "you" remembering this moment. In the memory you recognize yourself in another.

Alone in body and one in mind you journeyed to the membrane of this new world. Immediately, you were greeted by forces expressing as "slowed down" light, beings offering themselves in service to you because *they love you that much*. These were living forces and their essence embraced you within their gift of wholeness. The ancients called these forces of electricity and magnetism "angels" and remind us of the role that these forces play in our lives. It is through the holy union, the marriage between the angels of sun, water, air and earth that you are offered the stewardship of your body during the time that you are here. Your body can be nothing more than some combination of the very elements that make up this world, tuned to a very specific code called "life" within a very special template called "man." Your body is a gift to you from the forces of this world, the angels of sun, water, earth and breath because *they love you that much*.

In the innocence of living only light, in the joy that only comes from the surrender to life's offering, you began your journey descending into the world of "slow light" that separated your creations from the thought of your creations. Deeper, into this world of grid, time and space you journeyed through the shell of man, living the play between yourself and forces that you had never known before.

Immediately, you found your emotions and feelings pulled in two directions at once!

In a world where there had been only light, there was no choice because all motion led to the light. Now pulling at your new emotions and new feelings is something very different. Now within each moment lives a choice. Within each choice rests the opportunity to align with one feeling or another. Where does this pull come from?

Upon arriving at the densest portions of this new world, you are greeted once again. A familiar force of electricity, the "angel" of the light, you recognize immediately. It is the call of this force that has led you into this world of uncertainty, emotion and feeling. This is the force of Archangel Michael. Michael reminds you that his purpose in this world is to anchor all that is familiar to you from the world that you have known as "light." A formidable task by any standards, he has enlisted other electrical forces, legions of angels, to aid him in his task, providing certainty that light is always available in this world for you. Michael and the legions have offered 200,000 years of their lives in service to you, to this grand cycle of experience, *because they love you that much.*

As you pass, Michael reminds you that he is always with you, one heartbeat away, in service to you because *he loves you that much.*

Of your ancient friendship, he asks only one thing.
As you begin your new experience, he whispers
please, feel my presence.
Remember my essence.
Please, remember me!

You watch in silence as he fades from feeling.
Suddenly you are confronted with a second force unknown and yet familiar at the same time. As you acclimate to this powerful opposite you remember a masterful being from the great light at the hand of your creator. This force has the feeling of the Brightest of the Bright, Archangel Lucifer. Something is different however, something has changed. Lucifer reminds you that his purpose in this world is to anchor all that is *unfamiliar* to you, the opposite of all that you have known. He relates that he was "chosen" for this task because of his position of the Brightest of the Bright. His power alone holds the strength to anchor the opposite of all that light could ever represent. His world is now a world of "no light." He calls it darkness. He has no legions to support him in his task. How can he? What angels possess the strength to hold the anchor of darkness, and not get lost in the experience? Archangel Lucifer has offered you 200,000 years of his life in service to you. As you pass, Lucifer reminds you that he is always with you, one heartbeat away, in service to you, *because he loves you that much.*

Of your ancient friendship, he asks only one thing.
As you begin your new experience, he whispers
please, feel my presence.
Remember my essence.
Please remember me!

You watch in silence as he fades from feeling.

So you began your journey of density, magnetics, polarity, feeling and emotion. From a place of love, journeying into a world greeted by love, "gifted" your body through the great act of compassionate love, you began. As the memory of your journey faded, the wisdom of love's many expressions faded also. For countless generations of countless lifetimes, you endured what no angel had ever been asked to endure. Through your eyes of light, you have seen what no angel was ever meant to see. Through your body of emotion and feeling, you have felt what no angel was ever meant to feel. As a "dense angel" of this world, you have known unspeakable joy and the heights of physical ecstasy as well as unbearable pain. You have known yourself in betrayal and violation as those that you trusted pushed you to the very edge of who and what you believe you are, and then pushed a little harder, leaving you in the depths of knowing yourself alone and betrayed. Through your experience, one question has always remained...

I invite you to ask yourself...

IF
you were loving enough to recognize the song of light
as it beckoned to you before your journey;

AND
you were loved enough by the forces of this world to give
themselves to you as the holy alchemy of your body;

AND
you are loved enough for the two most powerful forces of light, Lucifer and
Michael, to give their lives to you for 200,000 years of this cycle of experience;

AND
you came to this world as a spark of your creator's love, greeted by the "angels"
of this world in a sacred gesture of love, experiencing the polarities of possibility
because they love you that much...

THEN
Do you love yourself enough to allow yourself your experience?
Do you love yourself enough to allow for the possibility
that all there is in this world is love expressed in forms
that we have never imagined, in the past?

The answer to the question is "yes"! I can say yes because you have already demonstrated your love. You have chosen to love in a world that has hated. You have chosen compassion in a world that has judged. You have chosen trust in a world that has lived in fear.

These choices are you, loving yourself, expressing your truest nature, remembering. You are doing it in a world that may not have always supported your choices. This is you rising above polarity while living in the world of polarity. What a powerful being you are!

Will you allow for the possibility of your power in your life? Will you allow for the possibility that you, in your skillful, unique and masterful way, have honored your creator through the experience of your life, becoming a living bridge for those that you hold most dear?

As I offer this possibility in this moment, there is a vision of movement in my mind's eye. It is a vision of you and I and everyone that we will ever know, or have known, stepping single file along a beautifully illuminated path. On either side of the path are rows and rows of angels, all of the forces that we have ever had the opportunity to contend with in these lifetimes. As we pass, each kneels, bowing in respect of what you and I have accomplished. We move forward, one by one to a point that becomes clearer as we get closer. At the head of the line, at the entrance to the gates of forever, stand the two most powerful forces of all. Immediately we recognize these forces as our dearest friends, the portions of ourselves that we have named Archangel Lucifer and Archangel Michael. They kneel, facing one another, and as you pass each raises his head, admiring you in awe of your earthly accomplishments.

You did not forget them.

They are friends, missing you because you are part of them. Weary, tears stream down their cheeks as you pass between them. They embrace one another, the powers of the lightest of the light and the darkest of the dark, equal in the eyes of the One. They are ready to go "home" through the path of forever. They refuse to go without you. They will not leave a part of themselves behind.

In this moment, you have an opportunity. Beyond the practice of a meditation or the doing of a prayer. I invite you to remember the sophisticated technology that lives as your being. This is the liquid crystal of your body powered by the program of thought, feeling and emotion. Will you allow for the alignment of these three powers within you as a single force moving you through the offering of life? Can you find it within yourself to allow for the possibility that there is a single force in this world, expressing many ways, and that force is the sole substance of all that we may know in this world?

Will you allow for the possibility?

In the allowing lay the healing! This is the healing of our illusion of separation. Without another force, there can be only the One. That One is you and me and the compassionate expression of our love. There is no separation. There is no duality. They are expressions of our ancient illusion. There is only "I" and I has many expressions in this life dream! There is nothing else "out there" other than you and I knowing ourselves in all ways.

Now we know.

We know that we choose equality over oppression.

We choose peace over the alternative to peace.

We choose life over non-life.

I'll ask you to give yourself permission to heal our illusion of separation. Regardless of what anyone else says, thinks, feels or knows, for you in this moment,

as you allow yourself the possibility that there is a single force in our world expressing as all that we know, you have healed the separation within yourself.

This is the moment! It is with you now. In this moment you may allow yourself to become the compassion that you so desire in your world, your life, your community and your family. The moment lives within you, now. Will you allow it? Someone must choose this moment to make it easier for the next to choose this moment. Someone must shift our pattern, redefining our programs of separation, trust and self worth. Someone must do it first.

I invite you to use the ancient Lakota Sioux code that was left to you to create the vibratory opening into the grids of human consciousness.

Iwaye cin wakan yelo.

(ee-wa yeah sin wak-kan yeah-low)

"The words that I speak are sacred"

Into the opening that you have just created, place the new code. Say these words to yourself, out loud if possible.

I remember union.

I heal our illusion of separation.

I heal our illusion within myself.

I choose Union.

Separation heals within me.

Feel the feeling of your Sacred Words. Repeat your codes again, and again. Say the codes as many times and as often as it takes, to "become" your healing. Stating these commands out loud sets up the vibratory pattern, the grid, providing access to the next person with the courage to allow their healing from within.

Now say them to yourself quietly within your mind. Allow your commands to rest silently within you, holding the sacredness of your allowing.

You will notice a feeling in your body as you say these words. Notice the taste in your mouth, the moisture of your tongue, the perspiration on your palms, brow, chest. Women often will flush under their chin, neck and upper chest. Each of these is a physiological response to the sacred words that you have just spoken. Each is an indication of shifts of energy, patterns of electrical charge that move within your body in response to the commands of your program. Healing the illusion of separation as thought, feeling and emotion will have a physical component.

If what you have just read had meant anything to you at all, even on a minute scale, then energy has shifted within your body. You may know of the shift as a change in sleep, bowel or dietary patterns. That shift, your shift, is a signal to creation to bring on an experience allowing you to demonstrate your new level of mastery. From this moment forward the opportunity now exists for something to occur in your life allowing your demonstration of the healing of separation.

Blessings to you in your skillfully created opportunity. This is your opportunity to demonstrate your highest levels of compassionate mastery.

SUMMARY

Within the context of *Walking Between the Worlds,* the Shift of the Ages, your relationship to the earth through your sacred circuit and inner technology of compassion, we may summarize our opportunity of this time in history as follows.

1. You are, and have always been, intimately connected to all that you see and experience in your world. Researchers have now digitally measured this relationship. Each cell of your body specifically, and all matter in general, attempts to hold a tuning to the reference vibrations of our earth home. Through your sacred circuit you touch all of creation and it touches you, as the gentle undulations of pulsed resonance.

2. As you approach the Shift of the Ages, you are asked to re-tune your body to accommodate the changing parameters of the Shift. These may be measured as decreasing planetary magnetics and increasing planetary frequency.

3. The codes that allow you the opportunity of change are the very gifts of relationship. Each relationship offers you the opportunity of emotion, feeling and thought. Each relationship, regardless of length or intensity, mirrors to you something of your feeling, thinking and emotion based beliefs. You will see and interpret the actions of others through the lens of your personal charges. Beyond the right or wrong of judgment, charge is simply your way of showing yourself beliefs that seek balance as you strive to re-tune your body.

4. Ancient texts left you clues, the vibrational technology that will allow you to accomplish your re-tuning gracefully. That science we know as compassion. Researchers have now demonstrated that genetic shifts, changes in the actual sequencing of DNA, may be accomplished by specific qualities of thought, feeling and emotion!

5. Redefining the spiritual parameters of light, dark, good, evil and the unconscious intent underlying your joy, as well as your pain, is your path that will allow you balance in your life. The science of compassion and the gift of the blessing are your tools to implement your science in daily life.

I believe that becoming our truest nature is the greatest gift that we could ever offer to ourselves, one another and our children. I feel that it is possible to remember and embody our gift in a heartbeat, "in the twinkling of an eye."

APPENDIX I

Definition and Discussion of the "Shift of the Ages"
Excerpts from the book,
"Awakening to Zero Point: The Collective Initiation"
by Gregg Braden

The nature of the Shift has been questioned, pondered, postulated, hypothesized and worshipped for thousands of years. Religions have developed surrounding what appear to be well-intentioned, though distorted understandings, of this elusive yet fundamental force of creation. The consequences of this shift transcend the boundaries of religion, science and mysticism. All are languages developed throughout history to understand creation, creative processes, the origin and ultimate fate of human life. Each represents a single portion of a much larger, more all encompassing truth.

The process of the Shift itself may be viewed as analogous to that of a very familiar shift seen on a daily basis. The change-of-state or phase transitions of water between any of its familiar forms provides a powerful metaphor for the Shift of the Ages. Water may be seen in any one, or a combination of, three forms or states as they are referred to: solid (ice), liquid (flowing water), or gas (vapor or steam). Chemically each of these forms of water is the same, H_2O. Structurally, the geometry of the molecular packing is different, allowing the compound of water to express differently under varying conditions. Illustrated through the use of a particular graph known as the Phase Diagram, the ability of water to express itself within each of these states is a function of temperature and pressure.

In general, the phase diagram indicates the following:
- At low temperatures within a wide range of atmospheric conditions, water expresses itself as a solid, ice.
  Chemically it is still water, H_2O. Structurally it has become more dense, the molecules are moving very slowly.
- As temperature increases and atmospheric pressure increases, water begins to become less dense and begins to express itself as gas or vapor (steam). Chemically it is still water. Structurally the molecules are moving more rapidly.
- As temperatures decrease and atmospheric pressures increase water is able to express itself as flowing liquid, water. Again, chemically the same. Structurally, molecules are more mobile than in ice, however, less mobile than in vapor.

Chemically, the water remains the same, H_2O. while structurally it expresses itself differently as a function of the environmental parameters of temperature and pressure.

Further examples of matter demonstrating a change-of-state may be found within the mineral kingdom. Many minerals exhibit varying external expressions, crystalline in nature, while retaining the chemical properties that allow them their identity, by definition. For example, the mineral fluorite is commonly found in large clusters of perfect cubes bordered upon its flat faces by other cubes. In the same deposit, fluorite may also be found expressing as the geometric form of the octahedron, an eight sided crystal reminiscent of two four-sided pyramids mirroring one another with the widest portion, the base, the plane of reflection. Chemically, both forms are identical, CaF_2. Structurally, they express differently as a function of the processes that created them.

Iron pyrite may be found in the field as discrete hexahedrons (perfect cubes) loose in the deposits or bound to other cubes. Again, in the same deposits, the pyrite may also express as the geometric form known as the dodecahedron, an approximation of the sphere with twelve faces. Chemically the same, FeS2, structurally different.

Conceptually, the phase diagram of water and the mineral examples are very accurate metaphors for the process of the planetary shift being experienced by earth and the earth/human interface. Chemically, earth remains the same, a "wrinkle" in the uniform fabric of creation expressed as crystalized carbon and silica. Structurally, it is the morphogenic expression of earth that is reflecting the Shift. The "environmental" parameters of earth are changing. Rather than the temperature and pressure expressed in our phase diagram, it is our environment of planetary magnetics and base resonant frequency that are shifting. As these parameters change in much the same manner as the temperature and pressure of the phase diagram for water, creation expresses itself in a different manner. Chemically, matter remains the same. Structurally matter vibrates faster, becoming less dense while maintaining its form.

Metaphorically, our bodies may be considered as a single compound, such as water, within a dynamic evolutionary environment. This environment has been predominantly governed by fields of planetary magnetism and frequency. For approximately the last two hundred thousand years earth has functioned within one specific zone, or range, of frequency and magnetics. All matter, all that human consciousness has known, felt, touched, created or un-created has occurred within the context of matter expressing within this range of frequency and magnetics. Catastrophic events throughout history have had a pronounced impact on human evolution through the interruption of these fields.

There has been, and still exists, another range of frequency or band of information, that has always lived within the range of earth's fields. This body of information has appeared as a zone of high frequency; available while not as easily accessible to each conscious being. It is into this new range of highly evolved information that both earth and humankind are moving into exclusive resonance. It is to these frequencies that each cell within the physical body of each individual is attempting to "map" itself. The migration into complete resonance with this new body of information, by definition a process called Ascension, is the goal of the shift.

Resonance to this highly evolved band of information is attained through intent and life conduct. Any relationship to this body of knowledge is one which must be achieved, using the tools of choice and free will applied as the processes of life. It is into the zone of experience offered through this new range of frequency, that the phase transition will carry earth. A function of conscious and intentional evolution, earth will support harmonic patterns of compassion, forgiveness and blessing. We have no name for this one, highly evolved body of information as yet.

It is to this zone of information that the ones known as "Buddha," "Jesus" and other beings of reference were in resonance. This was the gift of our reference beings, to anchor the map of life conduct leading to this information firmly into the consciousness of humankind. The map survives today because it was anchored in our presence, among us. The process of their lives became the living bridges, making the higher range of information, accessible to all of human kind.

A western physicist would describe this initial shifting of resonance as a dimensional shift. In Biblical terms, the act of consciously vibrating from one state-space into another is referred to as Resurrection. The living example of our Reference Being of Jesus of Nazareth demonstrated that through the conscious use of choice, free will and life conduct, humankind may collectively become more than any individual fear or perceived limitation.

The Shift is the term applied to the process of earth accelerating through a course of evolutionary change, with the human species linked, by choice, to the electromagnetic fields of earth, following suit through a process of cellular change.

The human aspect of the Shift may be consciously facilitated, even accelerated, through the use of choice and free will, associated with the ancient wisdom of the human mind.body.spirit relationship. This is the purpose of the Shift, the ultimate balance and healing of earth and all life forms that are capable of sustaining the energy of that healing. This is the shift to a new way of expressing the human form, through the lens of higher frequency. The shift is us remembering our potential as human. This is *Awakening to Zero Point: The Collective Initiation.*

THE NATURE OF STILLNESS: ZERO POINT

In traditional physics there is a general assumption that "things may happen" only in a space where there is the absence of a vacuum. It is within this space that the forces of temperature and pressures drive the systems of creation, producing events that may be observed and measured. Scientists typically use this principle embodied as an instrument to measure temperature in the laboratory. A glass thermometer indicates temperature through the rise and fall of a column of mercury within the vacuum of the sealed tube. As temperature decreases, the pressure of the gas within the tube decreases correspondingly. In theory, there is a point at which the pressure would drop to zero, with a corresponding drop in temperature yielding zero degrees on a scale known as the Kelvin scale.* Another term for this point would be that of absolute zero.

Following the guidelines of Newton's third law of thermodynamics,** traditional science has accepted the theory that it is not possible to achieve zero degrees Kelvin. A specialized study of physics, however, quantum physics, both allows for, and

* The Kelvin scale is an absolute scale of temperature, the zero point of which is -273.15 degrees C. It is at this point, in principle, that all molecules are at rest and become "still" as gases exert no pressure and occupy no volume.

** Newton's third law of thermodynamics states that at absolute zero, all molecules are perfectly aligned and motionless, with the degree of disorder (entropy) at zero. Traditional physics states that this is a theoretical point only, not possible to attain experimentally. Quantum physics, however, predicts and allows for continued motion through absolute zero.

predicts, fluctuations within a vacuum down to and including zero degrees Kelvin. The point at which temperatures reach absolute zero, with a corresponding decrease of pressure, is referred to as Zero Point: the amount of vibrational energy associated with matter at zero degrees Kelvin.

It is in the space of zero point that creation becomes very quiet and still to the observer, though energy is still in motion within the vacuum and experienced by the participant.

Earth is experiencing early stages of the events that will provide an experience of Zero Point, allowing the breakdown of thought constructs that are inharmonic with our "blueprint" of highest expression. In place of temperature and pressure, the parameters of magnetics and frequency are providing the conditions necessary to achieve Zero Point. Each individual now living upon the earth is an integral part of the Shift process, playing the vital role of midwife in the birthing of a new era of human perception and awareness. The intent of presenting *Awakening to Zero Point* at this time in this particular format is to offer the mechanics of the Shift, the inner workings of the event on a conceptual level.

You have been inundated for centuries with prophecy, prediction and warnings of catastrophic change within this period of history. You have been asked to accept and believe the information as it has been presented to you, as you have been told. The following section will provide you with the mechanism to know, from within, of the change that is occurring and present it in terms that you may relate to events in your daily life. From this you will begin to see for yourself, to understand why the changes are occurring and the interrelated nature of various aspects of the events. The experience of Zero Point is the goal of ancient meditative practices and is closely related to the Biblical term of Resurrection, as well as, an event commonly referred to as "The Shift."

The Shift is more than a hypothetical event to be viewed as something to occur during some distant geological epoch far into the future. It is more than a process reserved for mystical, esoteric theoreticians living recluse lives in remote locations of the globe waiting for the end of the world as we know it. The shift is a sequence of knowable, measurable processes and events that are already under way.

The Shift of the Ages has already begun!

MAGNETICS: THE FIRST KEY OF RESURRECTION

The Shift may be addressed from a variety of perspectives, each a valid language in its own right. Esoteric discussions will center around "moving toward the light" and the coming of the "New Age." An equally valid language that may be used is that of earth's changing physical dynamics. From the perspective of earth science, the changing paradigm is accomplished through a realignment of two digitally measurable, fundamental parameters; those of planetary frequency and planetary magnetics. These parameters alone have a far reaching and profound impact upon human consciousness, human thought and perception specifically, and the behavior of matter in general. Both of these parameters are changing very rapidly at present, having fluctuated dramatically in both the historical, as well as, the geological past. Each has a dramatic yet subtle effect upon the cellular body, human consciousness, and the manner in which that consciousness expresses itself.

In the college textbook, *Physical Geology* by Leet and Judson it is stated

"The cause of the earth's magnetism has remained one of the most vexing problems of earth study. A completely satisfactory answer to the question is still forthcoming."[1] The relationship between earth, the planetary magnetic fields, and cellular function of the body is a key component to the understanding of the conscious evolution and the process of the Shift. A conceptual knowledge of the magnetic fields of earth may be gained through the use of a simple demonstration. Consider a simple iron bar of any dimensions. The iron appears as dense with no magnetic properties. If an arbitrary length of conductive wire is wrapped around the iron bar in one direction, with any number of windings, and an electrical charge is passed through the wire in an arbitrary direction, an interesting phenomenon occurs. The previously non-magnetic iron bar becomes magnetized, developing a magnetic field with polar expression of North and South.

The next portion of this demonstration produces a very significant, and possibly unexpected effect related to the Shift process of earth. As the flow of the electrical charge around the iron bar is reversed, with the bar remaining in its original position, the first magnetic field is lost and a second magnetic field is generated in its place. This second field, however, has significantly changed the manner in which it is expressing the magnetic effect. It is now reversed.

Without changing the physical orientation of the bar, what was once the Northern most pole on the bar has become the Southern most and the Southern most pole is now the Northern most! Simply by altering the direction of the flow of electrons relative to the iron bar, the sense of the magnetic fields has reversed while the bar itself has remained in its original position. If this field is generated upon a flat surface of iron filings, the individual particles of iron will align themselves along the arc line of the magnetic field, so that the arc becomes visible. The lines of force on the flat surface will look like the lines of force that surround earth.

The key to the field of magnetics follows:

Electrons moving in a circular motion around a relatively fixed body of iron generate the field of magnetics.

The electrons of electricity are being guided along the pathway of the conductive coil, in a circular motion around the iron bar, generating a new field of force at right angles (ninety degrees) to the direction of the electron flow. This demonstration is a very good analogy for the physical dynamics of the Shift process that are occurring upon earth at present.

A generalized cross section of earth reveals that the planet is not uniform throughout. Rather, it is composed of zones, layers of material varying in temperature and density. Each of these parameters is a function of depth below surface and tremendous pressures associated with these depths. The outermost layer is referred to as the "crust" and provides the visible surface of the continents and oceans. The crust is a relatively thin layer averaging three miles thick beneath the oceans and twenty five miles in thickness as measured through the continents.

Below the earth's crust there is a second layer, averaging approximately 1,800 miles in thickness; the mantle. The material of the mantle is much denser than that of the crust and exists at such high temperatures and pressures that it is essentially a thick liquid. It is this plastic material from the mantle that "extrudes" itself onto the surface through openings in the crust such as volcanoes and lava flows.

Under the mantle material lies a thinner, yet more dense zone of material, the core. Scientists divide the core into two zones, the outer and inner core, estimated at 1,366 and 782 miles in thickness, respectively. The inner core is believed to be a plastic-like sphere, with the outer core a more liquid-like material, warmer than the core while cooler than the next mantle layer.

Within the iron and nickel core of earth, our iron bar analogy resumes. In the demonstration the movement of the electrons around a stationary core of iron produce the effect of the magnetic field. Earth's predominant field of magnetics has a simple dipolar shape, as if the planet had a huge bar magnet as its core. It is the rotation of earth around the molten inner core, that generates an excess of electrons (-e) within the crustal layers. Following the "laws" of classical physics, a proportional field of magnetics is generated at a ninety degree angle to the flow of electrons, yielding the shape of the donut-like magnetic fields. These fields, measured in units known as Gauss,** are a function of the composite rotation of earth around these iron cores in general, and specifically the motion of the outer core relative to the inner core. The more rapid the rotation, the greater the intensity of the field around the planet's iron and nickel core.

The movement of rotation is analogous to the previous example of electrical charge moving in a circular motion through a conductor wrapped around the iron bar. For this discussion, the mode of transport for the electron stream is not significant, be it the charge of planetary rotation or conductive copper winding. In each example, electrons are moving around a relatively stationary source of iron producing a field effect that is termed magnetic.

The implication is that the intensity of the fields of magnetism is a function of the rate of rotation. In other words, the more rapidly that earth rotates, the denser the fields of magnetism. The slower the planetary rotation, the less dense the fields of magnetism. This is precisely what is happening, at present, as well as numerous times throughout planetary history! Though alluded to in the ancient texts, evidence supporting the rotation/magnetic relationship is just beginning to surface in recent years. Nils-Axel Morner reports,

"Because the inner core is a good electric conductor and carries a large rotational energy, it is likely to have a strong interaction with the main geomagnetic field."[2]

In addition to the field of global magnetics, earth's rotation within an envelope of a multi-layered atmosphere produce an electrical charge that may be measured as *static potential*. The electrical charge builds to a certain value before it is discharged. Tesla

---

** After Karl Gauss, the unit used to measure magnetic flux density

discovered, and modern science now recognizes, that the system of earth and atmosphere essentially functions as a large spherical capacitor, with the surface, (ground) negatively charged through an excess of electrons. Layers of the upper atmosphere exhibit a positive charge, creating an electrical potential with an average value of 130 volts per meter over the surface of the earth. The phenomenon of lightening is a dramatic and beautiful demonstration of earth's attempt to reach equilibrium, balancing the charge between the atmosphere or ground. Global discharges of lightening involve approximately 2,500 strikes over a 100 square kilometer area per year, as part of an ongoing attempt by earth and the atmosphere to reach a perfect electrical balance. You are bathed in this electrical potential throughout your life, seemingly without effect.

It is this "trickle charge" of static electricity that is partially responsible for holding the magnetic alignment between your body and the patterns of your experience. Recent studies (*Science,* Vol. 260:1590, June 11, 1993) have validated the brain earth relationship through magnetics. An international team studying the phenomenon of "magnetoreception," the ability of the body to detect magnetic fluctuations announced that the human brain contains "millions of tiny magnetic particles."

The ancient texts tell us that the body seeks a harmonic balance with the earth. This balance is the goal of the life experience, and may be consciously regulated through non-polarized thoughts of forgiveness and feelings of compassion. The magnetic particles within the brain serve as a physical link; the static potential serves as the "trickle charge" holding the information component of the particles in place.

Our geologic record indicates that the magnetic fields of earth have shifted previously, at least 14 times in the last 4.5 million years,[3] as determined by magnetic measurements taken from extrusive rock cores. These are samples of earth material that was once molten and has been ejected to the surface, cooled and preserved the alignment of minerals sensitive to magnetism.

Additional evidence of a 180 degree polar shift relatively recently may be seen again in the work of Mr. Morner.

"Radiocarbon dates of carbonate concretions within the varves (sedimentary deposits) gave ages that suggested that the varves were laid down between about 13,600 and 12,800 BP (before present) with the transpolar shift occurring at about 13,200 BP. This means that the same transpolar shift is now also recorded from the Southern Hemisphere. This can hardly mean anything else than a di-polar nature of the shift."[4] (Parentheses are the author's.)

If the strength of earth's magnetic fields is, in fact, a function of core and mantle relationships, a reversal of the poles would seem to indicate that the motion of these bodies has slowed and reversed coinciding with the shift. If such an event did occur within the collective memory of humanity, is it reasonable to expect that an event of such magnitude would have been recorded?

Possibly. Apparently, there are records of at least one such event, in the collective memory of not one but two separate civilizations, when the rotation of the earth exhibited a very unusual behavior. In his book, *The Lost Realms,* author Zechariah Sitchin recounts narratives from these societies. The first is from the Peruvian Andes, the second from Biblical texts. Each provides an account of anomalous activity regarding earth's rotation, in the language of the time. During the time of Titu Yupanqui Pachacuti II, approximately 1394 B.C., there was a time of anomalous night when ,

"...there was no dawn for twenty hours."[5]

This event was not describing an eclipse, as none was recorded or predicted for that time by either Chinese or Peruvian astronomers. If the event were attributed to an eclipse, none has been known to last for such a long period of time. Something happened that was interpreted as immersing one portion of earth in night for twenty hours, nearly twice as long as should be possible. Sitchin theorizes that if such an event did occur, somewhere on the opposite side of the world an opposite event should have been recorded. The Concordance version of the Biblical texts records such an event in the book of Joshua, chapter 10 verse 13.

"And the Sun stood still, and the moon stayed, until the nation took vengeance on their enemies."

"...The sun stayed in the midst of heaven, and did not hasten to go down for about a whole day."

According to Biblical scholars, this event took place sometime shortly after 1393 B.C. Is this conclusive proof that the earth routinely slows its rotation to a standstill? Certainly not. These accounts do indicate, however, that there are times within the memory of human consciousness, as well as geologic time, when the rotation of earth has performed unusually.

In a later portion of this section, we will examine why the majority of records from a particular cycle do not survive the Shift. Here may be a clue. The only materials that may survive the disruption of planetary magnetics and base resonant frequency are those that are earth resonant. Regardless of what values earth parameters shift into, the materials are always "tuned" to those parameters.

At present, the indicators preceding such a shift are not readily recognized, although they are acknowledged. In the June 1993 edition of *Science News*, an article concerning magnetic reversals states that

"The task of finding an accurate reversal record seems to be all the more difficult because the magnetic field weakens considerably when it switches direction."[6]

The intensity of earth's magnetic field is dropping rapidly at the present time. Geologic records indicate that earth is declining from a magnetic high 2,000 years ago and the values have steadily dropped from that time to the present. The data indicates that the intensity of earth's magnetic fields is approximately thirty eight percent lower than it was 2,000 years ago.

Measurements over the last 130 years indicate a decline in magnetics from 8.5×10^{25} gauss units to 8.0×10^{25} gauss units, or an average rate of about 5% per one hundred years. As magnetics are a function of planetary rotation, a decline in the intensity of magnetics would seem to indicate a lessening in the rate of earth's rotation.

This is, in fact, precisely what is happening within the inner and outer cores of earth, as well as the overall rotation of the planet.

"In association with a minimum in the westward drift velocity of the eccentric dipole, which appeared around 1910, retardation in the rate of earth's rotation was observed." [7]

Twice in 1992 and at least once in 1993 the National Bureau of Standards in Boulder Colorado reset the Cesium-atomic clocks to reflect "lost time" in the day. Our days are becoming longer than the clocks can account for. "If we didn't do this, we'd eventually get out of sync with sunlight," according to Dennis McCarthy, an astronomer at the U.S. Naval Observatory.

The effects of global magnetics are not confined to individuals on a personal level. Variable planetary magnetics provide zones of experience where mass units of consciousness are drawn to feel or work out some form of common experience. When an individual or group consciousness feels that an area no longer feels appropriate, or resonates with them, they are describing the relationship of their body's sensors to those zones of magnetic density. The understanding of the nature of these fields is key to understanding mass migrations of large populations, human as well as animal, for no apparent reason. Additionally, these fields may explain the settling of ancient cultures in what may appear to be very unlikely locations such as Chaco Canyon, New Mexico, for example.

What, then, is the significance between fluctuating magnetic fields of earth and the Awakening process of the evolution of human consciousness? To understand this it becomes necessary to develop a working knowledge of the relationship between human consciousness and the magnetic fields of earth.

MAGNETIC TENSION: THE GLUE OF CONSCIOUSNESS

The energy referred to as *consciousness* is electromagnetic in nature. Our modern idiom would consider this information as a form of energy that is bound within the magnetic fields of our planet. Conscious essence may be considered as hierarchical grid upon hierarchical grid of this energy, forming continuous matrices of subtle frequency and geometry. It is within these matrices that magnetic influences provide a tension or stress field binding the essence of human consciousness as a framework of divine intelligence. These fields of information are bound to the earth sphere through a stabilizing "glue" of planetary magnetics. Please understand that it is the awareness of humankind, and not the life essence itself, that is used to interpret the three dimensional world, the self and ultimately the creator. Life essence does not "need" to understand. It is this awareness that is locked up within the fields of magnetics surrounding the planet. Through the structure provided as fields of magnetics, the meshwork of the conscious matrix is stabilized and secured in place.

You may view yourself as many things on many levels, and may be categorized and defined through the unique vocabulary used to describe yourself on each of those levels. Biologically you are bones, flesh, organs, cells, fluids, etc. Geometrically you are crystalline in nature. Each biological component of your body may be reduced to a substance of crystalline mineral. If you were to be scanned electromagnetically, you would appear as a composite wave form, a complex series of geometric patterns made of many individual wave forms from each unique biological aspect of your body.

Energetically, you are electrical in nature. Each cell within your body generates a charge of approximately 1.17 volts at a specific frequency for that organ. This unique vibration is termed a *signature* frequency. Each cell is in constant motion, the rhythmic oscillation of a subtle beat, generating its signature frequency. You are more than simply an electrical being, however. You are electrical and magnetic. In addition to the electrical charge generated by each cell of your body, there is also a magnetic field offset by ninety degrees that surrounds each cell. Viewed in three dimensions, the shaded area would come to you vertically from the page. The human body, as a whole, exhibits a composite magnetic field, the sum of each individual field from each individual organ, tissue or bone cell. Electromagnetic cells within electromagnetic beings. Two distinct though interrelated fields that determine, to a large extent, how you perceive yourself, your world and how you function within those perceptions.

The electrical portion of your body is "you," in your purest form. This represents "you" as information and energy. This is your seed core essence, you with no judgment, ego, fear or preconceived ideas regarding yourself, others or the world around you. The electrical aspect of you is what would historically be termed your *soul*. This aspect of you is not bound by dimensionality, planet or star. It is your soul that has traveled from a multitude of energetic systems to experience earth in this cycle of consciousness. It is your soul essence that will eventually leave the earth experience, at some chosen point in time, carrying the vibrational benefit of your earth lives on toward your new experience.

The magnetic fields surrounding each cell of your body may be thought of as a "buffer" stabilizing the information of the soul within each cell. This buffer creates "drag" or friction around each cell, effectively interfering with your ability to fully access that body of information. Earth's fields of magnetics have historically been your safety zone between thought and manifestation. Early in this cycle of consciousness, magnetics were high providing a distancing between the formulation of a thought and the consequences of that thought. The group body consciousness was relatively new, learning the power and consequence of thought. It was during this time that higher magnetics were desirable; both then and now it would be very confusing to have each thought and passing fantasy become manifest in your life.

Planetary magnetics were relatively high, insuring that to manifest something in this world, you had to be very clear and really want, or "desire" that which was being envisioned. Only then, could the seed of that thought be sustained long enough to be pulled down through the matrix of creation, crystallizing into something "real" in your world and your life. Now, as the intensity of the fields decrease, the lag time between a thought, and the realization of that thought, is decreasing proportionally. Perhaps you have noticed how quickly you are able to manifest in your world.

Lower magnetic fields provide the opportunity for change through the rapid manifestation of thought and feeling.

APPENDIX II

Definition and Discussion of the Platonic Solids:
Codes of Creation
Excerpts from the book,
"Awakening to Zero Point: The Collective Initiation"
by Gregg Braden

All patterns of three dimensional creation, including the human form, resolve to energy bonds resulting from some combination of five simple forms that have been the subject of scrutiny and debate for centuries. Religions have developed around the understandings of these forms, mystery schools devoted themselves to preserving the information for the use of future generations. The science of alchemy, often associated with the changing of lead into gold, is rooted in the study of these forms. Alchemists were concerned less with obtaining the actual metals, as with the transformation that the metals experienced in moving from one expression to another. Their transformation provides a beautiful metaphor for the process of earth's Shift at present. It is within this transformational process that the keys to conscious evolution may be found, for these keys provide the "map" of matter expressing as increasingly complex geometric assemblages. The basic patterns, literally the geometric codes of creation, are known today as the Platonic Solids and physically describe the volumes enclosed by these patterns.

A platonic solid may be defined as the surfaces delineating a very special, fully enclosed volume. All lengths defining any portion of the volume are equal, as are the values of all interior angles defining the corners. Conceptually, the solid may be thought of as a single unit cell of form, repeating until it falls back upon itself with adjacent, matching unit cells. Each angle formed by the meeting of the unit cells, and the dimensions of each side of the cell are equal. At present, there are five solids known that meet this criteria. Referred to as the five regular platonic solids, they are illustrated in order of increasing complexity as defined by the number of faces. (*Figure 1*).

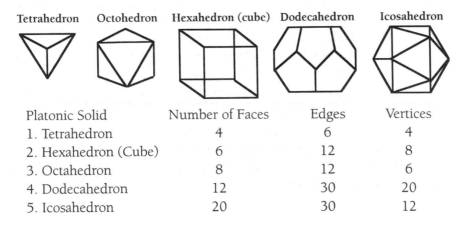

Platonic Solid	Number of Faces	Edges	Vertices
1. Tetrahedron	4	6	4
2. Hexahedron (Cube)	6	12	8
3. Octahedron	8	12	6
4. Dodecahedron	12	30	20
5. Icosahedron	20	30	12

Figure 1 *Schematic diagram of the five regular platonic solids.*

Walking Between the Worlds

The term "platonic" is a reference to the scientist and philosopher Plato and one of his best known works, the *Timaeus*. Within this work, Plato uses the tool of metaphor in the description of a universal cosmology based upon interlocking patterns of geometry. These patterns appear to have been known well in advance of Plato, however, as shown in the archaeological records of forms resulting from these patterns, that may be viewed in the Cairo museum in Egypt. Within the glass cases are finely crafted models dating to 3,000 years old; models of the forms referred to in the *Timaeus*. Pre-dating these forms are those kept in the Ashmolean Museum at Oxford, England,[1] estimated to have been "assembled" approximately 1000 years before Plato's time. Though not as finely crafted as the Egyptian forms, these models are quite obviously indications of an awareness of fundamental and geometric nature of the building blocks of creation.

For clarity, the mineral kingdom best exemplifies these natural expressions of energy along pre-defined guidelines of energy. The naturally occurring structure of the crystal, externally, is an outward expression of the planes of strength and weakness along which matter has aligned internal to the structure. Atoms combining to form the basic building blocks of the crystal as the first unit cell, define the appearance of the crystal for the remainder of its growth. An example of a common mineral.crystal sequence will help to illustrate this concept.

The mineral compound of table salt is represented chemically as sodium and chlorine, $NaCl$. The crystalline nature of salt, halite, is not readily apparent while it is dissolved in a solution of water, for example. At specific temperatures and pressures, halite may remain in solution indefinitely, assuming that the ratio of water to salt does not change due to evaporation. Under specific temperatures and pressures, sodium and chlorine will begin to combine, as long as atoms of each are available, and form the crystalline structure that is recognized as salt. This structure is based upon the platonic solid of the cube. The bonding of atoms along pre-defined patterns of geometry is referred to as patterns of packing or geometric coordination. Coordination describes the number of units (atoms, molecules, cells, etc.) that comprise the arrangement.

For example, "2" coordination describes a linear arrangement, with one of the elements residing at a point adjacent to the next ,

while the elements in "3" coordination will arrange themselves tangent to one another .

Packing patterns are expressed very clearly within the mineral kingdom, as geologists use these patterns to describe the bonding of atoms. The five common coordination patterns based upon the platonic solids are as follows:

Description	Geometry	Packing
1. (2) coordination	Linear	∞
2. (3) coordination	Equal-sided triangle	
3. (4) coordination	Three-dimensional triangle	
4. (6) coordination	Two four-sided pyramids	
5. (8) coordination	Cube	

Based upon these fundamental forms, geologists have developed a system of crystalline classification for all known minerals. The classification is divided into seven separate crystal systems based upon considerations of symmetry and external expression. The systems are further divided into thirty two distinct classes (not pictured) with each crystal resulting from a unique, external geometry, reflecting the ordering and arrangement of atomic patterns. All relate to, or are derived from, one or some combination, of the platonic forms.

APPENDIX III

Discussion of our "Message of Zero Point"
Excerpts from the book,
"Awakening to Zero Point: The Collective Initiation"
by Gregg Braden

Nearly 2,000 years ago a single event marked the beginning of a lifetime that would forever change the course of human history. The birth was that of a man, an extraordinary man, through the womb of a woman who had not given birth previously and was virgin at the time. From the onset, the event was marked with unusual circumstances. The arrival of a new star in the heavens was heralded as the long awaited sign of the arrival of a great prophet. The virgin birth, the fear of this sign by those in power and resultant deaths of thousands of Hebrew infants in an effort to nullify the prophecy of a savior are extraordinary events by any measure.

The unusual life of the man known as Jesus, the son of Mary and Joseph, is well documented through the very early years of his life. The young Jesus was recognized by the elders of the Synagogue as being very illuminated in the interpretation of the scriptures and their application in daily life. To date, the best records of the early years of Jesus are those found in the Biblical texts. The subject of controversy for hundreds of years, the discovery and subsequent translation of the Dead Sea Scrolls has validated the Bible in nearly every one of the chapters known as the "Old Testament." It is from the Biblical references that the life and teachings of Jesus are preserved and interpreted today.

Though distorted, the events of Jesus' life are documented in the open literature until the age of twelve, at which point nearly all Biblical references disappear for approximately eighteen years. The references reappear at age thirty, as he resumes a very public life of teaching and healing. The eighteen "lost years" of Jesus, though unaccounted for in the present form of the Biblical texts, may have been recorded in earlier versions prior to their reorganization by Constantine's Council of Nice in the year 325 A.D.[1] It was during this time that many significant biblical references were deleted and the remaining books reordered into present forms of the modern Bible. There are additional indications that these deleted books, stored in the Great Library of Alexandria, were lost in the burning of that structure in 389 A.D. References to the message and life of Jesus were so significant, however, that they were recorded and stored within other great libraries. Thus we have insights today into the life, teachings, travels and intent of this remarkable man.

Within the Jemez monasteries in the city of Leh, near the Cashmere region, are records of a great prophet that came from the holy lands. This prophet is noted because he was the first to excel beyond study, to the mastery of teachings of Buddha, Krishna and Rama. These records, the originals of which remain today in Lhasa, Tibet, detail the life of this prophet. His name was Ehisa, and he journeyed throughout India, China, Tibet, Persia and Egypt before returning to his home in Israel at the age of thirty, proclaiming that

"my father and I are now one."

According to the Tibetan records, the travels and studies lasted for eighteen years.

Possibly the most tangible, though controversial, evidence of Jesus that exists today are the remains of an image "burned" into a burial shroud. This woven relic is said to have wrapped the body of Christ Jesus following the crucifixion. Stored in Turin, Italy, the Shroud of Turin is made of linen measuring fourteen feet three inches by three feet five inches and has been the subject of debate, skepticism and mystery for centuries in regard to its authenticity. In October of 1978, a team of researchers at the Los Alamos National Laboratories, led by Ray Rodgers,[7] demonstrated that the image upon the shroud is the equivalent of a photographic negative, and is not painted or dyed into the fabric. Unexplainably, the image is literally burned into the cloth as the result of a high intensity flash of electromagnetic radiation originating from within the shroud.

The details of the shroud match, item for item, the Biblical description of the body in terms of the type and location of wounds to the wrist, feet abdomen and head. It is the opinion of Ray Rodgers, and his team of researchers, that the shroud is, in fact, an authentic image of the body of Jesus preserved through an unexplained process of intense biochemical radiation approximately 2,000 years ago.

Commonly, spiritual texts record the visit of a "white prophet" during a time correlating with the lost years and a message very similar to that which Jesus instilled into his followers following his reappearance. Native American traditions, for example, tell of a bearded white prophet who came to them and promised to return with a message from the "Father." The Hopi prophecy relates the story of "Bahana," the white brother who promised and has yet to return to those that he taught during his lifetime. He is regarded as the purifier and will spare from destruction those who have maintained the Hopi way of peace.[2] The fundamental premise of the Book of Mormon is that Jesus walked the Americas and anchored his teachings firmly in this portion of the world as well as his home land.

On his thirtieth birthday, the man known as Jesus of Nazareth reappears in the records during his initiation by John the Baptist. It is written that John, foreseeing the coming of Jesus as the messiah, had spoken to his followers saying,

> "I baptize you now with water for repentance, but he who is coming after me is mightier than I, whose sandals I am not worthy to carry; he will baptize you with the holy spirit."
>
> THE HOLY BIBLE, MATTHEW 3:11

As Jesus approached the river where John was performing baptismals, John immediately recognized him and spoke, saying

> "It is I who needs to be baptized by you, and do you come to me?"
>
> MATTHEW 3:14

Jesus replied "Let it be so, now."

It is during the years following his baptism that Jesus became known for his teachings and probably best for his miracles of healing and manifestation. In the face of his truth, those fearing his message were powerless to silence him - short of taking his life.

In attempting to silence his teaching, Jesus of Nazareth was executed under the direction of a Roman official, Pontius Pilate in the year thirty three A.D. The irony of this action may be seen in the intent. The execution, in an effort to silence, actually anchored the teachings and life of this man even more firmly into the conscious human matrix. In rising (Resurrecting), three days following his "execution," Jesus demonstrated a re-birth, an eternal life reaching beyond his apparent death and the fear that prompted it. In his resurrection, he also modeled a process that each individual will have an opportunity to experience within this lifetime. Earth's phase transition is the Resurrection referenced in ancient texts as "The Shift of the Ages."

Often in our literature we see the term "Christ" as a reference to Christ Jesus of Nazareth. The word "Christ," however, is actually a title conferred upon initiates of the ancient Essene Orders. Having mastered the teachings of this ancient order, the successful demonstration of their mastery was rewarded with the title of "Christ." From a number of religious and spiritual texts we are reminded of other highly evolved beings, other "Christs," preceded Jesus, some by thousands of years. Earlier Christs appeared as beings specific to a race or tribe.

Buddha, Akenaton, Shiva, Gogyeng Sowuhti, each planted seeds of our potential in human consciousness. Each paved the way for the next, preparing for a time in their future. A time of great change. With that change there would be a single messenger. This messenger would be the Christ for all of human kind, regardless of race or tribe or language. This messenger would be the Universal Christ. The message that he would carry was to be one of remembrance, human destiny and purpose.

The term "Christ" as used throughout the "Awakening To Zero Point" material, is a reference to the Christ Jesus of Nazareth. Inherent in the reference is the acknowledgment of all of the accomplishments of all spiritual forbearers that came before, paving the way and laying the foundation that allowed his message to be heard. This is a non-religious term referencing the man as his life-work without the rules and dogma that were established at a later time based upon distortions of his original teachings.

JESUS' GIFT TO EARTH

The gift of Christ Jesus to earth was in the form of a message to all of humanity. Though his message had been offered before, Jesus was the first to deliver and anchor his gift by virtue of his life experience. While each of the preceding Christs had a similar message and could have served as a Universal Christ, it was Jesus that became the Universal Christ, choosing to emerge into this world as most of humanity has emerged, in a manner that humanity could relate to. Rather than appear as a fully realized, fully resurrected being of dazzling light instilling awe and possibly fear into those that would know him, he was birthed through the womb of his mother. By doing so he demonstrated that he was birthed and lived within the same parameters as those around him, with no apparent tools of divinity other than his faith. Jesus lived the life of his time, associated with the people of his time, learned a skilled trade and the use of economics, ate the food and slept in the homes of those around him. Recent evidence suggests that he married and possibly fathered at least one child, a daughter, following his resurrection.

Through his life he demonstrated that he possessed nothing more than any other individual, except the knowledge and faith of his nature and potential. Through the use of two very powerful tools, available to each man and woman, he was able to effect change within himself, the world around him, and ultimately transcend the perceived limitations of that world. The tools were the gifts of "Absolute Choice" and "Absolute Free Will."

Etched into the memory of earth is the belief that the being known as Christ Jesus died for the "sins" of humanity. It is taught that through some mysterious process, known only to a few, the death of this man upon the cross served as a sacrifice for all of humanity and that through his sacrifice, all of humanity now has the opportunity to follow in his footsteps as perfected beings.

Jesus did not die for the sins of the earth or the people upon earth. Jesus did not die at all! In death the message would have been lost. Christ Jesus anchored the wisdom of birth, through resurrection, and that is very different from death. To those of his time not knowing or understanding the process, however, it may appear as death followed by the reversal of death.

Jesus was executed because the consciousness of earth allowed his execution, the result of intolerance for his message of empowering love. The innocent consciousness to whom he had come to deliver the tools of completion, those that he loved so much that he descended into dense matter to guide them toward completion, were the very souls that provided the environment, setting the stage for the events that followed. It was those individuals, in their ignorance, through attempting to "kill" our Universal Being of Reference, that effectively sealed his message of love, compassion and forgiveness into our conscious matrix.

Using the tools of choice and free will (expressed as fear, guilt, anger and ego) it was the peers of Jesus that ended his experience upon earth. In doing so, they effectively sealed his ability to perpetuate the message that he had come to deliver. Through his execution, Jesus demonstrated that there is no "death," only varied forms of life-force expression. Today, Western physicists term the shift of matter from one expression of itself into another a change-of-state. Jesus re-appeared whole, complete, healed and very much alive, as a resurrected being in complete resonance with a higher expression of creation. The phase transition of resurrection allowed those of his time to see Christ as an angel of light.

The gift that Christ Jesus offered to this world was the anchoring of his awareness firmly into the conscious matrix of all humans present at that time, as well as those yet to come. Through his womb birth and life experience, others saw, felt and experienced the love of Christ Jesus in their own lives. His execution and subsequent resurrection served then, and continues to serve, as a "living bridge" between the grids of every day, and those of a much higher expression of the same matrix, the Grids of Christ or Universal Consciousness. Through the use of choice and free will in the manner in which he conducted his life, Jesus demonstrated that resonance to all grids is not only possible, but also acceptable. He further demonstrated that there is no judgment from creation itself against any one individual for actions or deeds resulting from the use of choice and free will. There is no day when the weight of "sin" will prevent an individual from moving into a higher form of expression or "heaven."

There is choice, and the consequence of choice, expressed and mirrored as the patterns life. The greatest factor of limitation lies within you, and how you judge the consequences of your choices. It is you that determines your destiny. It is you that determines how, and to what degree, you progress along the evolutionary path to move beyond the illusion of limitation, to the reality of freedom.

The choice to evolve is determined by you rather than a high panel of regulatory beings. Certainly highly evolved beings, guides and Ascended Masters are with you throughout your life.path.journey. The primary tool of your journey, however, is your life process. The choices that you make on a daily basis are the components of this tool. How do you feel about yourself and your choices? How do you feel about other individuals? How do you treat others in day-to-day relationships-on the street, in the stores or office place?

You are concerned less with the outcome of each choice, as each offers a path of experience. Rather, it is through the very process of the rich and varied experiences that you are creating the eventual outcome of your evolutionary path. You are doing so in this very moment. Your use of absolute choice, and your application of absolute free will to carry out your choice, determine the energy that you exude as the result of a particular experience. It is to this energy that creation responds, without prejudice, without judgment or bias. The pattern of energy simply "is."

The manner in which you conduct yourself outwardly provides the mirror as to the degree of resonance attained within, to higher grids of compassion and non-judgment. You are learning to "un-plug" from the old grids of polarity that have held the belief systems, the laws, the rules and dogma that were ingrained into your memory over periods of thousands of years. As you "drop" the old programs held within these grids, you "plug in" to a new body of information. Christed grids of loving compassion have always been available within our conscious matrix, though perhaps not easily accessible.

Your ability to accept positive change, your openness to new ideas and concepts, your willingness to "drop" an old pattern that no longer serves you in exchange for the opportunity to create something new to fill the void. These experiences are you "un-plugging" from old grids. To the degree that you are able to allow new and life-giving patterns, to that degree will you find a strengthening of your connection with life. These are signs of a new wisdom. Your thoughts, beliefs and the manner through which you express those thoughts and beliefs are your tools of change. Thought, feeling and life conduct are your keys to the grids of the "Christ Consciousness" of life. It is to these grids that Christ Jesus anchored his bridge of compassion making this information accessible in the present lifetime. Building this energetic bridge is the purpose that Christ descended to our world, lived, was crucified and resurrected for nearly 2,000 years ago.

This was the gift of Christ Jesus, the gift of eternal life through conscious thought, feeling and conduct. He demonstrated to us, within our presence, how we may intentionally achieve a greater expression of ourselves. We call our shift Resurrection. His gift was demonstrated through life in a world that was not openly accepting. Into the midst of judgment and fear he anchored his divine wisdom, bridging the old to the new. You are living that path, now, within your lifetime.

THE TIMING OF JESUS' APPEARANCE ON EARTH

Through his living example, as well as his teachings, Christ Jesus provided a reference point for each human, reminding us of the possibilities which may be accomplished within a particular lifetime. His gift was a message of hope, remembrance and empowering love. He was welcomed with mistrust, disbelief, fear and non-acceptance. Not only was the message misunderstood during his lifetime, even today the interpretations of Christ's teachings have remained a source of debate and controversy - especially to those relying upon modern interpretations of the Biblical texts. Many modern interpretations are inaccurate, non-sequential and incomplete representations of teachings, in some cases recorded hundreds of years after the actual events themselves. Though growing in number and providing greater detail, our access to original accounts of this period in history are becoming inaccessible to modern scholars for a variety of reasons.

The Dead Sea Scrolls for example, have been recovered, restored, translated and now legal precedents are assuring that many will remain "closed" to nearly everyone, with the exception of a select few. In the summer of 1993, the Jerusalem Court awarded the copyright of a particularly significant text, the 2,000 year old MMT scroll, to Elisha Qimron of Ben Gurion University of the Negev.[3] Without these scrolls, and other texts (such as the original Biblical books of Enoch, Protevangelion, Christ and Abgarus, Nicodemus, Laodiceans, The Apostles Creed, Philippians, Philadelphians, Romans, Trallians, Letters of Herod and Pilate, Hermas, Magnesians and others), tangible records of the teachings of Christ appear to remain inaccessible.

Though the actual words of Jesus' message may not be seen directly, the vibrational equivalent his message remains. Anchored through Christ's life of demonstration among us, his teachings are both available, and accessible to those choosing to allow themselves resonance to the grids of those truths.

Why did Christ appear at the time, and in the manner in which he did?

What was his intent?

Was he successful?

A schematic view of Christ's appearance on earth in relation to our overall cycle of experience provides insight into the timing, as well as the geographic location, of his point of entry.

Earth, today, is living the completion of a cycle that began nearly 200,000 years ago. Another way of describing the timing of Christ's birth two thousand years ago is that it was two thousand years before the end of this cycle, 2000 A.D. An event occurring two thousand years prior to the completion of a 200,000 year cycle indicates that approximately ninety nine percent (198,000 years) of the cycle has completed. Note how much of the cycle occurred before the birth of Christ. The intent of Christ's emergence onto the earth plane was to serve as a trigger, reminding us of the evolutionary process that was at hand. With ninety nine of the cycle completed, this entry point appears to be an optimum time for this reminder. If it had come too early in the cycle it may not have been understood. Arriving too late in the cycle may not have provided consciousness time to assimilate his teachings.

Consideration of the relative intensity and location of global magnetic fields provides yet another indication as to the timing of the birth of Jesus in relation to planetary cycles. You may recall that, in general, relatively lower magnetics provide a greater opportunity for change, while higher values of magnetics provide a buffer of "interference" and less of an opportunity for change. Christ Jesus chose a time of relatively high planetary magnetics to introduce his message.

Why?

Why did he not choose a time in history when earth would be open and accepting of his offering and message of hope? Why did he choose to anchor his message in the Middle East?

To answer these questions, it becomes necessary to re-examine the intent of Christ's descent to earth. His gift was in his life. He lived his truth in the face of a world that was largely unaccepting, or suspicious of, and did not support his message. To firmly anchor his wisdom it was necessary for him to model his truth, to demonstrate the power of his faith and love for earth, in a manner that could not be disputed in his time. He used the actions of those who did not support him to work in his favor, by allowing the amplification of his message through their own fear! Their actions proved that the message of Jesus the Christ was valid, as they forced the test. This was precisely the opposite of their intent to silence through death. To have offered this message in a world of low global magnetics, a world of acceptance and lenience, the gift would have had neither the potency, nor the lasting effect.

Interestingly, though earth was experiencing generally high values of magnetics, a contour map of global magnetics indicates that the Middle East was, in fact, experiencing relatively low magnetics. The net effect of this may be seen in the following:

For the time in history that the Universal Reference Being of Christ Jesus chose to deliver his message, he chose the best possible place on earth with a high population density, relatively accepting of new ideas and relatively low magnetics, in the knowledge that these same conditions would seal his fate as a man, while anchoring his message into the human matrix.

In viewing the texts and doctrines of our history, there appears to have been an assumption made early on in our cycle, regarding the nature of human evolution. That assumption presumes that human progress occurs more or less uniformly, in a linear fashion, over time. That is, while not every individual within each race would arrive at the same plateau of understanding during the same period, within humanity as a whole, there would be a uniform increase in the conscious aspects of awareness. Within the same cycle however, there is, and has always been, the variable of an unknown factor. This factor may best be described by considering the relationship between the element of "human" and the behavior of human within the framework of "choice" and "free will."

The question: "Will humanity progress over time of its own accord, with the tools of choice and free will, without 'divine' intervention? Will humanity progress in a life affirming manner relative to its conscious evolution (collective vibration) over time..."

As of this writing, the answer is unknown, as the cycle is incomplete. With less than 6 years remaining, however, all indications point to a tremendous shift in human perception and understanding. To the degree that shift occurs, we may assume that the answer is "yes."

Throughout the cycle at various "milestones" of evolutionary progress, there have been surges in the evolutionary curve as a reference being "anchored" concepts of one-ness, without separation. Conscious evolution, as defined by the critical mass of con-sciousness required to trigger resonance with the next portion of the grid, is evolving in accordance to a geometric rather than a linear curve. Appearing as a slow progression over long periods of time, the process is augmented with sudden and abrupt increases in com-posite consciousness, in a relatively short period of time. The conscious mass as a whole is evolving so rapidly at the present, that the ancient prophecies predicting selected indi-viduals surviving the experience of the Shift into the new reality deserve re-examination.

Each person living within the envelope of earth's magnetic fields at the time of the Shift will experience the process of dimensional translation - in Biblical terms the Res-urrection and Ascension. Each individual will have a choice as to how they experience the process; consciously or un-consciously, awake or asleep. This was the message that Christ brought to this world, and with the message the tools of conscious Resurrection and Ascension.

THE MYTH OF SIN

Ingrained into the memory of the earth is the belief that each individual blessed with the physical experience begins from a lesser state of spiritual development; a state attributed to having "fallen" from a more evolved level of evolutionary progress. The term applied to life - choices resulting from the fallen state is that of "sin." Modern translations define sin as "A transgression of a religious or moral law."[4] The Latin trans-lation for "sin" offers a very different perspective. In Latin, sin simply means "separa-tion." This being the case is it possible that our sensing the illusion of separation has led to the concepts of sin that we embody today? A common premise in many religious and spiritual belief systems is that each individual has been predetermined to be a lesser spiritual being due to the very birth of that individual into the earth experience. Further, it is taught that all must, individually and collectively, strive to redeem them-selves from the wrong doings of life in the eyes of a creator. Additionally, we are told that no matter how hard one may try, it will not be possible to attain the degree of spir-itual evolution demonstrated by the universal Christ of Nazareth.

Following is a partial summary of common misconceptions perpetuated through distortions of the original teachings.

Myth 1   You are born into sin and have the opportunity of the earth experience to redeem yourself in the eyes of your creator, approaching, but never reaching the evolutionary state of the Universal Christ.

Myth 2   You are a fallen angel, flawed from birth by virtue of the fact that you were born into the earthly experience.

Myth3   Because you are fallen, you will require an intermediary, someone
to act in your behalf, to intercede for you, with your own creator.
Myth4   Your life-plan is a mystery to you; that the course of your fate is
predetermined by a plan that you are incapable of comprehending.

Today, as the close of this cycle nears, unprecedented numbers of individuals are turning away from the traditional religions based in these distortions. Though the specific reasons may vary; in general each is discovering through his/her unique experience that the relatively modern religions, based in fear, ritual and dogma, do not provide the tools to address the challenges they are asked to face on a daily basis. Traditional beliefs do not serve them as they are faced with the unprecedented challenges inherent in the shifting energy of the close of a cycle; their own fears, "failing" relationships and waves of emotion that have never been experienced before.

Religions based in distortion do not meet their needs, because they are rooted in the fundamental premise that each is helpless and powerless - unable to influence the outcome of events within and outside of themselves. It is for these reasons that today, in the closing years of this cycle, so many search to find a more meaningful expression of what is felt within. The search has led them into the "non traditional" belief systems of the ancient, indigenous and forgotten peoples of the earth.

Though the words may be different, there are underlying threads of continuity within the ancient traditions and the actual teachings of the Universal Christ — not the interpretations of the translated and fragmented Biblical texts seen today. Among those threads of truth, consistent within the Egyptian, Native American, Buddhist, Tibetan, Essene, early Christian and ancient mystery schools are these fundamental concepts:

Non Myth1   You are a part of all that you see, with the
opportunity to live in harmony with creation, as
opposed to controlling and ruling creation.
Non Myth2   You are not a fallen angel. You are here by choice,
having consciously chosen to descend into the earth
experience for some specified period of time.
Non Myth3   You are an extremely evolved, extremely powerful
being. You creator and experience the consequences,
of your patterns of thought feeling and beliefs.
Non Myth4   You have direct access to your creator through
yourself as a "spark" of creative intelligence that is
responsible for your very existence.

You are, and have always been, equal to your angelic counterparts, viewed as such by all except yourself. You are the creator of your world(s), and as such you are a part of all that you see and all that has ever been. You are the Alpha and the Omega - the beginning and the end, all possibilities existing as potential; awaiting the opportunity of coalescence provided through your thoughts-your choices.

COMPASSION

Possibly the greatest gift that you may develop, as well as the greatest challenge that you may encounter in moving toward a high state of personal mastery, is the ability to experience life through the eyes of compassion. compassion may be demonstrated as your ability to accept an experience for what it is, rather than what your judgment and bias will make of it.

To experience compassion is not an invitation to callousness, void of feeling and emotion. Quite the opposite, it is through the very act of allowing yourself to feel that you are guided toward that which you judge. As compassion feelings and emotions become the tools from which you access the reasons behind the intensity of emotion. Following is the mechanism.

Within each cell of your body exists a biological and electrical potential, created through differing charges of fluids on either side of the cell membrane. The brain regulates these potentials by maintaining an acid and alkaline balance (pH)* throughout the system. When you have an experience, and a feeling or emotion associated with that experience, you are quite literally experiencing the shift of electrical charge. What you are feeling, in that moment, is actually the shift of the pH balance within the brain and the resultant shift of electrical potential across cell membranes throughout the body. Emotion is what the electrical charge within the liquid crystal covering of the human body feels like.

It is this shift that polarizes the experience into a positive, negative, good or bad relationship, effectively preventing a neutral viewpoint. As your electrical potential shifts, you radiate into the world the frequencies of that which you continue to have a charge upon. Your charges will be seen as your judgments. Drawn by these frequencies, you will pull into your reality those individuals, circumstances and events that will provide the opportunity to experience your judgments. These are the mirrors of that which you judge, not necessarily that which you are.

You may begin to see the tremendous, yet subtle, power inherent within the ability to allow for all possibilities within a given situation. Interactions with others, especially now in this time of psychic fine tuning, when there is a tendency to empath, may appear to be "emotional roller coasters" in the absence of neutrality. You may begin to see, as well, why the charge cannot be falsified. Masking the outward emotion alone cannot alter the inward pH shift of the body. You are unable to deceive yourself on the level of the cell. For this reason, close and honest scrutiny of relationships, acquaintances and situations will yield direct insight into your present state of bias and judgment.

Within ancient temple sites, such as the King's chamber in Giza, the towers of Southern Peru and the kivas of the American desert Southwest, are found structures that provide an environment within which an individual may access him/her self within a zone of neutral charge. Through the "passive dynamics" of the structure's geometry, magnetic fields (the glue) binding the grids of fear, judgment, bias and ego are significantly decreased. The decrease in magnetics mimics similar processes that may be generated through specific thought streams, such as those taught through the

* A pH of 7 is neutral. An increase indicates greater alkalinity. Decreasing from 7 indicates greater acidity.

mystery schools and Zero Point Meditation. The net result of the process is direct access to the electrical essence of self in magnetic conditions very close to null. These are Zero Point conditions. Though effective, these are examples of an external technology intended as a tool, to induce a Zero Point experience. Though valid, the tool is not necessary. Christ demonstrated the gift of inner technology, the tools, with which to accomplish the identical process, from within.

One of the greatest, and possibly least understood, messages that Christ Jesus anchored into this conscious matrix is that of demonstrating love through compassionate allowing. Loving unconditionally another, while allowing him or her the latitude of their own experience. This becomes possible through the knowing that each individual comes to earth in a unique capacity, from varied backgrounds and modes of expression, and that all are equal in their response to the challenges of life. To the degree that any aspect of another's experience is judged, to that degree do we remain in the polarity of separation and the charge of that very judgment. The Universal Christ shared the secret to compassion in the following:

> *"Three are the dwellings of the Son of Man, and no one may come before the face of the (One) who knows not the angel of peace in each of the three. These are body, thoughts and feelings."* (parentheses are author's)
>
> ADAPTED FROM THE ESSENE GOSPEL OF PEACE[1]

Scholars that have spent their lives in the study of Christ's teachings are well aware that Jesus spoke and taught in parables, stories and through living example. This was the language that he gauged to be acceptable in his time. To turn the other cheek is not a literal command to allow unmitigated harm to yourself or others. It is simply a tool, one of many, that may be used to experience an event for what it is; for the experience. Allowing yourself, or another, the experience without charge is one aspect of the internal technology of Zero Point.

Though the vocabulary, culture and society have changed, the message that Jesus of Nazareth left to you is just as valid today as it was 2,000 years ago. It is a message of inner technology. This technology is a vibratory science that is the root of, and supersedes, all that we may engineer and build outside of ourselves. Through his life and Resurrection, Christ's experience was a metaphor for you and your life, as you attempt to live your truth in a world that is sometimes unaccepting of new thought and new ideas. Through his execution, he modeled for all of humanity a process that each will go through individually, as well as collectively. In the closing years of this cycle, every life form existing upon the earth will have the opportunity to experience the dimensional translation as earth's shift from a third to a fourth density experience. Earth's opportunity mirrors our opportunity to choose Zero Point awareness and resurrection rather than death.

TRUTH AND THE FORCE

Throughout the many and varied facets of human history, there has remained one constant, expressed as a subtle yet powerful force, driving the process of life forward. This force is experienced within each individual as the will to continue life. Driving each person, and the collective whole, forward toward some goal, a point of resolution for the life experience. To many, the resolution is anticipated as some thing, some event to make the experience of life worthwhile and complete. It is this something that has provided the momentum for consciousness. This is the inertia of will that perpetuates our experience. Somewhere within the remote memories of our past, the meaning of this force kept itself alive as flashes of insight. We see these flashes as glimpses of divine patterns of expression, perhaps as a dream or familiar emotion. A message of some kind, pierces through what appears to be a barrier into the awareness of human, to remind mankind of himself, his meaning and purpose. Evidence of that force may be seen throughout history as the relentless search for truth and knowledge- a search consisting of many lifetimes at the cost of many lives. What could be the foundation of such a desire? What drives our search to "know"?

In and of itself the knowledge of life may be meaningless, perhaps incongruent streams of information to be stored and accessed at some later date. It is the living of the knowledge that becomes an expression of the search, our wisdom, providing meaning to our life experience. Within the context of the wisdom inherent within you, through the experience of your life, you are compelled to remember in your own terms the purpose of life. From that purpose, from that knowing, stems the reason to continue. You begin to feel, on some level, that you are approaching a time when something within you life will change. This change may become a time when all of the knowledge gained throughout all of the joy and all of the pain from all of your lifetimes will apply. Some describe this feeling as a sense that they have been in training all of their lives, getting ready for "something." Something really big.

The outward expression of these feelings historically has appeared as inconsistent, at times unfathomable, extremes of experience. The reality is that each of the six billion (plus) humans incarnated at present, through unique and individualized experience, is expressing precisely the same pattern of energy. As a group consciousness, we must experience the extremes to know the balance. Each life experience becomes another lens from which to view the wonder, mystery and possibilities of life. Each individual fills a particular niche, purely through the uniqueness of themselves, within which to express the feeling of a shared and awesome force.

What is this force?

The energy, driving each individual toward some point of resolution, is what many call the "will" to continue. Perhaps more accurately, our will to return to the One from which we have come. The "force" is the force of life, Life Force, Chi, Ki or Prana. By virtue of its very nature, life is compelled to re-assemble the fragments of itself, time after time following each experience, and return to the wholeness of pre-experience. "Will" is the name given to the patterns of consciousness striving to attain this state of balance and completeness. Within the third dimensional world experience, "will" is expressed through the physical body, the liquid crystal resonator within which spirit, as an energy form, may resolve itself. The force always has a message and the message is always the same. In its consistency, the message becomes a truth . Rather than a relative truth that works under some circumstances, the message is known as an absolute message of universal truth. The languages to express the truth are limiting by their very nature. The truth constant that drives the creative intelligence of will is this:

There is a Force within you, that is infinite and eternal, and can not be created or destroyed. Your life is the expression through which you may know that force.

Before continuing, stop and consider the statement that you have just read. You have heard it many times. Do you know it to be true? Do you feel it to be true? Do you believe and have faith that it is so?

There is, sometimes, a tendency to confuse the experience of life with the energy of life essence. The electrical patterns of your life essence will continue, regardless of the outcome of your life experience. Through the gift of life, however, you have been given an opportunity to express your essence uniquely, perhaps in ways that have never been accomplished before. Pause for one moment and allow the impact of the simple statement above to become a part of you. Should you find yourself in disbelief of this statement, you may want to ask why? What it is that has occurred in your life to "teach" you not to believe a universal truth?

From the perspective of the ancients and the teachings of the indigenous peoples today, there is no real life. There is no real death. From their perspective, the totality of our experience is that of a dream. Within that experience, life and death are "dreams within dreams," with no separation between the two. There is only the perception of different and varied experience and how we think and feel about those perceptions.

Consider precisely the same truth presented within the context of another language. Words and symbols represent a language that accesses another portion of your wisdom. Within the conceptual framework of western science, Life Force may be thought of as energy.light.information. This language sees life as an array of electromagnetic pulses arranged into orderly patterns of experience. The language of this science will tell you that:

Energy may not be created or destroyed. Energy responds to varied experiences by changing the manner in which it expresses it's form. The energy of life force permeates all of creation, transcending the boundaries of dimensionality and time. Life Force is essentially infinite in nature. The now-famous equation of Einsteinian physics, from earlier in this century, equates mass to energy and states this truth very explicitly:

$$E = M C**2$$

E = energy, M = mass and $C**2$ = the velocity of light multiplied times itself. This equation, in an equally valid language of mathematics, states that as matter accelerates, its mass begins to expand. Upon approaching the speed of light, the mass expands to the homogeneous state described as that of infinite.*

Matter as a group vibration, accelerating into another group vibration, to become a new expression, that of light! Two very different languages, expressing precisely the same truth. One language is very intuitive and right brain oriented. The other more analytical and left brain oriented. Both are equally valid. It is this truth that drives the will, the desire to attain a state of development that will allow for an eternal life.

You know this truth within yourself. You know that your essence may not be created or destroyed. You have to have known this or you could not have navigated yourself through the matrix of creation, propelling your essence into the crystalline form that you call "body" for the experience of your life. You must come to terms with this truth within the context of your own life and the uniqueness of your experience. To give the gift of yourself, in wholeness and completeness, you must know yourself within the context of all possibilities, all the extremes. All of your joy, all of your pain, all of your anger, rage, jealousy, and judgment; those precious feelings are your gifts to help you to know yourself. Your unique experience allows you to push the boundaries of who you believe you are, as you approach the reality of what you are truly made of. In that knowing, you have the opportunity to see yourself in situations that you may never experience again. These are the extremes that will help you to know and re-define your point of balance. They are constantly shifting.

Though it may be masked within the distractions and rationalizations of a day-to-day three dimensional world, it is the indestructibility of the soul that provides the momentum to get up every morning and go on, continuing the life experience. You "know" of the eternal nature of consciousness on a deep level, it is encoded within the light patterns of memory that reside within each cell of your human body. Eternal life is based within eternal truth; an absolute within each cell of the creation matrix. The patterns of your truth are whole and complete unto themselves, expressing within each cell of existence. At the same time, those individual patterns are part of a much greater whole. The pattern continues. This, then, is the holographic law. Life Force is eternal and recursive in its existence. Non-destruction of consciousness is the law of creation - you cannot separate or un-create that which is eternal.

This is the message of the ancient prophecies. This is the basis for the texts dating before history, the foundation for each religion, sacred order, sect and mystery school. The essence of who you are, in the absence of fear, judgment, ego and any other interference patterns of this experience, is eternal. The world that you have created for yourself, your life, family, friends, and career, your surroundings, your behavior patterns are the result of your feelings and beliefs. Your world is a temporal pattern of energy that you have created to serve you within the context of your life-pattern-blueprint, to see yourself from many viewpoints. All are in support of this time in history, when the sum of all experience focuses upon now; the transmutation of yourself and earth into a more refined pattern of expression. The blueprint states that not only will you survive, but this process is your very purpose. You have come to this world to learn a new expression of the creative frequencies of your life.

The Shift of the Ages is your new life, born of a new wisdom. Please, use the gift of your life wisely.

---

* Recent studies indicate that the speed of light is not a constant, with electrical signals recorded traveling at over 100 times the accepted speed of light (186,271 miles per second).[3]

REFERENCES

Acknowledgments

1 Kahlil Gibran, *The Prophet*, Alfred A. Knopf, Inc., New York, 1977.

Preface

1 Dan Winter, *Alphabet of the Heart: The Genesis in Principle of Language and Feeling*, Waynesville, N.C., p.38-50.

2 Vladimir Poponin, *The DNA Phantom Effect: Direct Measurement of a New Field in the Vacuum Substructure*, Institute of HeartMath, Boulder Creek, Ca.

Introduction

1 Tom Hansen, *Trying to Remember*, Freedom Press Associates, Freedom, New Hampshire, adapted from cover

2 Eugene Mallove, "The Cosmos and the Computer: Simulating the Universe," *Computers in Science*, Vol. 1, No. 2, September/October 1987.

3 McCraty, Atkinson, Tiller, Rein and Watkins, "The Effects of Emotions on Short-Term Power Spectrum Analysis of Heart Rate Variability," *The American Journal of Cardiology*, Vol. 76, No.14, 1995, p.1089-1093.

4 Gregg Braden, *Awakening to Zero Point: The Collective Initiation*, Laura Lee Press, Bellevue, Wa., 1994.

5 *The Essene Gospel of Peace*, Book Two, Compared, Edited and Translated by Edmond Bordeaux Szekely, Third Century Aramaic Manuscript and Old Slavic Texts, I.B.S. Internacional, Matsqui, B.C., Canada, 1937, p.45.

6 *The Essene Gospel of Peace*, Compared, Edited and Translated by Edmond Bordeaux Szekely, Third Century Aramaic Manuscript and Old Slavic Texts, I.B.S. Internacional, Matsqui, B.C., Canada, 1937, p.19.

7 Joseph Rael, *The Sound Beings*, Exclusive Pictures/Heaven Fire Productions, Video, 1995, Van Nuys, Ca.

8 *The Essene Gospel of Peace*, Book Four, Compared, Edited and Translated by Edmond Bordeaux Szekely, Third Century Aramaic Manuscript and Old Slavic Texts, I.B.S. Internacional, Matsqui, B.C., Canada, 1937, p.30.

9 *The Essene Gospel of Peace*, Book Two, Compared, Edited and Translated by Edmond Bordeaux Szekely, Third Century Aramaic Manuscript and Old Slavic Texts, I.B.S. Internacional, Matsqui, B.C., Canada, 1937, p.109.

Chapter I

1 Carlos Castaneda, *Journey to Ixtlan, The Lessons of Don Juan*, Washington Square Press, New York, 1972, p.61.

Chapter II

1 Translation by Doreal, *The Emerald Tablets of Thoth*, Source Books, Nashville, 1994, p.79.

2 Tim Wallace-Murphy, *The Templar Legacy & The Masonic Inheritance Within Rosslyn Chapel*, "The Friends of Rosslyn," Rosslyn Chapel, Roslin, Midlothian EH, p.50-51.

Chapter III

1 *The Essene Gospel of Peace*, Book Two, Compared, Edited and Translated by Edmond Bordeaux Szekely, Third Century Aramaic Manuscript and Old Slavic Texts, I.B.S. Internacional, Matsqui, B.C., Canada, 1937, p.31.

2 *Oxford American Dictionary*, Avon Books, New York, 1980, p.172.

3 *The Essene Gospel of Peace*, Book Three, Compared, Edited and Translated by Edmond Bordeaux Szekely, Third Century Aramaic Manuscript and Old Slavic Texts, I.B.S. Internacional, Matsqui, B.C., Canada, 1937, p.70.

4 James M. Robinson, *The Nag Hammadi Library in English*, Harper San Francisco, 1990, p.129.

5 Kahlil Gibran, *The Prophet*, Alfred A. Knopf, Inc., New York, 1977

6 Dan Winter, *Alphabet of the Heart: The Genesis in Principle of Language and Feeling*, 'Can the Human Heart Directly Affect the Coherence of Earth's Magnetic Field?,' Commentary on HeartMath Institute Data Power Spectral Measurements of EKG vs. the Earth's ELF Resonance, Dan Winter, Waynesville, N.C., p.58-64.

7 James M. Robinson, *The Nag Hammadi Library in English*, Harper San Francisco, 1990, p.131.

8 Joseph Rael, *The Sound Beings*, Exclusive Pictures/Heaven Fire Productions, Video, 1995, Van Nuys, Ca.

9 Translation by Doreal, *The Emerald Tablets of Thoth*, Source Books, Nashville, 1994, p.34.

10 *Dances With Wolves*, TIG Productions, Inc., Orion Pictures Corporation, New York, 1990.

Chapter IV

1 Robert Boissiere, *Meditations With the Hopi*, Santa Fe, 1986, p.112.

2 *The Essene Gospel of Peace*, Book One, Third Century Aramaic Manuscript and Old Slavic Texts, Compared, Edited and Translated by Edmond Bordeaux Szelely, I.B.S. Internacional, Matsqui, B.C., Canada, 1937, p.10.

3 Ibid, The Unknown books of the Essenes, pp. 45-60.

4 Dan Winter, *Alphabet of the Heart: The Genesis in Principle of Language and Feeling*, 'Testing the Effects of Heart Coherence on DNA, and Immune Function,' Waynesville, N.C., pp. 56-57.

5 Dan Winter, *Alphabet of the Heart: The Genesis in Principle of Language and Feeling*, 'Can the Human Heart Directly Affect the Coherence of Earth's Magnetic Field?,' Commentary on HeartMath Institute Data Power Spectral Measurements of EKG vs. the Earth's ELF Resonance, Dan Winter, Waynesville, N.C., pp. 58-64.

6 McCraty, Atkinson, Tiller, Rein and Watkins, "The Effects of Emotions on Short-Term Power Spectrum Analysis of Heart rate Variability," *The American Journal of Cardiology*, Vol. 76, No.14, November 15, 1995, pages 1089-1093.

7 Rollin McCraty, William A. Tiller and Mike Atkinson, *Head-Heart Entrainment: A Preliminary Survey*, Institute of HeartMath, Boulder Creek, Ca.

8 Glen Rein, PhD, Mike Atkinson and Rollin McCraty, MA, "The Physiological and Psychological Effects of Compassion and Anger," *Journal of Advancement in Medicine*, Volume 8, Number 2, Summer 1995, pages 87-103.

9 James D. Watson, Matrix of the Human Genetic Code, Adapted from *The Molecular Biology of the Gene*, Third Edition, W.A. Benjamin, Inc. 1976.

10 Dan Winter, *Alphabet of the Heart: The Genesis in Principle of Language and Feeling*, Waynesville, N.C., pp. 58-64.

11 J. Travis, "Mutant Gene Explains Some HIV Resistance," *Science News*, August 17, 1996, Vol. 150, page 103.

12 Ibid

13 Clare Thompson, "The Genes That Keep AIDS at Bay," *New Scientist*, New Science Publications, IPC Magazines, Ltd., King's Reach Tower, Stamford Street, London, April 6, 1996, p.16.

14 Ibid

15 J.Raloff, "Baby's AIDS Virus Infection Vanishes," *Science News*, Vol.147, April, 1995, p.196.

Chapter V

1 James M. Robinson, *The Nag Hammadi Library in English*, Harper San Francisco, 1990, p.129.

2 Ibid, p.136.

3 Ibid, p.126.

4 Ibid, p.136.

5 Ibid, p.134.

6 Ibid, p.132

7 Upton Clary Ewing, *The Prophet of the Dead Sea Scrolls*, Tree of Life Publications, Joshua Tree, Ca., 1993, p.114.

8 Kahlil Gibran, *The Prophet*, Alfred A. Knopf, Inc., New York, 1977.

9 James M. Robinson, *The Nag Hammadi Library in English*, Harper San Francisco, 1990, p.134.

10 *Meetings With Remarkable Men*, Gurdjieff's Search for Hidden Knowledge, Corinth Video, 1987.

Chapter VI

1 Alex Grey, *Sacred Mirrors, The Visionary Art of Alex Grey,* Inner Traditions International, Rochester, Vermont, 1990.

2 *The Essene Gospel of Peace,* Book Two, Third Century Aramaic Manuscript and Old Slavic Texts, Compared, Edited and Translated by Edmond Bordeaux Szelely, I.B.S. Internacional, Matsqui, B.C., Canada, 1937, p.69.

3 Alan Cohen, *The Peace That You Seek,* Somerset, New Jersey, 1991.

4 Ibid

Appendix I

1 L. Don Leet, Sheldon Judson, *Physical Geology,* Prentice-Hall, Inc., 1971

2 Stig Floodmark, *New Approaches in Geomagnetism and the Earth's Rotation,* University of Stockholm, symposium, Sweden, 1988, "Earth's Rotation and Magnetism," Nils-Axel Morner.

3 L. Don Leet, Sheldon Judson, *Physical Geology,* Prentice-Hall, Inc., 1971

4 Stig Floodmark, *New Approaches in Geomagnetism and the Earth's Rotation,* University of Stockholm, symposium, Sweden, 1988, "Earth's Rotation and Magnetism," Nils-Axel Morner.

5 Zecharia Sitchin, *The Lost Realms,* Avon Books, 1990

6 Richard Monastersky, "The Flap Over Magnetic Flips," *Science News,* Vol. 14, June 12, 1993,

7 Tsuneji Rikitake and Yoshimori Honkura, *Solid Earth Geomagnetism,* Terra Scientific Publishing Co., Tokyo, Japan, 1985

Appendix II

1 Robert Lawlor, *Sacred Geometry, Philosophy and Practice,* Thames and Hudson Ltd., London, 1982

Appendix III

1 *The Essene Gospel of Peace,* Book Four, Compared, Edited and Translated by Edmond Bordeaux Szekely, Third Century Aramaic Manuscript and Old Slavic Texts, I.B.S. Internacional, Matsqui, B.C., Canada, 1937, p.30.

BIBLIOGRAPHY

Boissiere, Robert. *Meditations With the Hopi,* (Santa Fe, 1986), p.112

Braden, Gregg. *Awakening to Zero Point: The Collective Initiation,* Radio Bookstore Press, (Bellevue, Wa., 1994), p.29

Castaneda, Carlos. *Journey to Ixtlan, The Lessons of Don Juan,* Washington Square Press, (New York, 1972), p.61

Cohen, Alan. *The Peace That You Seek,* Somerset, (New Jersey, 1991)

Dances With Wolves, TIG Productions, Inc., Orion Pictures Corporation, (New York, 1990)

Doreal. *The Emerald Tablets of Thoth,* Source Books, (Nashville, 1925), p.34

Ibid. p.79

Ewing, Upton. *The Prophet of the Dead Sea Scrolls,* Tree of Life Publications, (Joshua Tree, Ca., 1993), p.114

Floodmark, Stig. *New Approaches in Geomagnetism and the Earth's Rotation,* University of Stockholm, symposium, (Sweden, 1988), 'Earth's Rotation and Magnetism,' Nils-Axel Morner

Gibran, Kahlil. *The Prophet,* Alfred A. Knopf, Inc., (New York, 1977)

Grey, Alex. *Sacred Mirrors, The Visionary Art of Alex Grey,* Inner Traditions International, Rochester, (Vermont, 1990), p.62

Hansen, Tom. *Trying to Remember,* Freedom Press Associates, (Freedom, New Hampshire, 1995)

Lawlor, Robert. *Sacred Geometry, Philosophy and Practice,* Thames and Hudson Ltd., (London, 1982)

Leet, Don and Judson. *Sheldon Physical Geology,* Prentice-Hall, Inc., (1971)

Mallove, Eugene. "The Cosmos and the Computer: Simulating the Universe," *Computers in Science,* September/October (1987), Vol. 1, No. 2

McCraty, Atkinson, Tiller, Rein and Watkins. "The Effects of Emotions on Short-Term Power Spectrum Analysis of Heart Rate Variability," *The American Journal of Cardiology,* Vol. 76, No.14, (1995), p.1089-1093

McCraty, Rollin and Tiller A. William and Atkinson, Mike. *Head-Heart Entrainment: A Preliminary Survey*, Institute of HeartMath, (Boulder Creek, Ca.)

Meetings With Remarkable Men, Gurdjieff's Search for Hidden Knowledge, Corinth Video, (1987)

Monastersky, Richard. "The Flap Over Magnetic Flips," *Science News*, (Washington, D.C., June 12, 1993)

Oxford American Dictionary, Avon Books, (New York, 1980), p.172

Poponin, Vladimir. *The DNA Phantom Effect: Direct Measurement of a New Field in the Vacuum Substructure*, Institute of HeartMath, (Boulder Creek, Ca.)

Rael, Joseph. *The Sound Beings*, Exclusive Pictures/Heaven Fire Productions, Video, (Van Nuys, Ca., 1995)

Raloff, J. "Baby's AIDS Virus Infection Vanishes," *Science News*, (Washington, D.C., April, 1995), p.196

Rein, Glen PhD and Atkinson, Mike and McCraty, Rollin, MA. "The Physiological and Psychological Effects of Compassion and Anger," *Journal of Advancement in Medicine*, Volume 8, Number 2, Summer (1995), pages 87-103

Rikitake, Tsuneji and Honkura, Yoshimori. *Solid Earth Geomagnetism*, Terra Scientific Publishing Co., Tokyo, (Japan, 1985)

Robinson, James M. *The Nag Hammadi Library in English*, Harper San Francisco, (San Francisco, 1990), p.129

Ibid, p.126

Ibid, p.129

Ibid, p.131

Ibid, p.132

Ibid, p.134

Ibid, p.136

Sitchin, Zecharia. *The Lost Realms*, Avon Books, (1990)

Szekely, Edmond, B. *The Essene Gospel of Peace*, series, Compared, Edited and Translated by Edmond Bordeaux Szekely, Third Century Aramaic Manuscript and Old Slavic Texts, I.B.S. Internacional, (Matsqui, B.C., Canada, 1937)

'The Unknown Books of the Essenes,' 1937, p.45

Ibid., p.31

Ibid., p.69

Ibid., p.109

'The Essene Gospel of Peace,' 1937, p.10

Ibid., p.19

'The Teachings of the Elect,' 1981, p.30

'Lost Scrolls of the Essene Brotherhood,' 1986, p.70

Thompson, Clare. "The Genes That Keep AIDS at Bay," *New Scientist*, New Science Publications, IPC Magazines, Ltd., King's Reach Tower, Stamford Street, (London, April 6, 1996), p.16

Travis, J. "Mutant Gene Explains Some HIV Resistance," *Science News*, (Washington, D.C., August 17, 1996), Vol. 150, page 103

Wallace-Murphy, Tim. *The Templar Legacy & The Masonic Inheritance Within Rosslyn Chapel*, "The Friends of Rosslyn," Rosslyn Chapel, Roslin, (Midlothian EH25 9PU, Scotland), p.50-51

Watson, James, D. *Molecular Biology of the Gene*, adapted from the 'Matrix of the Human Genetic Code,' Third Edition, W.A. Benjamin, Inc. (1976)

Winter, Dan. *Alphabet of the Heart: The Genesis in Principle of Language and Feeling*, (Waynesville, N.C.)

'Can The Human Heart Directly Affect The Coherence of Earth's Magnetic Field?,' pp. 58-64

'Testing The Effects of Heart Coherence On DNA and Immune Function,' pp. 56-57

GLOSSARY

BLESSING. An ancient verbal thought code offered to release the charged potential upon an emotion or event. Blessing an action, event or circumstance does not indicate a condoning or agreement with the event that has passed. Rather, the blessing serves as a vent to release the emotional charge, acknowledging the divine nature of the experience. Blessing an event, in effect, states that

> "I acknowledge that what I have witnessed or experienced is divine in its nature and part of the One, though I may not understand or know of the reasons or mechanisms underlying the event."

The gift of blessing is that it allows the individual to move on with life's offering. In it's divinity, the experience is viewed within the overall context of the One, neither good nor bad and still part of all that may be.

CHARGE. A strong feeling as to the right, wrong or appropriateness of an outcome is our charge upon that experience. Technically, charge may be measured as an electrical potential surrounding an expectation, act or situation. Created as an event is judged and labeled through the eyes of polarity as good, bad, dark or light, the charge is often sensed as feelings of anger, sadness or frustration. The holographic mirror of consciousness assures us that we will experience our judgments (charges) so that the judgments may be redefined (reconciled) allowing us to move forward in life without the hindrance of that particular charge.

COMPASSION. The single-word expression of a specific quality of thought, feeling and emotion; thought without attachment to the outcome, feeling without the distortion of an individual's life bias and emotion without the charge of polarity. The science of compassion allows the witnessing/experience of an event without the polarized judgment as to the rightness or wrongness of the event.

CREATOR. One, who knowing the principles of "God," creates life from non-life. Apart from the procreation resulting as the union of sperm and egg, creation is the act of bringing together non-living compounds within an electrical environment, to producing living material.

EMOTION. Emotion is the power that you place into your thoughts to make them real. It is the scalar potential of emotion, combined with the scalar potential of thought, that produces the vector experience of reality. The waves of scalar potential produce the interference pattern of your vector reality. You experience emotion as sensation flowing, directed, or lodged within the liquid crystalline form of your body. The electrical charge that pulses through your body as life force provides the sensation of emotion. Emotion may be experienced spontaneously or as the result of a choice to be. Emotion is closely aligned with desire, the will to allow something to become so. As you truly desire to replace hate in your life with compassion, you will sense the power flowing from your lower energy centers as a warm tingling sensation into your chest and heart centers.

ENTRAINMENT. The alignment of forces, or fields of energy, to allow maximum transfer of information or communication. For example, consider two elements adjacent to one another and each is vibrating. One is vibrating at a faster rate while the other is vibrating at a slower rate. The tendency for the element of slower vibration to synchronize and match the element of faster vibration may be considered entrainment. To the degree that the match is accomplished, we say that entrainment has occurred or the faster vibration has entrained the slower vibration.

ESSENES. An ancient brotherhood of unknown origin, who chose to separate themselves from the masses of their time to live the purity of traditions that had been left to them by their ancestors. Located primarily around the Dead Sea and Lake Mareotis in the first century, A.D., the teachings of this mysterious brotherhood have appeared in almost every country and religion, including Sumeria, Palestine, India, Tibet, China and Persia. Some Native North American tribes trace the roots of their ancestors to the clans of Essenes just after the execution of Jesus.

The ancient Essenes were communal agriculturists with no servants or slaves. They lived a structured life without meats or fermented drinks, allowing life spans of up to 120 years or more. Among well known Essenes were the healers of John the Beloved, John the Baptist, Elijah and Jesus of Nazareth.

FEELING. Feeling may be defined as the union of thought and emotion. As you experience sadness, hate, joy or compassion, for example, you are experiencing feeling. Feeling is the sensation of emotion, coupled with the thought of what you are experiencing in the moment.

The liquid crystal resonator of the heart muscle is the focal point of feeling. It now becomes apparent why the body responds so well to love and compassion. Through love and compassion the heart is optimally tuned to the earth, allowing the circuit to express fully and completely.

Examples of feeling:
When you feel love, you are feeling your thought of what the object of your love means to you coupled with the emotion of your desire.

GOD. The matrix of intelligence underlying all of creation. This principle provides the vibratory template upon which all of creation is "crystallized." The principle of God represents all possibilities and lives as each expression of masculine and feminine expression. From this perspective, the God Force is a living, vibratory pulse that lives in the spaces between the nothing and is inherent in all that we may experience in our world.

HOLOGRAM. A recursive pattern of energy (geometric, emotional, feeling, thought, consciousness or mathematical) that stands whole and complete unto itself while serving as a portion of a greater whole. For example each cell of the human body is whole and complete unto itself, containing all of the information required to create another human body. At the same time, it is one cell of a much larger whole, the body itself.

By definition, each element of a holographic pattern mirrors all other elements of the pattern. This is the beauty of the holographic model of consciousness. Change introduced anywhere in the system is mirrored throughout the entire system.

RECONCILE. Within the context of Walking Between the Worlds, to reconcile an event or circumstance is to find a place of balance within where the event makes sense. Reconciliation of an event does not indicate a condoning or approval of what has happened. It simply allows for an acknowledgment within the individual so that they may move forward in life. The act of blessing, acknowledging the divine nature of life's offering, is an example of reconciliation.

RESOLVE. The removal of a charge upon an event, circumstance or situation is the zeroing out of the electrical potential that judgment has placed upon the event. We say that the event has

been "resolved." To resolve the charge upon an event, for example, is to redefine the meaning of that event, refining the meaning until a true neutral feeling is reached. Neutrality is a biochemical expression of resolution.

RESONANCE. An exchange of energy between two or more systems of energy. The exchange is two-way, allowing each system to become a point of reference for the other. A common example of resonance is illustrated with two stringed instruments placed on opposite sides of the same room. As the lowest string of one instrument is plucked the same string on the second instrument will vibrate. No one touched the string, it is responding to the waves of energy that traveled across the room and found resonance with the second string. In our text, we speak of resonance between systems of energy such as the earth and the human heart, or two individuals "tuning" to resonance through emotion.

SCALAR POTENTIAL. A quality of energy described as having not been dispersed or dissipated. Scalar energy may be thought of as energy that is fully enabled and waiting to be used; a potential force available for activation. Upon activation, the potential becomes "real," or a vector quantity, that may be measured as magnitude and direction.

SHIFT OF THE AGES. Both a time in Earth history as well as an experience of human consciousness. Defined by the convergence of decreasing planetary magnetics and increasing planetary frequency upon a point in time, the Shift of the Ages, or simply The Shift, represents a rare opportunity of collectively repatterning the expression of human consciousness.

The Shift is the term applied to the process of Earth accelerating through a course of evolutionary change, with the human species linked, by choice, to the electromagnetic fields of Earth, following suit through a process of cellular change.

THE ONE. A non religious term in reference to the matrix of intelligence underlying all of creation. This principle provides the vibratory template upon which all of creation is "crystallized." The principle of The One represents all possibilities and lives as each expression of masculine and feminine expression. From this perspective, The One is a living, vibratory pulse that lives in the spaces between the nothing and is inherent in all that we may experience in our world.

THOUGHT. Thought may be considered as an energy of scalar potential, the directional seed of an expression of energy that may, or may not, materialize as a real or vector event. A virtual assembling of your experience, thought provides the guidance system, the direction, for where the energy of your attention may be directed. Without the influx of emotional energy into your thoughts, they are impotent and powerless to create. In the absence of power, your thought may be considered as a model or simulation of how or where your power may be directed. Fantasies, "what ifs," affirmations, and "I choose to," are examples of the beginning of a thought. These processes will determine where you focus your attention.

ABOUT THE AUTHOR

Author, lecturer and guide to sacred sites throughout the world, Gregg has been featured on radio and television programs nationwide. Following the publication of his book, *Awakening to Zero Point: The Collective Initiation,* he has been a popular guest and keynote speaker for conferences, expos, and media specials regarding ancient wisdom, planetary change and the role of relationships within the context of these changes.

Professional careers as an earth scientist and aerospace engineer have provided Gregg with the tools to offer his powerful seminars with clarity and relevance. Two near death experiences early in life provide the intimate language to express his message of hope and opportunity.

Gregg provides his powerful message of compassion as a series of one, two and three day seminars. Each workshop is a multimedia experience of sight, sound, feeling and ceremony as you are skillfully guided through your memory of the vibratory technologies of compassion, emotion and relationships.

ABOUT THE ARTIST

An accomplished decorative and fine artist, Melissa Ewing Sherman has explored the techniques of visual expression for more than fifteen years. Inspired by impressionist and Renaissance masters, her work reflects her love of art history as well as her travels throughout Europe and Egypt. Melissa's trompe l'oeil and decorative finishes are seen in distinguished homes and residences throughout South Florida.

Her interest in Sumi-e and Chinese brush painting led her to study with the late Glory Brightfield. The Oriental ink paintings found at each chapter's beginning are created as a meditative preface for the message that follows.

The solitude of northern New Mexico's mountains and South Florida's coasts serve as home and inspiration to Gregg and Melissa between their travels. Additionally, as the timing and conditions allow, they lead journeys to sacred sites in Egypt, Peru, Bolivia, Tibet and the American Desert Southwest.

SCHEDULES

Gregg's extensive lecture and travel itinerary have necessitated the development of an office to assist with the volumes of daily correspondence. Your questions and comments are important. He and his staff work closely to honor each request and inquiry. Thank you in advance for your patience. For inquiries regarding dates, locations and specifics regarding seminars, workshops and Sacred Journeys, please address your correspondence to:

Sacred Spaces/Ancient Wisdom - H.C. 81 Box - Questa, New Mexico 87556 - Attention: Schedules
or call 1-500-675-6308

You may write to Gregg Braden and Melissa Sherman
c/o Sacred Spaces/Ancient Wisdom - H.C. 81 Box 683 - Questa, New Mexico 87556 - Attention: Personal

SACRED SPACES/ ANCIENT WISDOM NEWSLETTER

If you would like to receive a complimentary issue of 'Shekinah Newsletter' write to:

Sacred Spaces/Ancient Wisdom - H.C. 81 Box - Questa, New Mexico 87556 - Attention: Newsletter

TO ORDER BOOKS AND RELATED MATERIALS

For a free catalog and to order additional copies of this book, the study guide, the workbook that accompanies this material and other publications by Gregg Braden contact:

Radio Bookstore Press - PO Box 3010 - Bellevue, WA. 98009-3010

To order books, tapes and videos,
call 1-800-243-1438 outside the US and in Seattle 1-425-455-1053
or at our website at www.lauralee.com

Awakening to Zero Point: The Collective Initiation
by Gregg Braden

There is a process of unprecedented change unfolding within the Earth. You are part of the change. Without knowledge of the artificial boundaries of religion, science, or ancient mystic traditions, the change is characterized as dramatic shifts in the physical parameters of Earth accompanied by a rapid transformation in human understanding, perception, and experience. This time is historically referred to as "The Shift of the Ages." As science witnesses events for which there are no reference points of comparison, ancient traditions say that the timetable is intact; the events of "The Shift" are happening now. Each event carries with it a similar message, and is a by-product of something much more significant than the event itself.

| #5590 | Book - Softcover - 248 pages | $17.95 |

The Isaiah Effect: Decoding the Lost Science of Prayer & Prophecy
by Gregg Braden

Of all the Dead Sea Scrolls, Gregg finds the Isaiah Scroll of particular interest. Gregg examines aspects of the Isaiah prophecies, ancient Hopi, Mayan, and Egyptian texts, laboratory studies on the power of prayer, and emerging ideas from quantum physics. He finds clues to the mystical power of "active prayer" -- a lost art that is key to choosing our future. This is what Gregg calls the Isaiah Effect.

| #5588 | Book - Hardcover - 276 pages | $23.00 |

Awakening to Zero Point: The Video
Presented by Gregg Braden

This fully-illustrated, multi-media presentation is a message of hope and compassion. Gregg presents evidence that we are collectively preparing for an evolutionary leap. He draws from the records of ancient cultures, new scientific research on the connection between our emotions and DNA, and geological data on Earth's cycles. One cycle of great interest is the strength of Earth's magnetic field; science does not yet acknowledge the subtle but profound effect this and other cyclic conditions have on us. Previous cultures have either experienced these cycles, or similated them at sacred sites and temples, leaving us a "road map." As these cycles converge now, we are allowed graceful access to higher states of consciousness.

Gregg details: How to change the patterns that can determine how and why you love, fear, judge, feel, need, and hurt. The cause for dramatic shifts you may be experiencing (radical changes in sleep patterns and dream states, perception of time "speeding up" and intensified emotions and relationships). The direct link between what you feel and how your body codes genetic information. How to affect positive enhancement of your own physiology.

| #7401 | 2-VHS Videos, 3 hrs 40 min | $39.95 |
| #7405 | 2-VHS/PAL, European Format | $49.95 |

Walking Between The Worlds: The Audio Book
by Gregg Braden

A five and a half hour audio presentation by Gregg Braden, based upon the book and seminar *Walking Between The Worlds*. Gregg finds evidence to support ancient texts that speak of compassion as a "path" allowing a life of vitality, longevity, and freedom from disease, in new scientific studies that suggest direct links between the emotion of compassion, our DNA, and the immune system. Gregg revives the "Science of Compassion" in a sequence of emotional, logical, and vibratory "codes" and asks: Is Emotion our forgotten "switch" that can turn on our genetic codes at will? What are the verbal "equations" for compassion, left to us over 2,000 years ago? Do we have a "seventh sense," one that links our experience with the way that we "feel" about our experience?

#6113   6 - audio cassettes 5 1/2 hrs $39.95

Walking Between the Worlds: The Video

Presented by Gregg Braden

Gregg Braden further explores the understanding the inner technology of emotions by heavily detailing the Essene Mirrors of Relationship. The ancient knowledge of compassion may be one of the few viable approaches for creating a better environment for self-knowledge - now and in the future.

#7402   2 VHS Videos - 4 hrs $39.95

Beyond Zero Point

Gregg Braden

Gregg offers scientific research essential to understanding the prophecies of the Hopi, Essenes, Mayans, Egyptians, and others. Experience how the outer world mirrors the inner conditions of our consciousness and transcends ordinary awareness.

#6114   Audio Cassettes - 2 $18.95

The Lost Mode of Prayer

Gregg Braden

Gregg delves into libraries lost to the West nearly a millennia ago. The Essenes were but a single link in a secret chain of ancient wisdom holders. Gregg finds in their records, an esoteric practice of focusing thoughts and emotions to directly influence the physical world and those around us.

#6115   Audio Cassettes - 2 $18.95

INTERVIEWS ON AUDIO CASSETTE

The Collective Initiation

Gregg Braden

Highlights: Humankind is fast approaching a collective evolutionary leap. Sacred sites and ancient texts suggest that previous cultures constructed temples which simulated the geophysical parameters that hasten higher consciousness. Evidence that these same cycles (Earth's diminishing magnetic field and rising base frequency) are converging today.

#1122   Interview on Cassettes - 2 $13.50

Decoding Crop Circles

Gregg Braden

Highlights: Gregg views crop circle designs as glyphs, symbols meaningful in the languages of genetics, physics, & sacred geometry. He offers an interpretation for the message of the circles.

#1259   Interview on Cassettes - 2 $13.50

The Physics of Emotion

Gregg Braden

Highlights: Emotions may serve as a "switch," turning on or off specific DNA codons. Why our lives are the continuation of spiritual initiations begun thousands of years ago.

#1357   Interview on Cassettes - 2 $13.50

Tools for Inner Technology

Gregg Braden

Highlights: Many cultures had specific insights into emotion as a means to accelerate spiritual growth. Gregg details "the Science of Compassion" of the ancient Essenes.

#1437   Interview on Cassette - 1 $7.00

Technology to Tune Emotions

Gregg Braden

Highlights: New technology may be imitating a lost ancient technology and therapy. Gregg looks at heiroglyphs and other clues that a lost technology was used to tune emotions to specific frequencies, with specific postive effect.

#1676   Interview on Cassette - 1 $7.00

Earth Magnetics and Ancient Wisdom

Gregg Braden

Highlights: Anomalies in Earth's magnetic field demonstrates the wandering of magnetic North. Airport ground control recalibrates instruments to align with North. Gregg cites references from previous cultures on how they saw similar anomalies unfolding long ago.

#1684   Interview on Cassettes - 2 $13.50

Advancing Humanity

Gregg Braden

Highlights: Gregg cites case studies of children and others whose immune systems strengthened in response to illness, that science cannot yet explain. Studies of individuals who seemed to benefit from spontaneously transformed DNA. Did these individuals "activate" certain DNA codons through compassion?

#1906   Interview on Cassettes - 2 $13.50

DNA Transmutations

Gregg Braden

Highlights: Gregg discusses the latest findings in genetic science that confirms our DNA can and does change according to specific conditions in the environment, and in response to emotion. Positive and negative emotions act very differently upon our DNA. We can choose how we respond, emotionally, to the events around us, and we can activate positive emotions intentionally. The effect on our physiology when we do.

#1938   Interview on Cassette - 1 $7.00

The Power of Prayer

Gregg Braden

Highlights: Gregg looks for confirmation of wisdom expressed in ancient texts from the Middle East, Tibet, Peru, and the American Southwest in laboratory experiments on particle physics, remote viewing, and the power of prayer.

#2001   Interview on Cassette - 1 $7.00

Revival of Lost Spiritual Techniques

Gregg Braden

Highlights: Through a language that we are just beginning to understand, we are reminded of two empowering technologies that allow us to determine the conditions of our bodies, and the future of our world. Join Gregg as he addresses these topics, updates us on his recent journeys

RADIO BOOKSTORE PRESS PO Box 3010 Bellevue, WA 98009-3010

to Egypt and Tibet, and shares his latest findings on the "lost" Dead Sea Scroll that unexpectedly resurfaced in late 1999.

| #2004 | Interview on Cassette - 1 | $7.00 |

The Emotion is the Power
Gregg Braden

Highlights: It's all in the feeling, the emotion, explains Gregg, and ancient cultures from the Essenes to the Tibetans to the Inca knew this. He details how we today can incorporate this understanding of the art of manifesting and the power of prayer into choosing our future among all the possible futures lying dormant. You'll enjoy Gregg's real life examples of this in action, from praying for rain to conversations with Tibetan mystics to his own close of the day ritual.

| #2033 | Interview on Cassette - 1 | $7.00 |

VIDEO PRESENTATIONS

The Hidden History of the Human Race: The Video
Produced and Directed by Richard Thompson

Computer generated illustrations and graphics, with commentary by Richard Thompson, co-author of the books *Forbidden Archeology* and *The Hidden History of the Human Race*. He presents a controversial challenge to rethink our understanding of human origins, identity and destiny: How science suppresses anomalies that run counter to the current favored theories. Why the scientific method dictates exploration of all theories suggested by all the evidence. One theory, suggested by almost half the artifacts we have so far of human antiquity, is that humans like us have lived on Earth for millions of years. This is also the view of the ancient Vedic texts and tradition.

| #7120 | VHS Video - 1 hour | (Special Price) | $24.95 |

Secrets of the Bird Tribe: Lost Stargate Artifacts & Spiritual Teachings
by William Henry

An illustrated lecture presentation. William Henry interprets the symbol of the bird man as ancient winged extraterrestrial beings and their stargate artifacts, and stargate myths of Moses, Nebuchadnezzar and other historical figures in line with the An-nun-aki of Zecharia Sitchin's research. Henry offers startling new insights into the ancient secrets for cleansing the human soul, purifying the human heart and the means to increase our spritual vision to perceive the gateways which prophecies predict will soon be opening.

| #7780 | VHS Video - 1hr 45min | (Special Price) | $19.95 |

Sacred Living Geometry
by Callum Coats

Illustrated lecture with Callum Coats, who spent 20 years researching Austrian ecologist Viktor Schauberger. A fascinating and in-depth look at Schauberger's ahead-of-his-time environmental theories, observations of Nature, and technical devices, which hold immense promise for the future.

| #7590 | 2-VHS Videos - 3 hrs | (Special Price) | $34.95 |

The Science of Innate Intelligence: The Role of Belief and Thought Mechanisms in Health
by Bruce Lipton
In this illustrated lecture, Bruce Lipton demonstrates how our thoughts and perceptions actively affect our health and behavior. Discover new information about the biology of consciousness, including its actual molecular mechanisms. Explore how knowledge of consciousness mechanisms can be employed to redefine our physical and emotional well being. Learn how our perceptions have been directly linked to the production of gene-altering mutations. Find out how our development and learning experiences produce life "filters" and how you can play a positive role in the alteration of these processes. This two part video presentation, featuring captivating, scientific, well referenced material, has been approved for Continuing Education Credit for health care providers.

| #7431 | 2-VHS Video - 2 hrs 30 min | $59.95 |

The Code - Video
Carl Munck
An illustrated lecture presentation, this homespun video was produced by Munck. Decoding a mathematically based key to ancient temples, from Stonehenge to the pyramids of Egypt and Mexico. Using illustrations and simple math equations, Munck describes how pyramids and earthen mounds around the world might "know where they are."

| #7610 | VHS Video - 2 hrs | $24.95 |

The Code: Parts 2 & 3
Carl Munck
Archeocryptography school is again in session as *The Code: Parts 2 & 3* continue here on one video with Carl Munck as your guide and teacher. Geomathematical logic, as well as contemporary science, demonstrates that the ancients measured and mapped the Earth. Part 2 - Matrix West: structures in N. & S. America Part 3 - The Pi Pyramids: the relationships of many structures and Pi.

| #7611 | VHS Video - 1 hr 45 min | $24.95 |

ADDITIONAL BOOKS

Friar's Map of Ancient America 1360 AD
by Gunnar Thompson
Anthropologist's collection of extensive evidence of voyages to North America long before Columbus. The story of Nicholas of Lynn and the Franciscan Map of North America. Includes: North Atlantic Voyages, Legendary Isles, Roger Bacon's Inventions, Ancient Astronomy, Solomon's Mines, & the Biblical Ophir. **Special: FREE Interview Cassette ($7.00 Value) included with the purchase of this Book**

| #5113 | Book - Softcover - 304 pages | (Special Price) | $19.95 |

Lions in the New Land
Gunnar Thompson
The story of a mysterious English friar whose passage through time altered the course of world history. In the 14th century, the friar traveled from England, to Norway, Iceland, and the Northern Regions in the service of King Edward III. The friar's assignment was to survey isles of the North Atlantic in an effort to find the lost, overseas colony of King Arthur. This project, entailing discovery of the Western Hemisphere, was first proposed by England's premier scientist—Roger Bacon in 1266.

| #5114 | Book - Softcover - 225 pages | (Special Price) | $12.95 |

RADIO BOOKSTORE PRESS PO Box 3010 Bellevue, WA 98009-3010

ORDER FORM

Book
Other titles Gregg Braden references in his seminars and workshops.

ITEM#	DESCRIPTION	PRICE
5640	Book of the Hopi	13.95
5645	The Book of Enoch	11.95
5637	Crystal & Dragon	19.95
5592	Emerald Tablets of Thoth-The-Atlantean	15.95
5591	Nothing In This Book is True	14.95
5594	Something In This Book is True	14.95
5601	Ancient Secret of the Flower of Life - Vol. 1	25.00
5602	Ancient Secret of the Flower of Life - Vol. 2	25.00
5630	Sacred Geometry	15.95
5635	Sacred Mirrors	29.95
5593	Nag Hammadi Library	21.00
5600	Essene Gospel of Peace [set of 4 books]	22.00

Video

ITEM#	DESCRIPTION	PRICE
7410	Mathematics for Lovers	20.00
7411	Cymatics III: Bringing Matter to Life	25.00
7412	Cymatics IV: Cymatic SoundScapes	25.00
7414	Cymatics: The Healing Nature of Sound	30.00
7590	Sacred Living Geometry [2-VHS]	34.95

Music

ITEM#	DESCRIPTION	PRICE
8050	Chaco Canyon - CD	16.95
8051	Chaco Canyon - Cassette	9.95
8100	Eternal Om - CD	16.95
8101	Eternal Om - Cassette	10.95
8060	Macchu Picchu Impressions - CD	16.95
8061	Macchu Picchu Impressions - Cassette	9.95
8111	Music for the Native Americans -Cassette	11.95
8110	Music for the Native Americans - CD	19.95
8065	Ocean Eclipse - CD	16.95
8070	Where the Earth Touches Stars - CD	16.95
8071	Where the Earth Touches Stars - Cassette	9.95
8130	Jungle of Joy - CD	16.95
8080	Higher Ground - CD	16.95
8081	Higher Ground - Cassette	9.95
8120	Beautiful World in Existence - CD	15.95
8121	Beautiful World in Existence - Cassette	10.95

SHIP TO:

PHONE:

ITEM#	DESCRIPTION	PRICE	QTY.	TOTAL

TOTAL =

SHIPPING/HANDLING =

SUBTOTAL =

WA Residents SALES TAX 8.6% =

GRAND TOTAL =

Credit Card Information

❏ Discover ❏ Visa
❏ MasterCard ❏ American Express

Card# _____

exp. date _____

name on card _____

signature _____

International Shipping Charges

PREPAID ORDERS: Due to the wide variety of products we offer, it is near impossible to pre-determine a fair international shipping charge for every situation. To ensure check customers are charged the correct cost of shipping, please e-mail (customerservice@radiobookstore.com), fax or call for the shipping charge. To pay by check, send an international bank money order payable in U.S. funds, drawn through a U.S. bank.

CREDIT CARD ORDERS: will be charged cost of shipping.

Videos are NTSC - American Format unless otherwise noted.

Shipping & Handling Charges

If the total falls between:	Add: US	Canada
0 - $9.99	$2.00	$ 5.00
10.00 - 24.99	$3.00	$ 7.00
25.00 - 49.99	$4.00	$ 9.00
50.00 - 74.99	$5.00	$12.00
75.00 - 99.99	$6.00	$14.00
Over $100.00	Free	$16.00

www.radiobookstore.com Phone 800-243-1438 (425) 455-1053 Fax (425) 455-1231